YOUTH UNCHARTED

THE MACMILLAN COMPANY
NEW YORK · BOSTON · CHICAGO · DALLAS
ATLANTA · SAN FRANCISCO

STEPHEN LAWFORD

YOUTH UNCHARTED

NEW YORK
THE MACMILLAN COMPANY
1935

SET UP BY BROWN BROTHERS LINOTYPERS
PRINTED IN THE UNITED STATES OF AMERICA
BY THE FERRIS PRINTING COMPANY

TO

LARA

AUTHOR'S ACKNOWLEDGMENTS

To my regret it has not been possible for me to make due acknowledgment in each and every case as regards sources of information or quotations used in this book. When this occurs, it is because they were first used by myself in letters or diaries, and I am now unable to trace their source.

I therefore tender the necessary apologies and thanks to my unknown benefactors as well as to those whose names I have been able to remember.

My grateful thanks are due to Edward Phelan for wise advice, and particularly for permission to use the four lines which close this book.

CONTENTS

ix

PART III

NEAR EAST

"I saw the Ottoman's fortress—austere and darkly impending, high over the vale of the Danube—historic Belgrade. I had come, as it were, to the end of this wheel-going Europe, and now my eyes would see the Splendour and Havoc of the East."—EOTHEN.

PART IV

SOUTH AMERICA

"In America the Geography is sublime, but the men are not."—EMERSON, *Conduct of Life.*

CONTENTS

ENVOI

"But in spite of all temptations
To belong to other nations,
He still remains an Englishman."

SIR W. S. GILBERT, *Pinafore*.

INTRODUCTORY EPISTLE

"Never mind the Why and Wherefore."
W. S. GILBERT.

GENEVA, 1935.

MY DEAR IVAN,

There is a French proverb to the effect that a father is a banker provided by Nature. Except, perhaps, in England, bankers are by now somewhat discredited, but, even though this be so, it seems likely that for a few more decades one must continue to listen to them and to read their letters with apprehensive attention. So you must listen to me, and I hope that you may be interested in what I have to tell you.

For it is my fell purpose to treat you as if you were a casual and sympathetic stranger met by chance on the upper deck or on a Balkan railway station, and inflict on you the story of my life. It pleases me to imagine that you may in the future have journeys, joys, adventures, troubles, states of mind and experiences similar to those I had in the past, and that comparing them you may find we have something in common.

Such is my intention, long cherished as we crawled, you to boyhood and I to maturity; yet reflection leaves me still appalled by the difficulties and dangers of autobiography. There is the tendency to embroider the fading fabric of the past. *"On est toujours tenté de s'attendrir sur soi-même et de se peindre tel que l'on voudrait être,"* as somebody said. I shall try my best to

xiii

escape from this tendency, for the classical writers, whom I have searched in quest of a little reasonable elasticity, are all against anything but the most complete truth-telling.

The Opium-eater is most categorical. "It would," he declares, "vitiate the interest which any reader might otherwise take in this narrative if for one moment it were supposed that any features of the case were varnished or distorted. From the very first I have been faithful to the most rigorous law of accuracy—even in absolute trifles."

"Je n'ai rien tu de mauvais, rien ajouté de bon," asserts Jean-Jacques. I hope I meet them both with the Recording Angel in the Vale of Jehoshaphat.

In view of these definite instructions I shall not fail, as they say in official correspondence, to use every effort to keep well within the limits of the authentic. If, as regards conversations reported verbatim and often reproduced from letters intended either to pierce the financial carapace of an affluent uncle or the evasive heart of some indifferent maiden, I may have neglected in each and every case to obliterate the results of having formerly taken the Ciceronian counsel, *causam aspergere mendaciunculis*, then excuse my tender pruning. If they are not absolutely within the severe formulæ already quoted, they are true enough.

Whilst earnestly endeavouring to avoid being sucked down by the Charybdis of falsification, I shall put forth an equal effort to escape the horrid rocks of exhibitionism and lack of reticence, for I am no Stendhal and could not hope to interest you in my purges. Indeed, I agree with Lamartine who, when he began his *Confidences*, declared that he would not imitate Rousseau, for, said he, "the *Confessions of Rousseau* without his genius would be a sewer." Similarly, Montaigne could talk about his colics, and by his genius raise them almost to the level of the pains of a protomartyr, yet were I to attempt it I fear that only a dreary odour would result. So I doubt if there will be anything over-intimate in these letters, for excessive self-revelation is to my mind a form of pornography, and pornography is rather like garlic: just a suspicion makes a tasty dish, and just a little more makes a foul neighbour. As my first housekeeper used to say—she was a Macedonian and had lived in all sorts of *ménages*—"it all depends on how much you rub the bird."

In conclusion, I may add that if, when you read these letters, you find that some of my admonitions concord but ill with what you remember of my actions when I was emitting them, you must excuse me, and remember that "*les vieillards aiment à donner de bons préceptes pour se consoler de ne plus être en état de donner de mauvais exemples.*"

Now it is time to finish this introduction, which I have spangled with quotations to show that, even if I do like to talk about myself, yet I am always ready to listen to others, and to remain

Your affectionate

FATHER.

All the persons mentioned in this book actually
existed. I have, however, thought it advisable to
change the names of a few of them.

PART I

A SHILLING A DAY

"Glory is the sodger's prize,
The sodger's wealth is honour."
                                   BURNS.

CHAPTER I

LOVE ALL, 1914

I

I SHALL not describe in detail to you the time when I was "a lovely white unwritten book," my early boyhood, upbringing and education. Your grandparents and uncles may be relied upon to do that accurately and at length. They do not know, however, that, when I was at a preparatory school in Sussex, I spent the whole of one Sunday afternoon in terrible fear devising formulæ of complete repentance for all my sins, because I was quite certain that the end of the world was due for five o'clock. There was a fog, and the science master, an unrecking enthusiast, had discoursed of the nature of fog and had said—he was a Scot—that the Day of Judgment would, in his opinion, be preceded by a sudden obscurity caused by the appearance of "fine par-r-rticles of mist," the product of some head-on and planetary collision.

Nor are they aware, these relatives of yours, of a broken word of honour concerning a promise not to accept a passenger flight in one of the early Caudron biplanes which, cautiously circling the aerodrome near our house, enshrined for me all adventure. They are sure, however, to tell you of episodes relating to creaking cupboards in dark bedrooms and panic flights from neighbouring dogs.

This was the period in which I acquired a habit that has stayed with me, and which has had a certain effect on my career. I used deliberately to cultivate the practice of day-dreaming. You might like to hear a little of these pre-War daydreams of mine so as to be able to compare them with your own. Furthermore, they were in my case, as in that of many others, a sort of psychological introduction to the wave of patriotism which started me on my journey.

It is rather alarming to think that you may be taught at school to analyse them, and that as a result of such analysis you may decide that your father suffered from an Œdipus complex, a tendency to masochism or something similarly Freudian; but I suppose I must bear it; and even if he did, I can assure you it never worried him!

A favourite dream of that period was that in which I was enabled to intervene as a result of having overheard—usually on the top of a bus—a conversation between two would-be assassins who were contemplating a *coup*, and was therefore in a position at the last moment to preserve a visiting monarch from being blown up at Victoria Station.

There were a good many variants of this, and I used to spend quite a lot of time and ingenuity in debating with myself the relative advantages and disadvantages of sitting on the bomb and losing a leg, as compared with those of receiving the knife-thrust intended for the unconscious back of the visiting poten-tate. I usually opted for "a knife-thrust through the fleshy part of the arm." This, in contemporary juvenile shockers, was the accepted formula for the escape from violent combat of persons whose immediate extinction was not required by the exi-gencies of the plot, but who could hardly expect to get off scot-free. I remember dubiously feeling my stick-like arms, and wondering if there was enough flesh on them to allow of this compromise.

On the other hand, an instinctive appreciation of the reasonable used to prevent me, even in my imagination, from thinking that I could obtain any major benefit free, gratis and for nothing, except, perhaps, the labour of imagining it and the lost time involved. Vaguely I realized that something for nothing was not usually a tenable theory, and my preoccupation was to try to define the relative proportions of glory and grief in such a way as to form a blend that would ensure a satisfactory preponderance of the former without too great a disturbance of the eternal verities.

There were other forms, which involved the rescue from drowning of crippled old ladies, the stoppage and subjection of runaway horses, the salving of half-fried infants from burning houses and the disposal of itinerant mad dogs, either by the wily ruse of enticing them into a room and shutting the door on them, having previously turned on the gas, or more simply by a frightful hack with the gardening spade.

But perhaps the most glamorous of all was the one in which I was unjustly accused of a number of heinous crimes—as a result of which I was spurned by the girl of my heart and treated with every possible manifestation of public contumely. My regimental buttons were removed at a court-martial; I was publicly insulted in my club—I had several; the most terrible newspaper articles appeared about me; I received insulting letters by every post, and one Sunday I even had a specially comminatory sermon preached for my exclusive benefit by the old vicar, who had known me and loved me since I was a child.

Of course, all the time I was bearing the load of another's guilt, being bound in honour not to betray him. The guilty one, in case you should want to dream this dream, is usually the vicious and depraved younger brother of the heroine, to whom she is attached by a maudlin and entirely unreasonable affection. Something, you see, has to be unreasonable in order to produce situations like this, and you will generally be right in putting the blame on the female.

As I grow older and continue this practice somewhat less frequently, I find that the character of my dreams has become less romantic and more material. I am willing to dispense with imaginary suffering and do not insist too much on the necessity of achievement by sacrifice. I find that the joy of imagining even the well-rewarded rescue of a visiting President or Commissar—monarchs are getting too scarce—is gradually being replaced by the comfortable glow induced by the inward contemplation of the conquest of material independence consequent upon the fortunate selection of a lottery ticket issued under the auspices of a reasonably stable South American Government. In fact, during the recent depression, like Jonathan Swift:

> *"I've often wished that I had clear*
> *For life, six hundred pounds a year,*
> *A handsome house to lodge a friend,*
> *A river at my garden's end."*

.   .   .   .   .

As I look back to those days just before the War it seems to me that never again will the world appear so normal and regular. In the sphere in which I lived until I reached the age of seventeen there was a sort of solidity, a dependable and disciplined routine of life for the many, which has not yet been regained in Europe, Asia or America. The family washing was sent out every Monday, and snowy white and starched I found my share on my bed on the following Saturday. There was always marmalade for breakfast. The relationships of the various Royal Families were always discussed by my mother with such visitors as dared to compete with her in knowledge of them.

It seemed as if nothing could happen very seriously to disturb the peaceable state of affairs in England. Diplomats fussed and worried about abstruse questions with a remote bearing on the European situation, such as the failure of the proposed N'Goka Sangha Consortium and the integrity of the Sanjak of Novibazar; my father used to have long talks with his friends all about the Ball Platz, the Sublime Porte, the Quai d'Orsay and what Isvolsky really wanted; but any wars that actually broke out were more or less confined to Turkey and the Balkans or to the Afghan frontier. To me, then, studying for a scholarship at Oxford, the whole business of international politics seemed much more a sort of aristocratic game played by fussy foreigners under the impression that it was important than anything which could possibly react upon my private affairs.

"All unconscious of their doom, the little victims played." I played as much as I could. What was I like then? I was small but very wiry, active and fairly good at games. I stooped a little and wore glasses, being short-sighted. Not a romantic figure from the outside, but somehow I always felt that strange things would happen to me. Slight: reasonably well dressed, and at times inclined to dandyism. Very shy, particularly with women and girls, about whom I thought a great deal and whom I invested with the most impossible qualities.

In short, in 1914—like the great majority of my generation —I was a convinced romantic.

II

I read of the declaration of war at the local tennis club. I had just finished a rather strenuous set, and having given up the court to what looked like being an interminable ladies' four, had strolled down the street to meet the newsboy whose excited and raucous cries I had heard. It was the six-thirty edi-

tion of the *Evening News* that informed me that everything was
going into the melting-pot. I went back to the club, and saw
that the ladies had abandoned their court and were in the grip
of the club bore who had just come down from Whitehall.
They were listening to him eagerly. Obviously the occasion
was serious.

Almost in a flash I became utterly, completely and mysti-
cally exalted, and so were thousands and millions like me. Mark
you, I had no hate for the Germans. I did not know any, except one of the boys at the tennis club, and him I disliked only
because of the painstaking way he would endeavour to play on
my backhand. I did not personally think that any Englishman
was necessarily equal to four foreigners. I was mortally afraid
that I might not be the equal of one when the time came.

The violation of Belgium meant, to use an Americanism,
absolutely nothing in my young life. But even if it had been
the violation of Birmingham, where dwelt my wealthiest and
favourite aunt, I could not have been more exalted than I was.
The War meant, I thought, adventure, romance and the possibility of proving oneself a man. Ordinary work seemed to
promise only the probability of proving oneself a proletarian.

Imagine, then, your father in August 1914, full of bunk and
illusion, or if you prefer it—and alas! I am not yet sure that I
don't hope you will—filled with the purest brand of patriotism,
yearning for opportunities of self-sacrifice and savouring a particularly inspiring dream which included the singlehanded capture of the Kaiser, his sequestration in an aeroplane, deposit
in the British War Office—where he immediately signed really
humiliating Peace terms—and a subsequent marriage with the
beautiful and well-born Red Cross nurse who had played a
secondary though occasionally heroic rôle of collaborator in the
exploit.

The question then arose as to how to make a start. I walked about London, proposing myself to the recruiting sergeants and regimental depots, but all to no purpose. The pick of the young men of England were also applying, and a smallish person below military age and wearing glasses, though lit by internal fires of terrible incandescence, did not seem to be able to command much attention, or indeed to be wanted at all.

My family, minus two of my brothers already mobilized— one with the fleet and one with the 1st Canadian Contingent— after mingling with the crowds that surrounded the War Office and Buckingham Palace, decided with admirable common sense that, as the rooms were engaged and would have to be paid for, Armageddon ought not to be allowed to interfere with my father's much-needed summer holiday.

The move suited me, as one of the less scornful of the recruiting sergeants, for whom, reversing the usual rôles, I had bought beer, had told me that I might have more chance of being able to join up outside London, since some of the County territorial battalions were still under strength. So off we went in August to the West Country.

We went to our usual hotel. Still consumed with patriotic fervour and unutterably sad because I could not join up, I loafed, bathed and played tennis. At the hotel were a doctor and his daughter.

The doctor was a keen tennis player. He had just won the local tournament, which, unaffected by the War, had come to its conclusion on the local courts, whence one could look down on the sea and the grey cruisers and transports as they came slowly round the point.

Very shortly after our arrival, I bicycled over to the nearest town where there was a recruiting centre. In I walked boldly and stated my wishes to a fat sergeant with drooping moustaches and sagging stomach, who was sitting at a table and dealing faithfully with a Cornish pasty. He looked at me dubiously, and still masticating, pushed over a form for me to fill up.

My sergeant studied the form at close range, and after another dubious look at me he disappeared into an inner room. After a minute or two he came out and said that the doctor awaited me. I went in, and to my surprise saw that it was my acquaintance of the hotel, who was, it appeared, deputizing for the regular military medico, who had been summoned elsewhere. He greeted me kindly and asked me to strip. This I did. If there is an occasion when my inferiority complex reaches its fullest expression or peak output and rears up to attain complete domination, it is when I caper naked in front of an official doctor. I blushed, coughed, jumped, bent from side to side, reflexed and breathed heavily while the doctor tapped, thumped and listened in.

As far as I could make out, no mortal weakness had revealed itself. Then I was told to take off my glasses and read some faint figures on a distant wall. I peered at them mistily, and though, as a result of previous experiences in London, I had been foreseeing enough to try to memorize them when I had first caught sight of them, my memory failed me, and I made a lamentable performance.

The doctor made a clucking noise and asked me the strength of my lenses. I told him, and he clucked again and dived into a book of regulations. At last he looked up.

"I'm very sorry. I can't pass you," he said. "You're fit enough and wiry, though no Hercules. Also, you're no more than seventeen, or I'll pawn my stethoscope. But your eyes throw you out."

"But, Doctor," I said with a gulp in a breathless hurry, while

the offending members filled with tears which I blinked back,
"I wear glasses, and with them my sight is normal."

He wavered.

"With a rifle I am quite a good shot," I went on hurriedly.
"I'm sure I could stick anything anybody else could." (Oh,
confidence of youth!) "Please make an exception and let
me in."

"That's the spirit," he said approvingly. "But supposing
your glasses got broken: you would be helpless and no use."

"Well," I replied, "that's certainly true. But I always carry
a spare pair, and to be on the safe side I could carry a third . . .
in my haversack, instead of that Field-Marshal's baton one
hears so much about," I added brightly.

The doctor turned things over in his mind.

I went on desperately. "Suppose a bullet did smash my
glasses; then the odds are that it would also penetrate my brain,
and in that case, as the minor disaster would involve a major
one, it would be of no consequence."

It will give you, my boy, some idea of the exalted frame of
mind in which I was when I tell you that this portentous remark
—which I had previously rehearsed so as to be able to produce it in an hour of need—did not seem at all humorous
to me.

The doctor grinned. "Not bad reasoning for a kid," he
said, "though specious. You may put on your clothes," he
added, as though my recent utterance had proved my right to
the insignia of a reasoning being. Then, with an air of one
coming to a final decision, he produced his judgment. "But it
won't do at all. Regulations are regulations."

My hopes fell to zero. But I persisted, and produced a
second speech, also carefully rehearsed for such an occasion.

"Look here, Doctor," I began, "I have been round all the

recruiting offices, and so far have been turned down consistently in favour of perfect physical specimens who may not have the courage of a canary or the intelligence of a louse. Don't you think that something, some rôle, is played by the spirit or the soul or whatever you like to call it? Have you not seen physically weak but courageous and strong-willed persons recover from diseases which have terrified and killed many a sturdy lout? After all, neither Nelson nor Bonaparte were very big, or very fit either, if the truth were known." This again was all part of a previously prepared line which I gabbled as convincingly as I could.

There was a pause while he studied my blushing face.

"There is certainly something in what you say," he said at last. "But the War Office . . ."

But I interrupted him.

"Please, sir," I said, "you won the local tennis tournament; don't you think you could actually test my physical fitness in the most practical way possible? Give me a game to-morrow morning. A single. The best of five sets. If you win, I won't worry you again. If I win, you pass me into the Army and give my Colonel a note to try me out for a bit." I stopped and waited breathlessly.

The doctor laughed aloud.

"Well," he said, "of all the cheek! But still, it's rather a sporting idea. I agree. After all, I'll be in France myself in three weeks, and if I know anything of official procedure, it'll take them ten years to find out who let loose such a warlike Jesuit on them. To-morrow, then, at nine."

At this juncture the door opened, and his daughter peeped cautiously round the door. I surreptitiously verified the buttoning of my trousers and blushed an even deeper hue.

"Hullo, Peggy," he said. "You know our young friend, I believe."

He then told her of the great trial by ordeal.

"How topping!" she said, glancing at me approvingly. "But the parent is very good and you'll have a job to win. In any case it's splendid of you to want to join up. My brothers have all gone. But they were much bigger than you," she added, and glanced at my already sufficiently disparaged form.

I burned with rage, love and a desire to show that size was a trifle, but actually said nothing.

"Very well," chuckled the doctor. "Nine o'clock to-morrow we meet in mortal combat. I need some exercise, and as it's Saturday I shan't have to spend my time looking at any more Titans in a state of nature."

I fled before he should change his mind.

The next morning was fine, and I was on the court at nine o'clock sharp. Very shortly afterwards appeared my opponent, in flannels, and accompanied by his daughter. With an exchange of salutes we tossed for sides, the doctor winning and electing to give me the service. After a preliminary knock-up the umpire climbed into her seat. Then began a match, every detail and stroke of which remains clear in my memory, owing, I suppose, to my exalted state of mind at the time.

I had observed the doctor's game when I watched him play his final. It was more cunning than fast. He placed beautifully, had a strongly cut backhand, was an accurate lobber and, though he seldom went to the net, when he did he was usually effective. My own game was more violent. I had a very strong forehand, a rather weaker backhand and was fairly severe overhead. Luckily, the court was dry and hard, which favoured my game more than his.

I collected the balls preparatory to serving. As I did so, a transport came slowly round the point. She was so close in that one could easily see some khaki-clad figures on her decks. I took heart, for this must be a favourable omen.

"Play," shrilled the umpire.

I tossed the ball high into the air and served as hard as I knew how, putting into the stroke all my annoyance with the medical profession which had so consistently barred my military ambition and insulted me of late. The ball flew over the net like an astonished swallow, and skimming the chalk of the service line, passed the doctor in a flash. He looked up with a wicked grin.

"Sorry," he said, "but I wasn't quite ready. Would you mind serving two more?"

Rage filled my heart. I mustered a crooked smile and said to myself, "Don't lose your temper or he'll beat you. Just hate him concentratedly."

But the umpire intervened.

"Oh, Daddy," she said, "you pig! Cross over at once."

"All right," said my opponent. "I only did it to annoy, because I know it teases."

He crossed over and we started in earnest.

It was a hard-fought set. The rallies were long. The doctor kept me going from one side of the court to the other. Sometimes I would come to the net so as to end the rally one way or another. At times I would get to forty-love by going all out for my strokes and then, thinking that the game must come my way, would play carefully: the doctor would creep up to forty-thirty, I would try a decisive shot, and mishit. And so it went on, deuce and vantage. We were each winning our service games, and I was thankful I had taken service, because thus I managed to keep ahead instead of having to draw level.

We came to five-four in my favour, and the doctor to serve. The first points of the game were evenly distributed, but then, owing to a lucky drive that grazed the sidelines, I came to set point. I was sweating freely, and as I dashed up to the net and shaped for a volley, a bead of perspiration fell from my forehead on to my glasses and I hit the ball out.

"Aha," said the doctor, meaningly, as I wiped the mist from the lenses and bound a handkerchief round my head to prevent a similar misfortune in the future. As a result of these adjustments I was a little insecure, and winning the game, he deuced the set. Five-all. I won my service game fairly easily. Six-five. Deciding that it was then or never, I stood up close to return his service, sliced my returns to his backhand and stormed the net.

He sometimes tried to lob over my head and sometimes to pass me on the wings. Fortune favoured us equally, and we won point for point to deuce. Then I made a terribly weak return, the result of changing my mind at the last second as to the sort of shot I should make. However, I had good luck, for the ball struck the net cord, and after wavering for what seemed many seconds, finally dropped on the doctor's side of the court. This gave me vantage, and the doctor took special care with his next lob as I rushed the net. He was a little too precise, however, for he gave me a little more time than I expected, and by making a frenzied leap I just managed to get my racket to it. The ball hit the wood and flew in a direction totally contrary to my intention and to the doctor's legitimate expectations. He made a great effort, changed direction and managed to spoon it up, giving me an easy kill. I apologized for the fluke, but inwardly I was overjoyed at having won the first set in what was certainly going to be a desperate struggle.

We wiped our faces on a towel which was hanging on the post. If I shut my eyes I can still see the initials of the hotel worked in red worsted on that towel.

The second set began. Try as I would, I could not get rid

of the feeling that he would certainly win it as a result of a subconscious relaxation on my part and an increased will to win on his. I could not overcome this feeling, and so it was. He won the first two games, and though I tried hard, I did not get more than three games in the set.

Thus we were set-all. The umpire had long since exhausted her shrill voice in an effort to call the score in a professional manner and now announced it in a hoarse croak.

The doctor then asked me if I would like an interval after the first two sets. I replied diplomatically that I was not in need of it, but that as it was usual we might as well take it. I felt that such a position would at once underline my resistance to fatigue and my willingness to oblige. That will show you how serious I was. The doctor grunted, lit a cigarette, and sat down on the grass. The umpire imbibed a gaseous liquid from a green glass bottle ingeniously sealed by a glass marble affair which I had painfully to remove by hammering my thumb on to it.

"Time," called the umpire when there was nothing left in the bottle.

We got up and resumed the struggle. I had nourished the hope that the pendulum effect which had lost me the second set would win me the third, but in this I was sadly mistaken. The doctor went ahead, seeming to have taken my measure and to have found his best form. I felt baffled and played mechanically, waiting for the tide to turn. But it did not, for the simple reason that I did nothing to make it, and returned my opponent's balls feebly and without malice. In consequence, he took the set at six-two, almost before I had realized the danger. This put him one set up.

I then proceeded to get savagely annoyed. "Blast him," I said to myself as we changed courts, "him and his neat, well-

placed strokes of just the right strength, his carefully cut lobs
and his placings which never seem to run him into any risk."

Realizing that he had succeeded in imposing his type of
game on me and that I could not compete with him at it, I
decided to go all out for my strokes. Luckily, the first two
fizzers I tried for I managed to get well in the middle of my
racket, and after that, I could do nothing wrong. The doctor
waited for my fireworks to exhaust themselves, but happily,
they lasted long enough to give me the set.

We were then two sets all. "What will happen?" I asked
myself. "Shall I go to pieces, or shall I be able to carry on in
my winning vein of the last set? After all, I have taken the
match to four sets. Stop that line of thought," I adjured myself savagely. "Why the hell do you have to think in that
despondent way? Try to get the idea in your head that you can
beat him and that he never ought to have got two sets at all."

Thus ruminating, I set off at a great pace. I won the first
game and thought that all was well, but the doctor encouraged
me to excesses and took the next two.

Smack, slash, slice, bang we went at it without relaxing,
while the sweat streamed down our faces. My throat got drier
and drier, and I began to wonder whether my legs would obey
the imperative commands of my brain. So we went to four-all.
I was keeping the ball low, and as a reward I got two net
cords which justifiably annoyed my opponent. I apologized
hypocritically, realizing that I only wanted another point to
get to five-four. The doctor produced a good lob but rather
short. I dashed forward and made as if to hit the ball as hard
as I could. The doctor insensibly retreated before the menace
of my preparation and at the last second I changed my mind
and cut the ball short just over his side of the net. The doctor
realized the position a second too late. His brusque readjust-

ment caused him to slip sideways. He grunted and swore, while I tried not to look too smug at the success of my trick.

The next game went to deuce after a great struggle by the doctor, who took it to forty-fifteen almost at once. Then he made a shot which I thought was in and which beat me completely. But the umpire gave it out—bless her wherever she is now—without the least hesitation. The doctor gave her a dirty look which she promptly rewarded by chanting "Deuce. Five-four in the last set, and Dad nearly done!"

But he wasn't. Deuce followed deuce. It seemed quite impossible to win two points in succession. The play dwindled into long rallies which, as the umpire disgustedly remarked, reminded her of the final at school between the head girl and the Maths. mistress. But we were both too hot and bothered to mind these remarks. At last the doctor squared the set, and we glared at each other and wiped our faces. We went to seven-all. Then I got the fifteenth game fairly easily, owing to the doctor serving two double faults: a thing which he only did once during the match.

At last I was up again. I followed my service to the net and won the first point. We came to thirty-all. I smashed the ball from the service court, and hitting it with the wood, just managed to steer it out of the doctor's reach.

"Fluke," said the umpire dispassionately.

"Never mind," said I to myself. "One more point and I'm through. What shall it be? Shall I go out for the stroke or resolve to keep steady? Courage or caution?" I opted for caution.

We started a long ding-dong rally, but I was slowly being forced to make inadequate returns. So I threw caution to the winds and went to the net. But the doctor had plenty of time, saw me coming, and lobbed accurately over my head. I tried to stop and run back, but I slipped and fell, knocking the breath out of my body. I lay sobbing for breath on the ground, and twisting myself round I saw the ball come down. It came down exactly in the middle of the base-line, and the chalk went up in showers. I heaved myself up with the conviction that I had shot my bolt, and that the doctor would now take the set and match.

But from the umpire's seat there came an excited shriek of "Out! Game, Set and Match!"

With that, the umpire scrambled down the ladder and fled in the direction of the hotel as though the Devil were after her.

But the doctor did not pursue her. He first looked astonished and annoyed: then a slow smile came over his face. Turning, he shouted abuse after the flying form and then looked at me and smiled.

"Look here, Doctor," I said; "that's not fair. It fell on the line. Let's finish it."

The doctor grinned. "Not for a thousand pounds," said he. "*Ce que femme veut Dieu le veut.* You win. I'll give you your certificate on Monday. But now let's go and have lunch and gallons of beer."

"Oh, sir," said I, with a full heart, "how sporting of you!"

Having broken the news to my parents, in the evening of the next day I met the umpire by appointment. It was the hushed close of a sunny day, and there was a gentle brooding melancholy in the air and a sense of destiny. The earth and sea were quiet and still, like an old married couple resting before repose after a laborious day. Only the sea made slumbrous noises like the gentle breathing of a sleeping child, as the oily swell rolled slowly up to caress the gloomy cliffs.

We wandered over the close springy turf and talked bashfully of all the marvellous things we were going to do. Of how wonderful it would be if I got wounded and climbed into an ambulance that she was driving. . . .

First the twilight and then the flashes of the lighthouse illuminated the pale cameo of her youthful face. . . . I thrilled with unutterable thoughts of glory and fulfilment. Consciously I tried to realize the exquisiteness of the moment and to savour it to the full. We lingered by the hotel gate and then wandered on by silent mutual consent. A black-faced sheep looked mildly and benevolently up at us as our faces met in a tremulous inexpert kiss. Then it resumed its search for better grass with an air of complete understanding. The next embrace we accomplished better, and there followed a flow of words, love, gratitude, apologies and vows of undying faith. I demanded a keepsake (do not laugh: this was 1914) and for some time "nourished a special lock of vowèd hair" which I kept safe until, as a result of my determination to wear it next my heart and the stupidity of the War Office who designed a Tommy's uniform without an inside breast-pocket, out it fell one day in camp when I pulled out my handkerchief. It was seized by the ribald soldiery, who made an obscene mock of it till I hit one of them with the stock of a handy rifle and fled from the tent in a sobbing rage.

After a long good night, she stole away to bed and I lit a pipe, sat on the turf, and went over the events of the day, slowly trying to fix them in my mind so that I should always be able to recall them.

Next morning, as I cycled off to war, she came to the hotel gate and waved. I looked round to get a last glimpse of her, and almost collided with one of those stone walls they have in the West Country instead of hedges. Righting my bicycle with a jerk, I rode on.

CHAPTER II

ROOKY

I

AND so, my son, in a state of great exaltation at the fulfilment of his dearest wish under such pleasing circumstances,
your father pedalled on that August morning through the
sweet-smelling lanes towards great events.

But as the memory of triumph and a hurried breakfast faded
with the approach of luncheon-time, I became apprehensive
and afraid lest something should go wrong in the second act of
this play, something which would compel me to beat an in-
glorious and heartbroken retreat from the Headquarters of the
Battalion to which I was journeying. Like a tremulous mediæval traveller fingering an amulet, often I put my hand in my
pocket to touch the signed Army form setting forth the carefully edited details of my physical perfections which the good
doctor had given me, until at length, perspiring and nervous, I
presented myself and my documents at the Armoury.

To my immense relief no awkward questions were asked,
and on production of the doctor's certificate I was duly attested
and given a number. Imagine my joy when I was handed a
complete suit of khaki from the regimental store. This was a
real cause for rejoicing, for in the very early days the existing
stocks of khaki were soon exhausted and many newly joined
and fiery warriors had their martial ardour damped by having
to perform their preliminary warlike exercises in what were

usually referred to as "civvies." This was a disadvantage from
many points of view, and when, later, on Salisbury Plain, I used
to watch the new recruits drilling in blue suits and cloth caps
under showers of rain from the skies and of invective from the
sergeants, who took full advantage of the strange attire of
their squads when it came to criticism, I rejoiced again at my
luck.

In addition to my uniform, I received various impedimenta,
including a knife (clasp one, general purposes, as the issuing
sergeant described it), a razor, some soap, a pair of ferocious
boots, two sets of super-scratchy underclothing, a pair of braces,
a button-stick, and various other small articles such as cleaning-
brushes, a housewife and a hold-all, and finally, a kitbag to
hold the lot.

Of all the "issue," that which most took my fancy was my
identity disc with my number stamped on it. I was told to wear
this round my neck. On assuming it I at once imagined my
posthumous identification by an itinerant general attracted by
the heap of slain surrounding my gashed corpse.

After all this, the sergeant took down certain details concerning my age, name, etc., which he called my "perticklers";
I was told to salute all officers in uniform. An anticipatory
and grateful Government gave me an advance of pay amount-
ing to ten shillings, which sum, together with the parting
parental contribution, made me feel quite wealthy.

My previous reading decided me that it would be in character if I were to offer the sergeant a drink. This I did, and was
uncompromisingly refused by the man who, it appeared, was
an ardent Baptist and a complete abstainer. He told me that I
was free for the rest of the day, but that I must report at nine
o'clock in the evening to proceed with a draft to Salisbury Plain,
where the Battalion was training. He adjured me not to get

drunk, and I never knew whether this was a result of my recent
invitation, a stock precaution in fulfilment of a special War
Office instruction, or a tribute to my apparent virility. I hoped
the latter, but was doubtful.

So I sallied forth in my new uniform in a state of great
pride, holding myself in such an impossibly stiff and ramrod-
like fashion that presently my unaccustomed muscles cried out
and I was forced to relax a little. My chief preoccupation was
with my puttees, which were new and stiff, and refused to
cling at all affectionately to the curve of my inadequate calves.

Shortly after leaving the Armoury gates I was accosted by
a harpy. She was not unattractive, and under her cheap rouge
and powder were the face and features of a healthy country
girl, whilst beneath an air of artificial gaiety one could read
the patience of a peasant.

"Do 'ee want to come with me, young chaap?" she asked
simply in a husky voice.

But though conscious of the historical obligations of a soldier's career, I was full of pride, patriotism and Peggy.

"No, thank you," I replied with a smart salute. . . . "You
must excuse me."

With that I tendered her the ten shillings which had just
been given me by the King's representative. It had seemed to
me that the occasion needed a gesture, and having produced
an adequate one, I walked on, disgustingly satisfied with
myself.

She took the note, but soon came running after me, and putting it in my hand, said to me, "You'm a vule, but God
bless 'ee!"

Majestically I strode on, trying not to look too obviously at
my reflection in the plateglass windows of the shops. In a
jeweller's window I saw a little model of a tennis racket in sil-

ver. It was not a very good imitation, as the handle was too long and thin and the head completely circular, but it was just recognizable, so I bought it and sent it to Peggy, accompanied by a card with, "From Private . . . , No. 3402" written on it and many crosses.

As I left the post office I found myself outside the Cathedral and stood looking at it with half a mind to go in and pray. I thought of those of my mother's ancestors—my father never claimed any, being sceptically inclined—who in mediæval times used to spend the entire night before battle on their tin knees on the cold flagstones alone with their virgin swords and discomforting reflections concerning the weight and efficiency of the new French battle-axe. Just as I was wondering which would be a good patron saint to choose, I was startled by a voice behind me saying, "Hallo! Noble pile, isn't it?"

I looked round, and beheld a dark young man with bright brown eyes, dressed in khaki that was as new as mine.

"Why," he said, looking at me quizzically, "it's the lad who spurned the flesh just before I did!"

"Did she accost you, too?" I asked.

"Why, yes," he replied. "I came out just after you. What are you doing till nine o'clock?" he went on.

"I was thinking of going to look at the Cathedral," I replied.

So we went in and bathed ourselves in peace. His name was Mitchell, and he was in his second year at Oxford. After supper at an inn we went back to the Armoury.

Very soon the roll was called and the draft of recruits fell in. Fours were formed somehow and, a miscellaneous crowd, we marched raggedly out into the street, carrying our kitbags and burdened with the weight of unfamiliar packs and equipment. Outside, there was a brass band and a vociferous gang of vicarious patriots.

The band blared, the crowd cheered, there was a word of command, and off we marched, a mounted officer at the head of the column.

In my four there were a Cornish miner, a Cockney who had served twenty years in the Marines and was rejoining, and a gap-toothed old tramp who stank abominably, and who was so drunk that he kept lurching and falling against me as he marched.

On we went, singing lustily, first Tipperary and then an obscene song started by the "old sweats." It was new to me, and dealt with the amorous adventures of Bill, a seafaring person who was obviously oversexed. The tramp kept lurching up against me, and after a little, disliking his contact, I fended him off vigorously. Thereupon he let rip a stream of the foulest language I had ever heard and much of which I did not even understand. Tom Green, the ex-marine, leaned across and struck him efficiently on the chin. The tramp fell into the gutter, vomiting. We marched on.

> *"It's a long way to Tipperary,*
> *It's a long way to go,"*

howled the draft.

"Don't you mind about that blanky illegitimate son of a female dog, young feller," said Tom Green to me, referring to the tramp. "No sanguinary right to use such 'orrible unseen language at all, 'e ain't. His edu-blank-cation must have been bloody well neg-blank-lected and he dunno no better."

> *"Paddy wrote a letter to his Irish Molly-O,"*

chanted the accompanying patriots antiphonally from the pavement.

"Yes, the Irish barstard," commented my mentor cynically.

"Probably told 'er to go to the doctor to get 'er aht of 'er trouble."

We marched on.

> *"Oh, and shall Trelawny die, my boys?*
> *And shall Trelawny die?*
> *There's fifty thousand Cornishmen*
> *Shall know the reason why!"*

boomed the band inspiringly.

"Poor bleeders," said Green. "Why, they won't even blanky well know the immedjit reason for their untimely ruddy decease if they go into action with that 'orrible imitation of a namachoor soldier on a fat 'orse in charge."

On and on.

> *"The girl I left behind me,"*

wailed the band as we neared the station. I thought of Peggy, and felt romantic.

"I wonder who's kissing 'er nah," said Green inexorably.

HALT!

We piled into carriages amid deafening cheers, and the train steamed slowly out of the station: the music, the cheers and the farewells grew fainter and fainter.

Puff-puff-puff-puff! Rattle-rattle-rattle!

In a carriage that smelt of beer, shag tobacco and feet, I sat up all night exchanging confidences with Mitchell.

II

Perham Downs, Ludgershall, Southdown, Tidworth, they were full of the youth of England when I got there that late summer of 1914. Sometimes, my Ivan, I wonder if some of the eager spirits that trained there with me then leave their Valhallas to revisit the windswept downs, and in files of fours swing along in ghostly route-march, returning to sit around the tent-poles, pipes glowing, and tell each other how they died and how before they crossed they lived short months in England on the Plain.

One day perhaps you and I will quit the haunts of peace and make a sentimental pilgrimage, and I will show you where my tent used to be. I could find it now. I will show you the site of the canteen where I used to stand the old soldiers drinks and listen to their tales; where the Y. M. C. A. concerts used to be held, and that part of the road from Tidworth where the traders had their stalls, and where I used to buy brilliant yellow cake made with cottonseed oil, and coffee of the most English, as your Aunt Tatiana used to say. The mere thought of them now gives me indigestion, but in those days in the early morning after physical jerks they were Lucullan.

That period was a blur of training and exercise that left me so tired every night that I slept like a log on Mother Earth till Reveille sounded. Gradually I got as hard as nails, as fit as a fiddle and as thin as a lath. On the whole, thanks to a wise distribution of occasional drinks, a proper humility and a desperate desire to do all that was expected of me, I got on all right, and in an astonishingly short space of time had settled down and knew my way about.

I suffered the usual verbal indignities at the hands of my sergeant instructors and of the coarser of my comrades, but I soon learned to hold my tongue and swallow their sallies in silent immobility. My beginnings were greatly helped by old Sergeant Shelton, a hard-bitten reservist from the Guards, who, to his great disgust, had not been allowed to go to the Front when he rejoined, being retained as recruit instructor instead.

He was very kind to me, and smoothed my path considerably

with his sound advice and tips. He was a master of invective in the classical regular army style, but one of the kindest, soundest and bravest men I have ever met.

Old Shelton would appear on parade, the acme of smartness, and for a moment would glare ferociously at his squad. He would then bark, "Shunasyouwershun" at them. No recruit squad was ever known to have come to attention quick enough the first time to enable him to dispense with the "Asyouwershun" which he had come to add almost automatically. He exercised the same sort of hypnotism on his squads as is exerted by popular comedians on their audiences. He had us hanging on his lightest word, and I have seldom wanted to do anything so much as I wished to fulfil his word of command in such a manner as to gain his very occasional praise.

I can easily recall and see him in his trim khaki, rows of medal ribbons, neat fierce waxed moustache, shining buttons, wrinkled polished boots, and swagger cane tucked under arm.

"Squad," he would shout in a tremendous voice. "At the first sound of the word of command . . . For inspection port hip. . . . Steady there, No. 3 in the rear rank, wait for it, WAIT FOR IT! For inspeckshun porrt HIP. 'Orrible! Bloody bad! Now listen . . ."

Then he would reel off the detail, and we would do it again. By this time he would appear likely to burst with rage at any moment. If the third attempt was not successful, he would run his bloodshot eye rapidly along the apprehensive ranks and seizing on some luckless wight would roar:

"You there. No. 5 in the rear rank. Left 'and firmly grasping the rifle at the upper band and at abart the level of the left breast, I said. Move yer left 'and hup and hout. 'Orribly lowbreasted you must be. Remind me of one o' them Zulu women, you do! STOP LAUGHING. You, there! No. 8 in the front rank! Fer 'eaven's sake tuck yer tummy in! I'll have yer sent to a maternity in a nambulance. Now try it again. At the first sound . . ." And so on.

A great man. I hope he survived and is living on his pension, with opportunities of comparing the present unfavourably with the past over an occasional glass.

Then there were the physical-training people. These were perfect devils, who made us run, hop, skip, jump and stab straw-stuffed sacks with the utmost ferocity. "In. Out. On guard," they would yell, and I, sweating, would go through the motions to be greeted with hoots of ignominy.

"What the 'ell do you think you're a-doin' of? You there, with the glasses." (I was always an easy mark.) "Put more beef into it! Anybody would think you were"—and here would follow a Rabelaisian image of some appropriateness. "Now, then. Through 'is bloody guts and out the other side."

In my tent there were twelve people, which was too many for comfort. On one side of me was my old enemy the tramp, who had been fished from the gutter, and who for alphabetical reasons was always near; and on the other, a mining student who was afterwards killed. Mitchell was in another tent. One night I came in late from a Y. M. C. A. concert and, stumbling in the dark, capsized all the twelve rifles that were piled round the tentpole. The tramp was foolishly sleeping with his head to the pole and all the rifles fell on his face. He awoke with a yell and began to blubber like a child. There was general disturbance. The corporal in charge of the tent shouted for order, and lit a candle. The rifles were rearranged. Moved by the sight of the old man weeping, I ventured an apology. Like a flash he turned on me.

"So 'twas ye. Ye blank, blank . . ." he shouted, and then, before in the dim light I could see what he was doing, he grabbed a bayonet, unsheathed it, and made a lunge at me which would certainly have finished my martial career had I not jumped quickly aside. As it was, the point went through my tunic and just scratched the skin. I smote him violently in the tummy and he collapsed in a heap.

Everybody woke up, and there was a lot of noise. But public opinion was on my side. Had I not recently received from home a large ham, cakes and chocolate which I had shared out equally with the tent? "Making friends with the gammon of unrighteousness," Mitchell had described it, when I enlarged on the good results of the division.

"Sneakin' old vule," said the corporal to the tramp. "Stab people, would 'ee? You'm vor aarderly-room to-morrow. Dirty vorrin trick."

Tom Green, who had constituted himself my special protector and mentor, then chipped in. He sat up, and regarding the prostrate tramp, apostrophized him:

"You old image. Lying a-vomiting and a-bringing hup like a whoremongering bleedin' biby."

The palpable absurdity of this epithet amused me so much that I went to sleep chuckling, and slept till Reveille. Mitchell and I at once adopted this incongruous expletive for general purposes.

Swearing is a curious thing. Before I joined the Army, I suppose I hardly ever swore. In about two months, however, I had an extensive and obscene vocabulary, and I am ashamed to say that a stubbed toe or a burnt finger still enables me to regain my old proficiency, so that I am always afraid of forgetting myself in the haunts of the highbrow and the virtuous.

Excursions succeeded alarms on the Plain. We were always being paraded in war kit and standing by to proceed to an unknown destination. Once we stood to for three hours, and apparently only just escaped joining Winston Churchill's Naval Brigade on their Antwerp adventure. The King inspected us and so did Kitchener and a host of War Office generals, but for a time nothing happened.

III

I was very friendly with Mitchell, who was in another Company, and also with Tom Green, with whom I would exchange beer for lurid reminiscence and soldierly wrinkles.

One evening Mitchell danced up. I have never since met anyone so peculiarly alive as he was. There was something faun-like and unworldly in his vitality. He seemed to glow with a life of his own and to have a capacity for full experience and enjoyment.

"Have you, soldier," said he, "a pusher?"

"No," said I. "What is it?"

"Don't you know," said he, "that 'pusher' is the generic term applied by the soldiers of this Wessex Division to their inamorata, long-haired chums, or lady friends?"

"Long-haired chum? I thought that was only used by a Yeoman addressing his steed," I replied. "But go on. Have you got one?"

"Yes," said he, "and a tarrable vine piece she be tu, as they say round here. *Tout ce qu'il y a de magnifique!* But, look here: she has a sister. Will you make a four? She won't play singles."

I agreed, and so that evening we swaggered out in our best uniforms and met Sally and Rosie. They were the two daughters of a Cockney sergeant-major who was stationed at Tidworth.

Mitchell took Sally and Rosie took me.

As we walked down a shady lane a closer fusion of the two figures in front and a glutinous noise made me surmise that Mitchell had kissed Sally. It seemed to me that I ought to do the same thing by Rosie. But . . .

"Nothing doing," said Rosie. "A kiss don't 'urt nobody, but we only just met, and I'm a girl as likes to go slow."

So we marched decorously through the country lanes hand in hand.

I asked Mitchell how he had progressed.

"Oh," said he, "she turned me down flat. Most devastating she was. 'Get a girl in trouble, would yer? No twilight sleep for me,' was the burden of her cry."

"What did you do?" I asked.

"Oh, I gave it up and resumed a less intimate rôle. She may be a piece, but she's certainly a piece of resistance!"

We often met afterwards and went to the cinema to laugh at Chaplin, and hold hands.

The day before we left for "an unknown destination" we met in the evening, and Rosie brought the exquisite Mitchell a cake which she had made. He was affected, and to cover his emotion, pretended not to be.

"Rosie," said he, striking an attitude and declaiming, "I shall always wear it next my heart. If on the gory field of battle I should fall pierced by a German bullet, you will at least have the consolation of knowing that the power of modern projectiles has never before been equalled. The body of Private Mitchell was found surrounded by heaps of enemy slain. It was afterwards discovered that the bullet which caused his decease had passed through one plum cake, several photographs of nude females, two Bibles, a mass of bills and his identity disc."

He went on:

> *" 'O moan and weep and keen and cry,*
> *Virgins and maids and such,*
> *For worms are crawling now close by*
> *The skin you loved to touch.' "*

"My! 'Ow 'e do go on," said Rosie.

" 'E is a one," agreed Sally.

We sat on a stile. All around was the smell of grass and fields and earth. The sun shone hazily through the dusty air. Great bees zoomed busily about on business. Up on the hill a distant lorry chugged steadily. A far-away bugle blew and the sun went slowly down. Its dying rays fell on the cake, which perspired gently through its grease-proof wrapping. Mitchell and Sally wandered away.

Rosie looked at me roguishly.

"Keep off the grass," she whispered, looking at it. A pause, and then, "Oh, well, as you're off to-morrow, we'll get off to-night."

I wish you the same luck, my son, when your turn comes.

I walked back to camp with mixed feelings. In the canteen I met Mitchell.

"Well?" I said.

He put down his glass, wiped his mouth with his sleeve.

"I have always such an aftermath," he said. "There is a Latin phrase . . ."

But it was lost in a beery chorus from the old sweats, who knew enough to drink while they could.

Curious times, my Vanja!

CHAPTER III

INDIA

I

At the end of September 1914 I started out *en route* for India, on the first of my travels. Since then, I have been travelling continually, and have been to a very large number of extremely interesting and distant places. You will seldom find them described, as I share Kinglake's objection to people who "ruin the ruins of Baalbek in eight or ten cold lines."

I have, however, done my best to learn about the countries I have been lucky enough to visit and to avoid the Anglo-Saxon detachment imputed to Mr. Phileas Fogg of *Around the World in Eighty Days*, who, if you remember, on one occasion "descended the entire splendid valley of the Ganges without even thinking of looking at it." When I descended the entire splendid valley in question, I did not play whist, as did Mr. Fogg, but gazed hard at the scenery. All the same, I cannot describe it to you. Unfortunately, the more one travels, the more Fogg-like one is apt to become.

These, however, were considerations which did not worry me when, after a frenzied day of packing up, standing to and general fuss and bustle, I found myself, in October 1914, in the bowels of a trooper bound for Bombay. Our martial ardour had been sadly dashed when we were informed that instead of leaping straight at the enemy we were going to be sent to the East to replace regular troops who were going to do the leaping instead. However, we were told that it would not be for long, that our service was more honourable than staying at home till we had completed our training, and that we should have a chance of seeing active service "somewhere in the East." It caused a lot of grumbling at the time, and a special pronouncement from Kitchener, to the effect that we should have the same honours as if we had gone to the Front, was made to pacify us. A promise which was not properly kept, I may add, but most of the grumblers were killed before the War ended, anyway.

I shudder now at the thought of having to repeat the discomforts of that voyage, but at the time my patriotic ardour was a sure shield against discomfort, which, indeed, I almost welcomed as evidence of sacrifice. This state of mind did not entirely disappear till the War had ended. The more I had to put up with the more I seemed to be justifying my existence and my admission to the status of "vir" and defender of the Empire. Also, I looked on everything as experience, which it is easy to do when young. It is harder now when one has had so much and the *rendement* therefrom is not so marked.

On the voyage, I drilled, did fatigues, managed to find a bridge four, smoked, slept, and ate what I could stomach. The food was scandalous, and I remember bribing a steward with ten shillings for the reversion of the officers' mess ice-cream bucket.

We always seemed to be being inoculated or vaccinated, or having quinine poured into us, and I felt that I was becoming a perambulating chemical formula.

When we were paraded for our first inoculation, just in front of me, in the file awaiting puncture, there was a big burly tin miner. We stood on the deck with our sleeves rolled up and— like "x" marking the spot—a dab of iodine on our arms, watched the doctor sterilizing his hypodermic in the flame of a little spirit-lamp. My miner turned to me, and in an agonized whisper asked me, "Whaat to 'ell 'e be a-heating lil needle for?"

I replied with great solemnity that it was essential that the needle should be red-hot before being stuck into one. As he stepped up to get his shot, he turned deathly pale, and fainting into my insufficient arms, bore me to the deck. I explained my joke to the doctor, and he reproved me with a twinkle.

At night I used to go forward, lean over the side of the ship, and watch the white water racing away into the darkness while the whole ship hummed and quivered as it drove onwards. I would try to read my future in the waters, and then, looking up at the black velvet sky, dusty with diamonds, I would be filled with a great surge of exultant expectation of imminent great events.

Stevenson said it much better. "The effect of night, of any flowing water, of lighted cities, of ships, of the open ocean, calls up in my mind an army of anonymous desires and pleasures. Something we feel should happen: we know not what, yet we proceed in quest of it."

Even now, after a good dinner in the restaurant car, I can recapture this zest as I return to my *wagon-lit* along the dim-lit warm corridors of the swaying Orient Express, and, as the train rattles through France or Italy on to the troublous and romantic Balkans, I can be so exhilarated that I start to sing under the kindly cloak of the noise of the wheels.

As I can never remember more than a few verses of the songs I do remember, and as I dislike being tied to tunes which I always render incorrectly, I often fall back on the printed public notices abounding in foreign trains, which I bellow with the maximum bravura, and how I like. "E periglioso sporgesi," I chant operatically out of the window, sure that no one can hear

me but myself and perhaps some lingering Roumanian plate-
layer, and then "Nicht hinauslehnen" in the tragic accents of
Gilda waiting for Sparafouchili to stab her. It is a magnificent
game to play by oneself, and I commend it to you. Once,
though, I leaned out of my window and was rendering in a
magnificent recitative "Sotto el lavabo se trova un vaso," a
phrase which, in my opinion, lends itself to such treatment,
when I realized that an attractive young woman was leaning
out of the next window to mine and thoroughly enjoying herself. Yes. I will get a lot out of travel, though the degree of
intensity is less.

I am beginning to realize that the chances of my being met
at the station by a mysterious veiled lady who will invite me
to her magnificent limousine and subsequent enthralling
adventures, based on my resemblance to the long-lost
Grand Duke or the Commander of the Ogpu, are not really
good.

After these intervals of wake-watching and star-gazing I
would go up on deck, where we were allowed to sleep, and
make up my hammock. Soon would come Tom Green, slightly
mellow from collaboration with the officers' mess waiters, and
Mitchell. I would lie and listen to Tom's yarns and watch the
sable sky and the Milky Way slide by the dark funnel.

Green was a remarkable man. He must have been about
fifty-two or fifty-three when I met him, which at that time
seemed to me a considerable age. He had been all over the
world in his service with the Marines. He had a distinct talent
for story-telling, and was an inveterate reader of newspapers
and novels, from which he had obtained a truly remarkable
vocabulary and facility of expression. He loved to talk in
clichés, and though he never lost a marvellous Cockney accent,
he had, through experience and study, acquired a good deal of

knowledge and almost an education. He was about 5 feet 10 inches in height, had sun-burnt, regular features, white teeth and a clipped military moustache. He was invariably neatly dressed, brave as a lion and very popular.

He would undoubtedly have risen in his profession had it not been that, at intervals of about a month, his normal somewhat heavy consumption of beer would rise to unparalleled heights, and he would end up in the guardroom, unless his friends got hold of him in time and dragged him forcibly away to sleep. He was extremely kind to me from the first moment that I met him, and he seemed to think that his superior experience and knowledge of various parts of the world would be recognized by myself, and I think it seemed to him that both Mitchell and myself would appreciate him more than those who had neither his experience nor our education. Tom would regale us with yarns from his woman-strewn path; there were musketry exercises, parades and fatigues. So the voyage passed uneventfully. We went through the Canal, glimpsed Aden and, after a brief scare about the *Emden*, finally dropped anchor in Bombay Harbour. After the usual inexplicable military delays, we got into troop trains and proceeded up-country.

II

At a wayside station in Baroda we stopped for a meal, and the Gaekwar's son came down with escort and band to have a look at us. I was rather pleased at this, because I had often read of the Gaekwar of Baroda in pre-War days as being a typical Indian potentate, and somehow the strains of his band seemed to underline and make real the fact that I had actually gone to India as a private soldier.

There then were the Gaekwar's bandsmen, dark, scarlet-uniformed and bootless, the sun shining on their polished brass instruments, their perspiring cheeks extended and the dust showing white on their brown feet.

I and my companions sat on the ground listening to the music and eating bully beef and biscuits. The troops made lewd and licentious remarks about those who were straining their guts to entertain them. It caused me pain and discomfort to hear their rude commentary, but the musicians of Baroda did not seem to mind, and grinned at us benevolently after their tune was done. I sat and let the music transport me to dreams of Begums, huge jewels in secret temples, beautiful Hindu maidens of vast wealth and temperament, Border fights, the Hindu Kush, the Pamirs and Central Asia.

This journey was destined to linger in my memory, because during it, for the first time in my life, I became definitely lousy. There were lice in the carriages in which we slept and lived, and some of them quartered themselves on me. It was a terrible shock at first, but, under the intelligent instructions of the experienced Tom Green, I soon got rid of them.

Now that the memory of the Great War is fading, and mass-deluding leaders tend to romanticize both international and civil war, it would perhaps be a good thing to take the younger generation—with the older surviving generals and politicians— and make them deliberately lousy and live in trenches for a week without hope of soap and water until they crawled.

As well as subduing the militarists, such treatment would also be efficacious as a useful corrective for some of our younger intellectuals and older doctrinaires who contemplate the disruption of existing society and the shooting down of the proletariat with such lighthearted abandon. As a reminder of common humanity and fallibility, a louse or two is hard to beat.

I do not know in what horrible civil welter, in what private adventure, in what war, in what cataclysmal breakdown of the

economic and financial system you may first make the acquaintance of these loathsome pale parasites, my son. But if you do—
perhaps as a civil war prisoner in some red, white or brown
prison—you may be comforted in the first shock of repulsion
and disgust by the thought that they are as old as humanity,
and that, accompanying the migrations, armies, navies, revolutions and pilgrimages of history, they have assisted at all the
most important convulsions of the world.

Catherine the Great, who was a queen of temperament, used
to have her would-be lovers medically examined before admit-
ting them to their exacting though well-remunerated duties.
One of these aspirants was once rejected by the Countess Bruce,
who served the Empress as a sort of preliminary tester of energies and excellencies, and who disqualified an otherwise well-
equipped young Guardsman because he was acting as host to
one of these insects. At least, so I read in a manual of Russian
history destined by the Bolsheviks to the "debunking" of any
atavistic young fervent in whom the previous accomplishments
of humanity under a capitalist system might have produced a
measure of dissatisfaction with the drab present.

So, should you meet them, Ivan, I recommend to you the
immediate adoption of Tom Green's method of exposing the
undervest and pants on a populous ant-heap, otherwise the
Commissar's wife may find that her class consciousness is not
sufficiently blunted to allow her to help you escape.

III

After some time in India I found myself promoted to the
dizzy rank of lance-corporal and in charge of a small rest-
camp perched up in the foothills of the Himalaya. With me
were Mitchell and Green and two tin miners, whom we used
to refer to as Boanerges, because they were so flatulent.

It was a pleasant interlude. The various detachments march-ing between railhead and the hill station used to burst over-night on to our quiet little mountain meadow with its bell tents and marquee waiting for them. Then for a night there was noise, bustle, beer, singing and twinkling lights. Next morning they would swing away up the mountain road shouting songs, and leaving us to clear up the orange-peel and litter and appre-ciate their absence.

Sometimes grizzled Regular Indian Army officers, either on leave, or going to France or to the Persian Gulf or the Frontier, would come to see what sort of people we were, and some of them would prefer to stay with us rather than at the dak bun-galow a little farther off along the tonga road. They were usu-ally somewhat unapproachable before luncheon, but soon would thaw and tell us tales of Frontier wars and old days in India. Sometimes they would take us out hunting with them, and on one never-to-be-forgotten day, I shot a panther in the behind with a service rifle. It got away, being only wounded, and I had to invent a fictitious night alarm by rifle thieves in order to be able to account for the expenditure of ammunition to a cold-blooded quartermaster-sergeant. The next time I shot at anything so large was in Bolivia, and I remember how the vision of Indian *khud* and valley came into my mind as I looked along the sights.

Some who afterwards achieved renown shared our tent, and others still who died. On the whole, a very fine lot of people, and not quite like any others I have met. India seemed to have stamped them.

In the wonderful hills we camped and dreamed, played, swam, fished and rode hill ponies. At night we played cards or talked interminably under the moon.

Our enjoyment of this idyllic interlude was marred by the

remembrance that fighting was going on at the Front. It was in vain that we comforted ourselves with the thought that one day we too should go, and that in any case someone had to do our job. Still, the fact remained that we were ingloriously comfortable and that others were dying.

It was wonderfully placed, that camp. "He who would try to describe in words the beauties of Himalaya is mad." But sometimes I can still recall and conjure up the unearthly beauty of Indian moonrise on the eternal snows. I can see Trisul and Nunda Devi shooting up and up into the void, where the stars winked like lights in lovely ladies' chambers. Another world it seemed was there, with all the horns of elfland blowing and certainly peopled by uncommon shades, the souls of great heroes and lovers.

Sometimes, when we rode out on hired hill ponies and took the road which led to the neighbouring hot-weather station, which was the civil headquarters, we would catch glimpses of Mrs. Hawksbee, Major Gadsby, Strickland and other Kipling-esque creatures out riding. I wonder whether you will read about them with the same interest as I used to in my youth. They would look at us curiously, for we were an undisciplined lot and certainly broke the Mulvaney and Ortheris traditions as regards our kit, which often contained relics of a former unmilitary existence, such as cricket blazers and ancient grey flannel trousers; Tom Green, however, was an exception, and with his quiff, topee slightly on one side, cigarette pendent from the upper lip, shiny boots and swagger cane, always looked the perfect Tommy.

One night, Mitchell came back very late for supper, and contemptuously refused the uninteresting minced cutlets which by soldier tradition had been kept hot for him. "Espud Cut-leys," our little native cook used to call them. Here, Ivan, I must tell you that one day we had caught his predecessor making these cutlets by the simple and primitive process of kneading the minced meat and the potato and flour into the requisite shape by putting the mess into his armpit and imparting a circular motion to his arm as he squatted in abysmal Asiatic filth. We chased him down the *khud* with maledictions, and subsisted on tins till the memory left us. Mitchell informed me that he had met an extraordinary individual called Mugton who had recently retired from the Supply and Transport Corps and was living in the neighbourhood. They had dined together, and we were to go again to his house the next night.

The next day we sallied forth in our cleanest uniforms, and I made the old gentleman's acquaintance. He was a fat, strange old man, clad in dingy duck and ringed like Saturn with a gaudy cummerbund. From this, attached by a piece of green silk, there hung a small Bible. He was obviously suffering from religious mania, but his cook was marvellous. He gave us an extraordinary meal, which could only have been properly appreciated by a personality composed of equal parts of Lucullus and Savonarola. It was a weird mixture of grace and gluttony and gloom and gusto. After each course we both gave thanks, he to the Deity loudly, and I quietly to the cook. We had a sermon with the sweet and a canticle with the coffee.

After this, we practised buckshooting on a very excellent miniature rifle range which the old gentleman had fixed up, and which he always had transported with him wherever he went. The buck were cardboard figures which careered across the target at a great pace. They were operated by an ingenious device, which was actuated by the opponent of the person who was shooting. Mitchell had told me that further invitations depended upon the old boy's victory, and when I operated the device, never were buck so slow and leaden as those that traced their plodding way across the target; and none so sprightly and lightfooted, so given to fitful movement, as when he did the same for me. By the exercise of these artless methods the old gentleman won easily, which pleased him mightily. When the scores were added up and he found himself at the top of the poll, he went down on his knees and publicly gave thanks that the Lord had not visited his many notorious sins and excesses upon his physical members.

The wife of this extraordinary and interesting person was a lady with a colourless personality, an overflowing bust and a fat chuckle. She reminded me of an elderly female cousin with whom I used to do duty dances at sedate *sauteries* in the parish hall at home, and who had a bunched soft bust which used to repulse my chin, the whole being contained by a brooch that scratched. Mrs. Mugton's waist was only distinguishable by the junction of her blouse and skirt. At times, and when she sighed, which she did often, a sort of hiatus, neutral zone or interregnum appeared, and this was covered by Heaven knows what undies or sundries of warm flannel. She was completely intimidated by her spouse, and her greatest pleasure seemed to be to listen to his views on Hell. At times affrighted—albeit pleasurably, it seemed—by the visions of worms and burns produced by the old man, she would shiver and vaguely protest the efficacy of faith and works as a shield and buckler against these horrors. I remember thinking that she ought to be an authority on bucklers, at any rate.

The daughter was a pale, intense scrap of a thing, who was comparatively untouched by the prevailing religious mania, and who was obviously impressed by the graceless and handsome Mitchell.

Old Mugton told me all about his conversion while Mitchell and the girl went for a walk in the garden and the old lady snoozed over her knitting. This, apparently, dated from an occasion on the Frontier when he had been left in the open for two days, having been shot by a sniper when riding alone. He said that, as he lay, the Apostle Paul had visited him, and after dealing sternly with illicit percentages levied on official purchases and various other difficult questions, had sealed him for the Lord and left him. I remember that his phraseology conjured up a vision of his plump and prostrate form extended over a mountain path while an angel bent over him busy with sealing-wax and wafer.

I went once again after this and listened to a long and frank dissertation on the lusts of the flesh and how to mortify them. After this, I gave up going, because such things always make me feel supremely uncomfortable, and because it seemed hardly decent to take advantage of his religious madness, eat his food and laugh at him. Mitchell, however, continued to frequent the house, and had an undoubted success with the daughter. Poor Mitchell. It was his last bit of luck before he died of dysentery in Mesopotamia, whither he went with a draft for which I unsuccessfully applied. What a death for that gay spirit! Just wasting away in discomfort and sobbing weakness. I know, for I almost went out the same way some time later.

IV

I was not left long in my little Paradise in the Hills, but before I left it I managed to get leave to go on various trips to some interesting places—Almora, Peshawar, Dera Ismail Khan and some others.

From Almora I sallied out with a friend on a country road that led eventually in the direction of Thibet, and though I never saw a Geelong Ringding Lama, yet I did see one of the more ordinary varieties in a brown robe with a prayer-wheel in which the Buddhist prayer—*Om, Ma, Ni, Pad, Me, Hum*—was whirled round many times a day, and I had the curiosity to enquire when I got back what it meant, Ivan, and this is the answer, if you can make anything out of it.

> *"Om"—of the heavenly world;*
> *"Ma"—of the world of spirits;*
> *"Ni"—of the human world;*
> *"Pad"—of the animal world;*
> *"Me"—of the world of tantalized ghosts; and*
> *"Hum"—*

I have forgotten, but it has something to do with Hell. It is the repetition of this prayer, produced by the spinning of the wheel, that shuts the doors of the various worlds and admits of untrammelled meditation, and I often say it to myself when I listen to the long speeches of the delegates to the Seventeenth International Preparatory Commission on the Unification of Methods of Instruction of Grandparents in Egg Suction.

I soldiered at Delhi, Lucknow, Bareilly and various other towns. I went on courses of instruction all over that vast and marvellous country. I saw Afridi tribesmen from over the Frontier, and I learnt to guard my rifle like my life; I saw how the Frontier was guarded, and many more things in India than I could tell you about.

Once, I remember, we sallied out from camp at Bareilly on an intensive course of field training, and marched all day along one of the great roads of India. White and dusty it was, but lined with trees which gave a pleasant shade when we "fell out on the left of the road." On either side were fields of paddy and rice. Natives clad in white flowing robes trotted along past us, singing tuneless songs in monotonous falsetto voices; ekkas crowded with Hindus and drawn by thin, miserable ponies, gharries, ox-carts, an occasional motor-car, and all sorts of conveyances, gave us their dust as we marched steadily on. My most constant souvenir of India is of route-marching along a never-ending road; that, and the curious, dusty, ammoniac smell of the bazaars.

As part of the baggage guard on that occasion, I was in charge of a supply and transport wagon, loaded with tentage, and driven by a turbaned transport driver who encouraged his two magnificent white oxen with throaty cries and, when this method did not bring results, by twisting their tails and taking a stick to their rumps. They were most tiring to march behind, as their progress consisted of a five-minute laze, during which we would fall well behind the main column, followed by a sharp trot to catch up.

Eventually, after a long and exhausting march, we came to our camping-ground. I had been practising my Hindustani with the driver, who had told me, in a mixture of his language and mine, that we were going to a ghosty place, where dwelt all manner of spooks and spirits. There had been a battle there in the old time, and even now, during the floods, the fields showed red with blood.

After I had handed over my supply waggon, I went to inspect a monument which had been erected to the memory of the British officers and men in the service of John Company who had been killed there in a battle with the Rohillas. To my astonishment, I saw that one of them, a captain, had the same name and initials as myself.

That night I was put on guard, and all night, in imagination, I saw shadowy Rohillas with large knives engage in mortal combat with old-fashioned British officers wearing funny-shaped sun helmets and mutton-chop whiskers. The result was that I mistook a wandering draught ox for a rifle thief, and roused the whole camp unnecessarily. It was some time before this incident was allowed to be forgotten.

Later on came unrest and rumours of an imminent uprising in the densely populated native city not far from our lines.

We marched through the town with fixed bayonets, whilst the natives in teeming thousands packed the filthy streets, and all business was for the moment suspended. I can still remember what a strange mixture of fear, hate, hostility, resignation and curiosity there was in the gaze of those sullen multitudes who so outnumbered us as the battalion marched by.

During this period I had a small detached post to guard near an old fort which had played a rôle in the Mutiny, and from which during the day one could sometimes see an elephant belonging to a local bigwig as it was marched along the road to and from its work. I used to like this place, where one could sit in the shade and see the life of India roll by, and have amusing conversations with all sorts of people about their having or not having passes.

One night, on this guard, I was coming back from posting a sentry when I heard a scuffle in the road outside. My heart pounded, but I dropped over the wall into the road and nearly skewered myself on my rifle and bayonet. In the moonlight I saw a little group of three natives attacking another native. As I came up, with my rifle at the ready, the assailants ran away. I approached the one who had been attacked, gingerly. He was swaying on his feet, and to my surprise, addressed me in unmistakably English English. He told me not to fire at the retreating figures, as I was about to, or turn out the guard, but to smuggle him behind the guardroom, let him sit down and give him a drink of water; which I did. He told me to make light of the incident with the guard, who were mostly asleep,

and to make no report at all. I did as I was told, as his voice
and manner were obviously trustworthy and authoritative. He
said he was on special work, but would not tell me any more.
After resting and washing his cuts and bruises, he asked my
name and disappeared over the wall again.

About two weeks later I got by parcel post a silver cigarette-
case with my name engraved on it and the inscription "For
common sense." I lost this later, or rather, it was stolen from
me by a hospital orderly when I was wounded. But on the
whole, I think I would rather have been told all about the
secret mission.

Once I went on shikar leave with John, my friend, and
Green. We found very little to shoot except a number of peacocks. I suppose that to shoot a sitting peacock—they used to
roost in the trees, and one could see them silhouetted against
the moonlit sky—is probably an unutterable crime in really
slaughterous circles, but it was rather fun, and they are not
bad to eat.

On the other hand, we raised the anger of the ryots, who
regard them as semi-sacred, and the whole village attacked us
with sticks and stones. Although we could have defended ourselves with our rifles and guns, yet I decided that hasty retreat
was the best policy. We felt rather guilty about the peacocks,
and had we added a villager to our bag, even in self-defence,
it would have been a horrible thing. So we ran away along a
dried-up water-course.

I tripped and fell, and some of the bank came away. Lo and
behold, I found myself gazing, as I lay and gasped for breath,
at the decayed and stinking face of a fairly recently killed and
half-buried man. His face and skull were battered in, and he
had evidently been buried hastily by the person who had killed
him; later, the river must have washed the bank away, so that

my fall had completed his disinterment. I got up and ran even faster. The pursuit checked on arriving at this grisly spectacle and made off the way it came.

For sport there were hockey matches with native regimental teams, railway sides and an occasional civilian side. There were mixed corporals' mess dances, to which came strangely speaking Eurasians with vivid quick-flowering—and even quicker fading —daughters, and where everybody drank beer and danced elaborately ceremonial dances.

One day, at the end of 1915, soon after I had heard that my brother had been killed at Ypres, it all came to an end. Pack-laden and surrounded by beery, sweating and singing fellow-soldiers, we swung and hiccuped to the station with torches flaring in the Indian night, the band playing the regimental tune and all the world out to see us go.

At last we entrained, and saw the last of India after a terrible cross-country journey. A marvellous country. I hope you will go there one day. I should like to go again, Ivan.

CHAPTER IV

THE EYE OF AL YAMAN

I

IN January 1916, the battalion with its baggage was spewed
out of the guts of a foul troopship—may you never, in the
Red Sea heat, experience the combined odours of camel flesh,
rancid butter, rotting vegetables, deck poultry and crowded
humanity—and landed at Aden.

If, Ivan, you take the trouble to look at the map and find
the narrow Red Sea, you will soon discover the mysterious coasts
of Arabia. It has always fascinated me to think that so near—
comparatively—to the great civilizations there existed apart and
unknown this secret veiled country with its fierce religion, its
untravelled burning deserts and its strange medley of tribes.
The Pamirs, Bokhara, Tiflis, Turkestan, Abyssinia and Amazon
—and I have been to or near to all of these—have thrilled me,
but Arabia Deserta and Arabia Felix, the Rub-al-Khali, Mus-
cat and Trucial Oman, with the names of their lovers and con-
querors, Doughty, Thomas, Lawrence and the rest, have always
contained for me the quintessence of romance, so that even now
in staid Geneva I feel sometimes like the subject of Walter de
la Mare's poem:

> *"Still eyes look coldly upon me,*
> *Cold voices whisper and say*
> *He is crazed with the spell of Far Arabia,*
> *They have stolen his wits away."*

51

Though I never trudged across the dusty Hadramaut or crossed the waterless Rub-al-Khali on a pedigree Bisharin camel, yet I did at times go into Al Yaman on a camel or a donkey—I always preferred the donkey—doing reconnaissances, and depending entirely on my wits, powers of endurance and rifle to escape from death at the hands of hostile Turks and the villainous and untrustworthy Arabs of the Hushaibah, the Awashib and the other "sanguinary Bidoos," as Tom Green described them. I have slept at night in deserted Arab watch-towers and stayed hid for hours in *hod* and *ghadir;* for many a blazing morning I have lain sweating and thirsty behind a *tel*, scanning the horizon through glasses for the sight of the enemy, and all the time with an uneasy feeling that he had worked round unseen and was between me and my honest picket of waiting comrades. Once he was, and Allah was merciful, for the "Bidoos" came back again in the evening without seeing me. I hastened them on with five rounds rapid, which was the purest swank and waste of ammunition.

I suppose, Ivan, that I should begin with the history of Aden, the eye of Al Yaman, and how we came to be fighting there. I fear that you must resign yourself to a few words about the history and background of the spot where Father—to use that magnificently brief and descriptive phrase invented by the troops—"stopped one," and shed large quantities of his hot and youthful blood upon the age-old desert.

It began with India and the trade route. We needed a harbour, a coaling station and a revictualling point for the ships going to India. At the beginning of the nineteenth century we tried Perim, a dry and rocky island. We still have it, and it is used as a coaling station, but it had no water and the harbour facilities were not good, so that it did not develop; then we tried Socotra, which we wrested from the local Sultan as a reward for his incredible obstinacy in refusing to sell us his domain. Socotra turned out to be full of fever and was later abandoned.

We watched and waited. Then Lord Palmerston did a deal with the Sultan of Turkey, and we obtained a treaty covering our right to unrestricted trade all over the Turkish Empire. Aden was then recognized by us as being part of the Turkish Empire. Consequently, we could trade in it. From having trading facilities we progressed to protecting our rights. The next step was easy. A pretext was arranged: the local Arabs were offered the choice of gold or steel; with heroic stupidity they opted for steel, but cupidity would have given the same result: the warships appeared, the guns roared, and Sultan Muhsin gave up the struggle and retired with his Awashib Arabs to the hinterland.

So in we came to Aden in 1859, and ever since then it has been a permanent garrison to which have come in course of time all the county regiments of England, the Scots, the Irish and the Welsh. As I wandered round the fortifications I would see carved in the wood or stone the names of Englishmen—Smiths, Browns, Atkinses, Cloughs, Cobbets—from all the shires. Usually there was a date, sometimes a girl's name, and often a terse comment on the place or climate.

Thus a footing was secured. It became necessary to secure the hinterland. To have occupied this would have been costly and difficult. So the local tribes were put under a Protectorate regime. The Protectorate covered—and still does—a narrow strip of land bounded on the south, to use the jargon of the textbooks, by the Arabian Sea from the Bab-el-Mandeb to Balhaf; on the east by the Hadramaut, and on the north by a vexed frontier which divides it more in theory than in fact from the territories ruled over by a scoundrelly yet picturesque

prelate known as the Imam Yahya of San'a. He still lives, and
only recently tried a fall with the formidable Ibn es Seoud,
who nearly but not quite swallowed him up.

In this territory there lived and roamed various Arab tribes,
whose rulers, Sultans, Ameers, Imams and Sheikhs, intrigued
with and fought each other under the Arabian sun, the mercy
of Allah and the "protection" of Great Britain.

The chiefs who were protected ranged from full-blown Sultans wearing turbans, bediamonded aigrettes, scimitars with
jewelled hilts, magnificent robes, and all the trappings of the
Asiatic potentate, to brown Sheikhs clad only in a loin-cloth
and the odour of sanctity.

In return for the protection afforded, they had to undertake
not to quarrel too violently with their neighbours, and more
particularly to refrain from diplomatic, financial, oil concession
or other flirtations with any wandering Commendatores, Mes-
sieurs les Colonels, Bimbashis, Palkovniks, Kommandants or
other emissaries of foreign Powers who might wish to entice
them into alliances prejudicial to our hold on Aden and the
route to India.

In 1905, when I was peacefully at school, the British came
to an arrangement with the Turks—then our stolid, fatalistic,
inefficient yet surprisingly tough and virile rivals in Islamic
Imperialism—by which the latter recognized the geographical
limits of the Protectorate. Such then was the Aden Protectorate
at the beginning of the Great War, with its various tribes: the
Subbiahas, who are brave and false; the Fadhlis, who are ruled
by the Sultan of Lahj, of whom more anon; the Awaleq, who
are primitive and tough, not even respecting Allah; the Wahi-
dis, the Alawis, the Awashib, the Aqrabis, and many other
freebooting sons of the Prophet. Away to the north-east was
all mysterious Arabia.

Early on in the War there had been minor operations on the

Island of Sheikh Saad, opposite Perim, and then one day in
the summer of 1915 the Turks, who had an Army Corps in the
Yemen, appeared in force near Lahj, not far from Aden. The
Sultan resisted, and a force was sent from Aden to assist him.
The result was disastrous. The Abdali Sultan was killed—it is
said by our side, in error—as he retreated at night, and a British battalion came near to complete disaster. Altogether a sad
story, particularly for the Sultan, mostly caused by the terrible
heat. The Turks nearly got Aden, and help was rushed from
India and Egypt. This arrived, and the Turks were driven
back into the desert. For the rest of the War, both sides contented themselves with holding down the other by means of
occasional operations and continual Frontier skirmishes which
sometimes could be dignified with the name of "serious operations." Our people called them "active defence," and no doubt
the Turks had an equally satisfactory formula for their despatches to Constantinople. Some of the Arabs fought on our
side, some on the Turkish, and a large number on both.

It was the merest sideshow when compared with the operations on the other fronts, and, of course, the risks of death and
mutilation were smaller, though they existed, as I discovered.
It had, however, some particular disadvantages, such as the
heat and the unpleasant habits of the Arabs with the wounded.

On the other hand, there was a sort of old-world atmosphere
about the affair which was not unpleasant. We had none of
your vast major operations in which whole Divisions were
thrown about like chessmen and where the average officer or
man was a comparatively unknown and unimportant cog in a
vast machine: we most of us knew what was going on and, so
to speak, all about it. We had no tremendous artillery bar-
rages—our largest gun was a six-inch howitzer, except for the
supporting guns of the Fleet—and there was no gas.

The Turkish Commander, Nuri Said Pasha, who was known

as the Turkish Bayard, and whom I afterwards met in Constantinople, was one of those Turks who supplied the material for the hazy British belief that the "Turk is a gentleman." However this may be, there is no doubt that Nuri Said was a good man.

He was a legendary figure amongst our troops and, indeed, amongst all the inhabitants of Aden. The story which I like best about him is one which he is supposed to have told to an English colonel after his surrender. This is what he said: "When my troops entered Sheikh Othman, I felt thirsty, and when I came to the first well I told a soldier to get me some water. The soldier asked me on no account to drink, because he said the English had poisoned the waters. I said to him, 'If the English follow this custom I will be the first to die. Give me a drink.'"

The Turkish soldiers against us were very tough customers, and even after the Turkish armistice was signed, they persisted in believing that the whole thing had been invented by the British Intelligence, and on they fought, and would not be persuaded until a very senior Turkish officer was rushed up from Constantinople in a British destroyer.

On another occasion we had the *Ben-Ma-Chree,* a seaplane ship sent down from Alexandria, and her airmen proceeded to bomb the Turkish camps and bases and the lonely Arab shepherds on the hills. The importation of this element of mechanical frightfulness into a previously gentlemanly war did not please Said, and he is reported to have sent in an elaborately worded note in French to the effect "that it is not in consonance with the best traditions of chivalrous warfare to use aeroplanes against an enemy that has none and is not in a position to get any. Any time that my colleague cares to assure me that not more than 2,000 British troops will be in a certain spot in the desert at a given time, I personally will guarantee that an equal number of my men will be there to oppose them and the matter can be settled decently." "Kick orf at 2 p.m.," said Tom Green when he heard the story.

There were many interesting rumours of this sort. Unfortunately, I was isolated and too obscure in my desert outpost to control them personally, and I never realized at the time what a tremendous handicap this uncertainty would be when it came to swopping war yarns after dinner with my slowly fattening comrades of the War, to yarning on the upper deck to a sympathetic audience of one, or to endeavouring to deal with your persistent curiosity and passion for "not fairy tales."

II

On arrival we were not, as we had hoped to be, at once sent out into the desert to strafe the Turks and Arabs, but to our disgust, kept in barracks at Steamer Point and the Crater. The Crater, where I was, was hot. The heat seemed to rise up and hit you as you came in from the port through the pass which divides the two parts of the city and which takes the form of a tunnel hewn through the solid rock. The sun shines down on the rock, dust and scoriæ, and these get hotter and hotter as the day goes on, and all night give out their stored calories so that it is impossible to sleep. As I used to trudge through the tunnel—near where the bones of Cain are said to rest—in marching order, escorting two or three enormous baggage camels which swayed grunting through the warm, damp gloom out into the bright sunlight, I used to feel like some Wellsian troglodyte tramping wearily over the lava beds of Mars in sullen obedience to a command from an impersonal intelligence.

Sometimes at night I would go up to the enormous water reservoirs which held over 9 million gallons, and which had been hewn out of the rock by some antique race—the Ghassans, said the Padre of the camp, who was an enthusiastic local historian—and meditate on the history of the place, on the Romans, or Ælus Gallus, the Abyssinians, the Persians, the Egyptians, and the Turks down to Captain Haynes, who captured Aden for the British and died in a debtors' prison in Bombay. I would try to reconstruct for myself as I sat in the warm moonlight a romance in the Rider Haggard vein, all about the White Princess of a lost tribe and the villainous high-priest who always bitterly resents the arrival of the brave young hero from the West.

The population of Aden was an amazing mixture. There were Arabs of all sorts and tribes; there were Parsis of grave politeness who had the provision shops; these had curious hats like coal-scuttles, and a few assorted names which they shared around between them—names like Bhicajee Hormusji, Cowasji Dinshaw, Eduljee Patel and the like. There were Jews, Bunnias, Bohras from India, Somalis with fuzzy hair always chewing their *arak* sticks, proud upstanding men. One could see an occasional Idrisi from Asir, dyed with indigo, with his long hair, looking like a woman, but actually the toughest of the tough; there were Abyssinians, coal-black Nubians, Warsangali, Dankali, men from Massawa, from Djibouti and Ethiopia, and all sorts of mixtures, sailors and divers from all the coasts of Arabia, pearl-divers from Bahrein, men from Berbera, slave-drivers from wild semi-independent States under vague French or Italian protection, where the trade in hashish, pearls and human beings flourished. They interested me enormously with their varying beliefs and customs.

Chance—a lift I gave him on a service lorry of which I was in temporary charge—threw me into contact with a young Parsi, who spoke good English and practically all the native languages. We formed a friendship, and when I could get away at night—often I fear illegally—we would go round the mysterious Arab haunts and native villages. We saw some strange things, and nearly had our throats cut on one occasion about which I shall not tell you much, except that it concerned one of the queerest marriage ceremonies I have ever seen, and took place in a little Somali village not far from civilized Steamer Point.

My friend's name was Cowasji, and he worked in a Parsi shipping company as a kind of supercargo.

He told me something of that strange and old religion, of Hormuzd and Ahriman: of how it originated in Azerbaidjan, "the land of burning fires." I thought of courageous little Cowasji when I went to Baku afterwards, and was told that Zoroaster had lived there, and that part of his religion, the worship of fire, the sun and the elements, was probably derived from the oil under the ground, which may also have been the cause of some of the miracles in the Old Testament; this, at least, was a favourite theory of little Cowasji's which we used to develop of a night.

He told me of the *sudra*, the baptismal shirt which Parsis wear, which is made in two pieces, and has a little bag on one side, the right, I think, and is a sort of symbolical deposit for all one's good deeds and thoughts. The Parsis are an ancient and dignified race, and Cowasji was a fine specimen combining a good business head, a capacity for study and research and a romantic mind which bade him seek adventurous paths.

Cowasji knew all about the local religions. He was an expert on Sufis, Shiahs and Sunnis, heresies, transmigrations of souls, *mullahs* and *walis*, whose tombs, often just rough heaps of stones surmounted by a flag, had stirred my curiosity. He told me of Aidarouth, the guardian saint of Steamer Point,

who could ensure a good catch of bright-coloured fish to faithful and devout fishermen, and whom I pictured as something
like the Jinn who surprised the fisherman by rising from the
bottle.

He it was who first told me something of Arab life, of the
tribes whose caravans I used to see coming in of an evening,
"as swells and swoons across the wold the tinkling of the
camel bell." The camels were roped nose to tail and looked
like strange birds on account of the forage which covered
their hinder parts and trailed down like plumage, whilst children and chickens sported on top of the load. He had visited
the indigo-blue warriors of the hostile tribes with whom we
had occasional skirmishes. He interested me in their habits,
and explained how they chew *ghat*, the leaves of a mountain
tree. It is curious stuff. I chewed some with him. It is like
privet, and the Arabs get the same sort of effect as the Boliv-
ians do out of the coca leaves. But I only got indigestion.

He had been to San'a and had seen the Imam Yahia, who
had a holy green umbrella, and still dispensed mediæval justice
under a tree, and he knew all about the Saiyids of Al Waht,
a very tough lot of holy men.

I liked young Cowasji, and I should like to visit him one day
at Aden again with you and revive some scandalous memories.
I wish him long life and good business before he retires to
his Towers of Silence.

There was another youthful person of a much younger civilization of whom I have a pleasant memory from Aden. I had
come in from the desert for week-end leave, and had been
with Cowasji to the bazaars. On my way back I met a young
American girl, who had come ashore from one of the mailboats,
which was waiting in the harbour for more than the usually
short interval by reason of some mechanical defect in the en-

gine-room. She was wandering about in the bazaars of the Crater, and had apparently lost her way. She was the first of the genus I had ever met, and I remember that her looks, vivacity, lack of side—she seemed to think it perfectly natural that I should not be wearing the uniform of an officer—made a great impression on me, as did also that American female habit of making one think that one is the only male on the globe. Be on your guard, Ivan; they do know about the others and don't really mean it. She wanted to see everything, so I took her to a cinema which had recently been started by a local Jew, to which the Arabs and Somalis and all the hotch-potch of the native population went in order to see the inanities of the Western world depicted on the flickering screen. About half-way through the performance an Arab from a desert tribe, who had come in to Aden with a caravan, recognized in the audience one with whom he had had a feud for many years. The opportunity seemed too good to be lost, so he crept forward through the crowded seats, and plunged a knife into the back of his enemy, who was peering intently at the antics of the infidels. This happened a few feet away from us, and in a moment there was a tremendous confusion. I had great difficulty in persuading my companion to leave while I could get her out, as she wished to stay to see the fight, which was becoming general and which she said she hated to miss. However, I did manage to hustle our way through by picking up a chair and driving onward with it in front of us. We then went to have lunch in the mailboat. She introduced me to her male parent, who, with magnificent disregard for Arabia and its wonders, had stayed on board and was drinking iced beer in his shirt sleeves.

"Say, Pop," said she, "look at my soldier."

To which Pop replied: "You sure have the gift of attraction, Sweetie." Then to me: "Howdy, General! Have some beer?"

So I stayed to dinner, and learned all about the home town, how Pop had made his money out of belt buckles—Pop's patent. Slogan: "It's a cinch." All about Sweetie's girl friends and her boys—their names formed an American Legion—and the times of all the boats and trains they were going to catch. We wandered on to the deck and found a secluded corner after dinner. I was led on just as far as she wanted me to go, turned down when I wanted to go farther, kissed, robbed of my regimental badge and finally dismissed, all in about an hour, and with an ease and technique that astonished me and which I still reminiscently admire.

A hurried good-bye from Pop, who had reverted to brandy, a handful of cigars, another quick clinch and I bolted down the gangway, looked round, saw a pert face lit up by the electrics, looking into her mirror, already forgetful and entirely absorbed in repairing ravages, avoided various military guards by devious detours, and was just in time to sneak into camp before "lights out" and smoke a reflective cigar, feeling it had been a good day.

III

After some time at the Crater I was moved out to various strong points in the desert and on the lonely coasts which had to be guarded. One night I found myself the corporal of a guard which had been posted on a desolate beach. It was hotter than I ever could have imagined possible, and I remember that, though it was night-time and there was a vague breath from the sea, I sweated—I was only wearing a shirt at the time —right through my webbing equipment. The sentry observed a *dhow* or *boutre* manœuvring about in the bay in a suspicious manner, and it soon became apparent that the crew had not seen us, and that they were preparing to land something. It might have been guns, hostile troops, a spy, ammunition, pearls or charas, or contraband whisky, or a nice black little female slave, as trade was done in all these commodities, in spite of the law and the prophets.

I had a brief colloquy with the sergeant in charge of the guard, who decided to send me back hotfoot to the nearest point to which I could get a message through to the officer on duty.

The moon had set, and I went off in a hurry towards the camp. I knew the way vaguely, and advanced, sweating streams. There is nothing like a mixture of heat, hurry, responsibility and vague apprehension to make the sweat flow. Soon I was wet through. I heard the sound of firing and hurried even more. I stumbled over all sorts of obstacles and went crashing over ditches, gullies, barbed wire and loose stones that gave an insecure foothold.

At last I came to a place which in the darkness I thought I recognized as being near my destination. I then became aware of unpleasant smells, after which I tripped up on a rope and fell on my nose, which bled. I lay for a moment and bitterly disliked the War. As I recovered, shaken and cursing, a long snaky neck with a fearsome antediluvian head and gnashing teeth, snapped at me from the darkness and uttered an eerie bubbling cry. I was so frightened at this manifestation that my heart stopped beating, and in spite of the heat I felt suddenly cold. Instinctively I dodged the horrid head and made a lunge with my bayonet, which glanced off the hard object it met. There was another ferocious gurgle and a formidable bulk reared itself up in the gloom. Then I discovered that I had disturbed a tethered camel from its beauty sleep. I retreated with the utmost cowardice until the camel was at the end of its tether—I was almost at the end of mine—and then gave it a vicious whack with the butt end of my rifle. Finally I roused the guard, which was not far off, and with a patrol we returned to the beach, where we found that the *dhow* had sheered off after attempting a landing, which had been prevented by the firing of a few shots.

Later on during a bathing expedition I saved the life of one of the people in my section who had got out of his depth. It was an unheroic performance, for he was insensible when I got to him, and I simply dragged him in by his hair for about twenty yards. I swallowed a lot of salt water, and Hichens, for that was his name, was afterwards resuscitated by an R.A.M.C. man who was with the party. Hichens was embarrassingly grateful, and I was compelled to drink too much beer in the canteen that night. He gave me a very elaborate pocket-knife, which I lost in the desert.

IV

At last we were ordered out into the desert on Movable Column, and things became more interesting.

For a start we were put on roadmaking and defence works. It was very exhausting in the heat. I remember taking over a fatigue party from an Irish corporal who had been in charge of a mixed gang of Somalis, coal-black Nubians and all sorts. When he handed over the duties, he gave me a large spade and the following advice: "They're good bhoys if ye trate 'em right. If ye sees 'em old-soldiering, thin spank 'em with the flat av the spade. They'll stand that. But nivver use the edge or they'll knife ye."

My general demeanour was hardly suited to such drastic demonstrations of authority. The Irishman was much bigger than I. So I preferred to look austere and aloof and practise a few choice remarks in Arabic. In my section I had with me a red-haired individual who, I discovered, was greatly feared by all the natives, because he was supposed to have the evil eye. I used to make him stand by me like a familiar, and by making a few passes in the air and directing the gaze of this lout who, whatever his eye may have been, had certainly an evil face, towards shirkers I could make the gang sweat much more efficiently than my fellow N.C.O.s. It was Cowasji who had aided me to discover this possibility. Tom Green was in my section and was a great standby.

I should like you to have seen your father in those slim and youthful days. We wore a strange uniform. We were clad in abbreviated khaki shorts and blue army shirts with the sleeves cut short. We had thick pith helmets to protect us from the sun, spine pads down our backs and anti-glare glasses, which were very pleasing to me, because as a permanent spectacle wearer I was no longer conspicuous. In defiance of regulations we had, in the *pagris* wound round our helmets, a tuft of brightly coloured flamingo feathers which, we hoped, imparted a dashing air. We had short puttees which came to just above our ankles, over which were rolled blue Army socks. About two feet of leg and thigh were thus exposed, and this, as were our hands and arms and faces, was tanned a deep mahogany, which I have never seen rivalled as to hue by even the most devout Riviera sun bather.

I found I preferred life in the desert to life at Steamer Point or Crater, in spite of the discomforts. I did all sorts of things, and perhaps one day I may be able to describe a little more fully for your benefit the various sorts of jobs I had and the incidents that took place as I wandered about in various capacities, all of them humble and none uninteresting. I was still fiercely patriotic, so that heat, sweat, flies and thirst lost much of their terrors.

For days I lived in an old Arab watch-tower from which all through the night we watched the enemy camp fires burning, and in the early morning, just as faint streaks of light in the gloom announced the imminent arrival of the sun, our inveterate foe, we crept out to advanced posts and exchanged a shot or two with enemy patrols: the sun would rise in more than Oriental splendour, and its burning rays would bring to both sides the conviction that enough information had been obtained; gradual retirement followed, and from nine to six the sun had undisputed domination: with dusk, touch would again be maintained, and then the sweating night hid us from each other.

These patrols were always liable to lose their way, and one which I had to take out I found particularly difficult, as my rendezvous seemed to be marked by no topographical feature at all; so I took a leaf out of the fairy tales and laid a trail of bully beef tins, on which I smeared a little luminous paint. After this, I led the section with complete confidence, and whilst others were marching on dubious stars which sometimes fell flaming from the heavens amidst the subdued jeers of the troops and the complete embarrassment of the officer, we always arrived on time and waited for the section which had to join us, with a comfortable feeling of superiority.

After short spells in hospital, due to attacks of jaundice and dysentery, I went back to the desert. I can never tell you all about that time, about the camels, the scouting in the desert, the alarms, excursions, the night marches; but sometimes nowadays, when I watch my little white golf-ball winging its way towards the yawning bunker, the romantic illusions of my youth return and I wonder if I was not better employed when I lay for hours in the burning sun behind a wilder sandbank and was amply rewarded by an exchange of potshots with the "Bidoos" and the Osmanli.

One evening, when we were in an old tower and expecting to have a "show" in the morning, I found, on my return from posting an outflung sentry, that Tom Green had come back from hospital. I was very glad of this, Ivan, for I had greatly missed him when an attack of dysentery had caused him to be sent back to the base for six weeks.

We were thoroughly bored with each other and Army rations and Tom had brought—gathered by devious arts—a whole collection of newspapers and things to eat and—risking a court martial for me—cheering things to drink, warm Italian vermouth and red-hot gin, in this instance. We were all packed up and ready for an early start next morning, so after waiting for the orderly officer to make his inspection—he was a cheery soul and knew we could be trusted to keep an eye on essentials and so was prepared not to worry us unduly—we decided to call it Saturday night.

We asked Green what had happened at the base and in the world, and after giving us the news, our raconteur was soon in full swing and the bottles got emptier and emptier, and I would have surrendered hopes of love and Heaven for a piece of ice. I reproduce his story, Ivan, as I wrote it down, so as to give you some idea of this remarkable man.

"Well, Corp and chaps," he began, "shortly after the amachoor Hescu-bloody-lapius 'ad hexamined me and 'ad arrived at the conclusion that I was sufferin' from serious diseases honourably contracted—which I am 'appy to say 'as never been the contrary with me, me being born lucky but not rich—I was removed from this contemptible and disappointing imitation of a sanguinary war and found myself bahncin' abart in a ruddy

basket strapped on one side of a nairy, hunsavoury and propa-
gating oont, me weight being counterbalanced on the other side
by a fat Farrier corporal from the Battery who was presumably
suffering from fatty decomposition of the patriotic nerve, 'im
'aving been found asleep when required for service and 'aving
pleaded in excuse a mixture of beri-beri and hover-fatigue,
coupled with a lack of green vegetables, thereby causin' a rush
of blood to 'is empty 'ead and the complete submersion of 'is
floating kidney which 'ad also been troubling 'im.

" 'E seemed, in addition, to 'ave all the symptoms of approaching maternity, and was proceedin' under hopen harrest
to 'ave it all looked into. 'E seemed to be in a bad way and
with hevery 'eave of the camel 'e 'ove halso and likewise
groaned 'ollowly. Mislikin' 'is clock and general hattitude, I
told 'im that in my 'umble opinion 'is only chance of escape
from being shot at dawn was to plead that the complication of
'is symptoms required the preservation in a glass bottle of 'is
diseased organs for the future instruction of young sawboneses
and pill shooters. In this way I 'inted 'e might atone for the
past.

"The suggestion, 'owever, did not please 'im, and so, with
'im vomitin' and me vichooperatin', we travelled along on that
blasted, puffin', 'eavin', whoremongering, eructatin', 'ump-
backed, stinking, illegitimate cross-eyed sore-assed camel for
what seemed ages in the 'ot sun, until in doo course we arrived
at the C.C.S., where we obtained the inevitable diagnosis of io-
blanky-dine and number nines.

"They labelled us up and took our particklers. We was then
transferred from camels to Fords, which bumped less but smelt
abart the same, 'avin' been used previously for the transport of
some of them miscalled friendly Bidoos, which, as you know,

Corp, armed with a gaspipe gun and a pair of somebody else's shorts, hindulges, under the command of a ruddy fool of a subaltern, in hambiguous operations between the front lines of ourselves and Johnny Turk, receiving subsidies from the intelligence orficers of both sides.

"We arrived at last at the base hospital, which was then being visited by a blanky group of tourists intent on hearin' the latest news from the seat of war before goin' on with their voyage. I was left alone for a minute while the sawbones had a conference to deal with the complicated symptoms of the Farrier Corporal, who, on nearing the 'orspital, 'ad become rapidly worse and 'ad begun to groan in a realistic and terrifyin' manner. In my 'elpless and labelled condition I was promptly accosted by an old lady with sun glasses, a green veil and a countenance similar to that of the sergeant-major just before he calls the battalion to attention.

" 'Soldier,' says she.

" 'Yes, Moddom,' ses I, always perlite.

" 'Tike this trac',' says she, 'andin' me one from a bagful she 'ad, 'which explains simply the first principles of faith 'ealing. Sit still,' she goes on, fixing me with an asterisk glare, 'and summon all the energies of yer mind to combat the symptoms of yer disease and they will disappear.'

" 'I doubt it, lady,' ses I. 'And in any case, I can't sit still much longer.'

" 'Why, indeed?' ses she.

" 'Because I got dysentery,' I said, and on that she goes."

Tom finished and a dark youth played subdued tunes on a mouth organ, and then, except the sentry, we fell asleep.

I was disturbed that night. I felt that rats were scampering over me. They were. I woke up with a start, and found that one had bitten right through the lobe of my right ear. I drenched it with iodine and suffered agonies of apprehension about the possibility of bubonic plague, blood poisoning and the rest. But next morning there was a counter-irritant in the shape of a small strafe, and I had other things to worry about.

CHAPTER V

CASUALTY

ALL of one sweating week we had been out on outpost duty in the desert: we were due to return to advanced base and to exchange bivouacs, old mud towers and the like for the comparative comforts of tents. Suddenly, eddies of rumour sprang up all round and died: then came gusts of information, and finally a steady breeze of instructions whistled through the hierarchy, so that we knew we were going out next morning on a stunt of some importance.

Tom Green opined that it would be the same as when H.M.S. *Euryalus* had arrived, and when, after tremendous preparations designed to synchronize the sea and land artillery arrangements into something approaching a creeping barrage, we, with some Indian troops and native levies, had sallied forth just before the light to attack a Turkish picket. The Turks, on that occasion, surprised at the size of the forces advancing against them, had decided, after a little long-range resistance, to imitate their Arab allies, fold up their tents and steal silently away into the desert behind. Just as they had put this into practice and were preparing a series of ambushes for us should we advance, the Navy began its barrage with 12-inch guns, weapons far larger than had ever been used, seen, heard or imagined on that front before. Either we had advanced too far, or the guns were worn, or the lieutenant had added it up wrong, but in any case, the first shell caused a huge yellow cloud—a pillar of fire in the desert—just in front of us on our left. The second seemed to

71

fall even nearer, and as Tom had remarked: "Us and our dusky hallies did a 'ell of a sight more creeping than the ruddy barrage."

The rumours became more definite. We were to take Hatum and the Carnatics were going to Jabir. Perhaps even we should penetrate to Lahj, drive out the Turks, reinstall the Sultan and make a splash.

I had been suffering from colitis or dysentery all day, and had made up my mind to report sick the next morning but, on hearing the news, thought I would try to participate.

Before Last Post, orders came round for a start in full war kit at three in the morning. Amidst excitement we turned in, and next morning, sleepy and cursing, we fell in and shuffled off in open fours in the cool starlight of a December morning. On we marched for hours over the sands, sometimes yielding and soft and sometimes harder and covered with sparse tamarisk and camel's thorn. On we went, and the sand got into our eyes, ears, noses, throats and rifles: there were occasional halts and whispered conversations with the spectral shapes of guides and officers.

"Lost again," we murmured. "Why the hell do our people never know the way?" At last we deployed and took up a position, being grouped in small columns. We awaited the first visibility. Would that I could describe in fitting language that wonderful dawn when delicate tinge gave way to pastel shade, and pastel shade to suffused red, and then the torrid sun burst with a roar of light over the sky and burnt out the lingering stars.

Then it began. Shells rumbled overhead like tube trains in tunnels, whilst the novices saluted them with reverences and machine-guns began their rivet-hammering on the flanks. Still we advanced in columns, and then, at a whistle from the platoon commander, extended into open order. I found myself with my section on the extreme left flank of all our line and between me and the open desert—with its limitless possibilities of enfilade —one Lewis gun. We advanced with short rushes, flopping down in the sand, and then dashed forward again. That is, we dashed for a little; then we ran; then we doubled; then we did anything which wasn't an obvious walk. Whee! Whee! Wheee!! The bullets fell and spattered up the sand. I remember trying to keep the sand out of my rifle and the perspiration off my glasses as we went steadily on. At last, through the red rays of the rising sun, I caught a first glimpse of the enemy line, which was surrounded by clouds of dust and smoke. As the shells burst around it figures could be seen in retreat.

I collected my section and gave a fire-order and we pumped away with our rifles. After this I ceased to be so excited and advanced mechanically, firing and giving ranges as I went. The enemy bullets seemed to be getting thicker, and we became more loath to leave friendly sandheaps for the open. But on we went. The platoon commander sent a man who, bent double, came to tell me not to advance the section more than another hundred yards or so, and that I should send out a winger to look after the flank and report any enfilade movements. I sent someone out. I then gathered the section behind a mound and we had a drink in the lull and let our rifles cool. Not long were we left in peace, but soon were waved onwards. Up to the next mound we struggled, which was, I suppose, too big, for the air around it seemed full of shells and bullets. It was probably a range mark.

We crawled to another mound and there came a lull. I left Green in charge and crawled over to the platoon commander, for whom I had respect. He told me I was doing well, on no account to leave the flank exposed—which sounded well, but was quite impossible to fulfil—and to keep pace with the advance.

Crawl back and on we went again. This was the hottest show I had ever been in, and the bullets whizzed and phutted, but their noise and the crumping of the shells did not worry me much. I felt it was unlikely I should be hit. One of the section got a bullet through his leg. He fell over with a yell, and as I ran to him he lay with an astonished face looking at a black hole in his brown leg. His neighbour bandaged him up and he hobbled back with the astonished look still on his bucolic face, like a ploughboy who had met Apollyon in a field. Then we passed the dead body of one of our scouts whom I knew. He had a hole in his forehead, but I hadn't much time to analyse my feelings about him and so passed on.

By this time the advance had ceased temporarily: the Turks and Arabs were still faintly visible and maintained a steady fire from their positions. The machine-gun, which was supposed to support our flank, had ceased fire for the moment. I made a cautious trip to the flank, but all seemed quiet and I gladly returned to the section. We started to snipe carefully at the enemy, and must, I think, have scored some hits; the enemy replied, and it was dangerous to expose oneself.

On the right the line went forward again and I took some little time to persuade myself that we must really leave our efficient, friendly, sheltering mound and take the open again. However, on we went, and when we got to comparative shelter I found that my haversack had been punctured by a bullet. Then for the first time I saw fairly clearly a bunch of five Turks on the flank and directed the fire of the section at them: we shouted to each other and yelled with excitement as they scampered—one limping—to cover. We swung outward to try to envelop them, and settled down again behind a mound.

Phut, phut came the bullets, and we chose another mound —this time a big comforting one—so big that I could even fire sitting, a great comfort after the prone position, which always made my elbows very sore. I had fired twice and was peering over the mound to see what was happening, when I suddenly found myself lying on my back after a violent blow in the chest which toppled me over like a rabbit. I sat up wondering, and felt a terrible pain in my right hand. I looked at it. There was a black hole in it and it was bleeding. "My God," I thought, as I felt the dull pain in my chest, "I'm perhaps mortally wounded . . . perhaps I'm going to die." I lay still and felt the world swim around me. I sat up and a bullet whistled by. "Oh," I said to myself again, "the next one *will* kill me. . . . What devilish things. . . . With what force they go through the air . . . fancy having to stop one with flesh and bone . . . how unfair."

Then Green appeared, bending over me.

"Stopped one, Corp?" he asked.

I looked at his sweating face.

"Yes," I said, "hand and chest, I'm afraid."

"Thank Gawd the —— bastards ain't done yer in," said Green, and proceeded to lay his rifle carefully down and look me over.

I insisted that I was hit in the chest and he said that I was not. He opened my equipment and swore jestingly to reassure me with a joke that I was "hintact but no blanky virgin." There was a hole in my equipment. He searched further, and amid volleying oaths he found a flattened bullet which had just bruised the skin. He held it up for my inspection. I told him to put it in my pocket. This he did, and then turned to look at my hand. The blood was welling from this. I felt a little better. We discovered that the bullet had glanced off the wooden stock of my rifle after piercing my hand and had then gone through my webbing equipment—luckily through a cartridge pouch which had no cartridges in it. A miraculous escape. Tom broke open his field bandage and emptied the iodine capsule over the wound. I yelled, but the pain cleared my brain. He then made a rough bandage. We consulted a bit. He wanted to go back a little with me, but I told him to take over the section, and that I would make my own way back. It seemed useless to go on, as I couldn't move my right arm and I felt as if I might topple over at any minute.

I hated this prospect and thought of the horrors of losing my way and falling into the hands of the Arabs. In some ways it seemed safer to stay with the section, but Tom persuaded me. He bade me a reluctant farewell, and went on with the section, over which, as the oldest soldier, he assumed command.

I lay back and tried to prevent myself from giving way to panic. I got up slowly and began to make the best of my way to the rear. Soon I came across some of our reserves who were panting along towards the firing-line. With them was a R.A.M.C. man, who made a sling for me, and gave me a drink of something or other which cleared my head.

The sergeant of the reserve platoon scribbled a message to his C.O., who was behind, and this I took over.

The reserves went forward, and I wended my way back with my arm in a sling and my rifle slung over my shoulder. By this time my shirt and shorts were all smeared with blood from my hand, and I must have looked a sorry sight.

The bullets and shrapnel still whistled and screamed, and to my nerve-shocked imagination it seemed as if each one might complete the work of its predecessor. The firing got hotter and I endeavoured to go faster. The result was that I tripped over some camel's thorn and fell forward and crashed on to my wounded hand. This gave me such exquisite pain that I lay despairing. Imagine then, Ivan, your father, not in the normal comfortable outline in which you first knew him, but thin, strangely dressed, covered with blood, prostrate and despairing on the sands, wondering how it would end, and . . . afraid.

I was afraid I would be caught by the Beni Abdali and mutilated. Would they, I wondered, realize that I did not believe in their material Paradise with its houris, and thus kill me quickly instead of slowly, and in such a manner as to render me, in their belief, unfitted for the joys to which they looked forward? I was afraid of losing my way and wandering in the desert till I died of thirst. Should I turn Mohammedan if captured?

I sat up. Then I remembered that I had in my bullet-holed haversack a medicine bottle full of brandy, gift of the faithful Cowasji. With my left hand I tried to extricate it. It was difficult to do this. I tried to assist the process with my injured hand, but as I moved the fingers a shock of the purest and most intense pain made me sit down and gasp and sweat. At this moment a shrapnel shell burst above and the iron hail scattered on the sand; a piece of something hard hit my right boot. Fortunately, the burst had been too high to be dangerous. But I saw the pock marks in the sand, and a round black bullet and something that looked like the inside of a clock—though whether I really saw this or imagined it, I do not know.

At last I extricated my medicine bottle, and pulling the cork out with my teeth I gulped away. I found some biscuit and tried to eat that, but my mouth was too dry and dusty to enable me to swallow. There was a lull in the firing and I smoked a cigarette. As I smoked, I wanted to leave the dust and sand and noise and blood, and lie on my back on the cool clipped grass on a lawn, listen to the impact of the balls on the rackets

and then go and have tea from a thin china cup and talk to a
neat cool girl in a white frock with a soothing interested voice.
After that, a bathe . . . to lie in the cool water, look up at
the blue sky and then at my pink toes as they stuck up out
of the water and the sea roared softly in my ear. . . . I got
up and walked on.

Soon I passed some more reserves, who glanced curiously at
my blood-stained shorts. "Caarpril's hit," said someone, and
asked what was happening. I gave my message to a sergeant,
and went on feeling more cheerful now that the way was clear,
and it looked as if I should not get lost.

A little farther on I met the C.O. with his orderly. He was
inspecting progress from a mound around which the bullets
still phutted. He called me over and, noticing my splintered
rifle stock, asked me what had happened. I gave him an account—a slightly vainglorious and rather inaccurate one, I fear,
of the proceedings—and he wrote a message and gave it to me,
telling me to give it to the first officer I met on the way back.
Then he offered me a cigarette, and with a cheery word walked
off blithely towards the line, swinging his swagger cane and
not worrying to take cover.

I began to feel vaguely cheerful—I was out of rifle range.
After all, thought I, I had done all that could be expected
of me, and I was walking honourably back with a message
and a wound to justify my exit. The platoon commander had
congratulated me and the C.O. had been encouraging. Then I
remembered that sickening moment when I had lain and
sobbed behind a mound, and not ventured and not dared even
to move for quite ten minutes, or an hour, perhaps. Who
knew? But after all . . . Was it not one of Kipling's people
who had remarked on the "shock" effect of a wound in the
hand? I must have lost a lot of blood. Thank Heaven no one

had seen me. But perhaps if there had been someone there I should not have given way. Self-respect is the basis of courage, but it is greatly assisted by an audience and the fear of ridicule.

Then I got rid of my message, and was shown the way to the Regimental Aid-post, where the doctor, with his assistants and two donkeys carrying his traps, was already installed. He came up cheerily with a sort of military bedside manner. I saluted him with my left hand—a little touch of the theatrical.

He felt my pulse and asked the orderly to give me a drink. After this I was told to sit down on a heap of packing stuff. The orderly told me that a shell had burst near the more bobbery of the two donkeys, which had promptly lit out for the desert, scattering dressings, medicine bottles and number nines all over the place. It had been recaptured, and was now switching its tail in a bored sort of way. There were a dozen or more casualties all bandaged up on stretchers: some were groaning and some were ominously still.

"Come along," said the doctor's corporal, and led me to the doctor, who asked me all about it while he undid the bandage. He told me to avert my face and not look at the hand, towards which I felt impelled by a fearful curiosity. I told him all about how the bullet had splintered my rifle, and showed him my punctured equipment, and finally the bullet. I saw him preparing the iodine swab and told him it had already been iodined.

"Oh, well . . ." said he, "a little more won't hurt."

But it did.

"Well . . . young fellow," he summed up, "it's smashed your hand up a bit. You're no more good here. You'd better go back with the next lot."

So I retired and sat down, listening to the firing, wondering whether they would have to take off my arm.

It was then about half-past one, and we had started at 3.30 in the morning. At about two, more wounded came in, and some were prepared for evacuation on a camel ambulance. I was told to accompany it with a native orderly, and a lightly wounded officer was put in charge of the party.

We were to go to the Casualty Clearing Station, which was some way back. Luckily, I knew the ground, as I had been on picket duty there the week before.

I did not much like the idea of setting out by ourselves, for I knew how quickly the positions changed in that sort of war, and for all I knew we might find ourselves walking back to the front again or we might get ambushed by Arabs. However, we set off across the desert in a comparative lull. When we got into the open, woolly puffs began to appear above us, and in a short time we were being fairly thoroughly shelled. I suppose the enemy thought we were supports and, as the Arabs say, "it is difficult to conceal murder and a camel."

The native orderly got panic-stricken and, flopping on the ground, refused to go on, calling loudly on his gods the while. The officer and myself threatened him, and finally he opted to risk the Turkish shells and go on. Otherwise . . .

During this scene the shrapnel bursts came nearer. The officer collected some of the bullets. He swore that he had found some of those glass marbles which are used as stoppers for ginger-beer bottles, but whether this was true or not I do not know. In any case, the Turks were hard up for munitions, and were reported to have their own amateur munitions factory established in an oasis in the heart of an acacia forest away back behind at Lahj. This officer also told me that his men had proof that the Turks were still using an old muzzle-loading gun that fired a solid cannon-ball which might be seen trundling over the desert.

The shelling ceased, and after a certain amount of obstreperous behaviour by the camel, which made me glad I was not on it, we eventually made our way to the Brigade Casualty Clearing Station situated in an old Arab watch-tower. Here we were well received. After being given tea we went before the doctor. He looked at my hand while I stared fixedly at the roof of the tent. He made the inevitable move towards the iodine bottle. I protested.

"Sir," I said, "first of all iodine from my field-service dressing was applied by one, Private Green, shortly after I was wounded. Then a lance-corporal of the R.A.M.C. put some more on. A further quantity was applied some two hours ago by a captain in the R.A.M.C. It is not the frequency of the applications—though they are painful—so much as the unfortunate fact that increase of rank seems to entail increase of dose, that I object to."

This, of course, I had carefully thought out while I was waiting, for making elaborate remarks in this vein was part of a studied technique I had often applied successfully to show I was not the ordinary Tommy.

The doctor, who was a Major in the I.M.S., looked at me curiously, burst into a loud laugh, and asked me who the hell I was.

I told him.

"Oh, well," he said, "a little more won't do you any harm."

So after a painful ten minutes, during which they soaked off sticking bandages and made painful probes, they tied me up all nice and white.

"Go in peace, Corporal," said the Major, "and tell the Colonel-Commandant at the Base Hospital that you have already been iodined!"

"Put it in writing, sir," I begged.

But he gave me a cigarette and sent me off.

Then off we went in a Ford ambulance driven by a smart young gentleman in the R.A.M.C. who stared haughtily at my blood-bespattered shorts. Soon we were bowling along a road I had helped to make a few months before. The motion was smooth and the pain in my hand had relapsed to a dull ache. I managed to fill a pipe, one-handed—later I became quite expert with my left hand—and smoked with some contentment. Soon we came to the base, and people stared at us curiously, for the guns could still be heard. Finally, we arrived at the Base Hospital. All was prepared for us. An Irish Sister took charge, and after shooing off the curious—including many wounded in the fields of Venus rather than of Mars—who had come to hear the news, she prepared the patients for the surgeon on duty.

"What about something to eat, Sister?" said I. "I'm starving; been up all night and not a bite to eat."

"Nothing doin' thin, Carpril," said she. "Ye'll just have to wait till the Major sees ye."

"And then, Sister?"

"Sure, they'll give ye some nice castor oil."

The doctor spent a long time on my hand, and told me that it would have to be operated on the next day. So I went to sleep on a clean white bed and slept for fourteen hours.

The next day the G.O.C. and the C.O. and the Company Commander and the Platoon Commander and Tom Green came to see me. I was congratulated on my handling of the section, which made me very proud, and then I "went to the pictures," as we used to say, that is, I was wheeled into the operating room and chloroformed.

After this I stayed at the Base Hospital for three weeks and had many operations on my hand. That was a period of anæsthetics, of counting drearily 96, 97, 98, 9 . . . 9, 100, 1 . . . 01, and then off I would go as the voices faded and the room became red and hazy. Next would be a painful wakening, sickness, wound dressing—how I used to dislike that, and what I used to call fuss and pus.

One day it was decided that I must go to Egypt. I went down to the port, and was put in a launch, and very soon found myself being collected by an upstanding Australian nurse with a pleasant face, and taken up the gangway into a clean white Australian hospital ship, where we seemed to have meat for every meal.

I stayed for a few months in Egypt, but they could not do anything for my hand, and so it was decided to invalid me home.

So I bade farewell to Arabia, but not to its fascination, and, as it turned out, to active military operations as an infantry soldier.

CHAPTER VI

OFFICER CADET

I

THE voyage home from Alexandria was uneventful till just before the end, when we were some fifty miles off Bristol. A big German submarine suddenly came up and fired shells and torpedoes at us. To do full justice to the enemy, I think I must add that I believe the ship I was in—the *Glengorm Castle*—had only recently been converted into a hospital ship, and had done various trips to Egypt before as a transport carrying troops and munitions.

I was down below when the shells burst and the torpedo passed astern, but it was soon evident that something was wrong. "There was no panic," as the communiqués used to put it, but . . . everybody ran about and hoarse shouts came echoing down. Then there happened the most humorous incident that I encountered personally during all the time I was a foot soldier.

In the bunk above me was a naval rating, who had been wounded in the Gulf, and who, with his bronzed face and beard, looked exactly like the tobacco and sardine advertisements. I had made friends with him on the voyage. I afterwards learned that he had the Distinguished Conduct Medal for notable gallantry in the Mesopotamia operations, but I did not know this at the time.

Well, Ivan, he pretended to be panic-stricken when he heard

the noise, and I had to look very closely before I discovered that he was bluffing. As I collected my scanty belongings preparatory to what looked like being a nasty get-away, I asked him what he thought our chances of being picked up were.

He replied, "Not so bad. But I 'opes to God we ain't picked up by them blanky Frogs."

I said I did not mind who rescued me, whether French or English, so long as someone did. To which my naval rating remarked, "You don't know nothing abart the 'orrors of war, you don't! Early on in the War I was in destroyers in these parts and a French transport was sunk. We went in to pick up survivors. I picked up two and, my Gawd, they kissed me something 'orrid!"

However, the submarine was chased off by a destroyer, and we finally landed in Bristol.

For a time I lived in various hospitals. I was clad in a blue hospital uniform, and in between operations on my hand, of which I underwent about a round dozen—none of them successful—I was entertained by vague Society women and preached at by old ladies.

I had a blessed spell of leave. So passed almost a year. Gradually the use of my hand came back, at first partially, and afterwards a little more completely, till one day they told me they could do no more, and that two fingers would always be useless.

I rejoined my reserve battalion on Salisbury Plain. It was in huts not far from where, three years before, I had sweated and trained under old Shelton. But now I was doing the training, and had squads of country boys to initiate into the horrors of gas. A boring and unpleasant interlude. I was marked in a category unfit for active service, as I could not dig trenches owing to my useless fingers. I caught pneumonia and nearly died.

In hospital I met a man from my old battalion, and learned that they had been in the fighting in Egypt. I have never met any of them again. Our ways have lain apart. I never saw Tom Green again, but I heard a story about him from a friend whose brother had joined the battalion after I had left.

It appears that he had been invalided home at last and put into a London workhouse which had been converted into a hospital. My friend was a surgeon there. Tom was in a bed next to a young recruit. One night, the Zeppelins or the Gothas raided. A bomb fell in the neighbourhood and exploded with a heavy German noise. The recruit woke up. Tom snored on. Another bomb fell nearer. The recruit leaned over, and shaking Tom by the arm said, "Tom! Wake up!"

Tom awoke.

"Wot the 'ell?" said he.

Crash fell a bomb in the courtyard, and a piece of metal came through the open window and ricochetted off the iron foot of Tom's bed into the wall with a ringing whine. Clouds of plaster and dust filled the air, and the young recruit thought his last day was come. Leaning over nervously, he asked Tom in a tremulous whisper, "Tom! Is that bombs?"

To which Tom replied, "Nah. Not bombs. Pamflicks!" and resumed his interrupted repose.

I have never seen Tom since, but I hope he has a little court in an English inn where the ale and the audience are worthy of him.

When the pus had been pumped from my lungs, back I went to my hut on Salisbury Plain, where I found someone else telling the boys how to put on their gas-masks. I was put in charge of the dining-rooms, and had to deal with enormous masses of vorticist stew and cubist piles of margarine. This was very dull.

I applied to go to France, but was told that my hand pre-

vented this. So I applied for a commission. I was informed
that I might get one in a Labour Battalion. So I waited. Then
came January 1918. The younger classes—boys of seventeen
—were pushed across to stop the German drive. I felt again
all my old fervour and fretted back at home. It was a horrible
period.

One day I was paraded on a special parade of all who had
put in for commissions. A Brass Hat came down from the
W.O. to see us. He glared at us fiercely and, accompanied by
the C.O., stalked in silent dignity down the lines.

"Fall out, all those who have not been on active service," was
the first order, and this disposed of about fifty of us. "You,"
barked our visitor, who bristled with hair and decorations,
"will go to France to-morrow."

Then this terrible man began a personal examination of all
of us who remained. He began with me, as I stood stiffly to
attention. The C.O. and the Adjutant, perturbed and anxious,
came up with papers and particulars for the different cases. But
the Brass Hat waved them aside ferociously. Consulting his
pocket-book, he glared at me and suddenly snapped:

"Corporal. Why the hell have you put in for a Labour
Battalion?"

I was so fed up with recent events, the misery of seeing
boys younger and less experienced than I march bravely off, and
the appalling boredom of the camp, that I was not overawed.
Further, I disliked his inference that I had specially sought a
Labour Battalion, so that I replied as brusquely as I dared.

"Sir, I was told that it was the only thing I could get into."

"When did you join up?"

"In August 1914, sir."

"There's nothing doing in Labour Battalions."

"Well, sir," said I shortly, "send me with the draft to France.
I've volunteered two or three times, but they won't let me go.

I don't particularly care about a commission, but if you had been in charge of a damned dining-room on this Plain for the last three months, you'd want to get out too!"

Here I thought the heavens would fall, and that I should be placed under immediate arrest and shot at dawn, but the Brass Hat merely broke into a sudden smile and said, "Steady," in a voice of thunder. After this, he asked for my papers. The Adjutant spoke up like a brick, and confirmed my previous statements. There was a brief colloquy, and finally the Brass Hat turned to me and said, "We'll be sending you soon to a Cadet School for an infantry commission. Your wound would be a handicap to you in the ranks, but as an officer it oughtn't to worry you. It's a special chance I'm giving you. See that you use it. And keep your cheek for special occasions like this one!"

I thanked him and he went on his majestic way down the silent waiting ranks while the Colonel followed him with an air of subdued apprehension, and behind him again the R.S.M., with corked-up blasphemies trembling under his bristling moustaches.

Soon after this we were moved from the Plain to Buncrana, near Lough Swilly, in Ireland, and I remember our crossing from Larne to Stranraer one foggy morning escorted by silvery blimps and lean destroyers.

Then after two weeks the Brass Hat kept his promise, and I was ordered to report to Oxford.

You may learn from this, Ivan, that fierce men are best faced fiercely.

II

I became a Cadet. In the long life of Oxford we were, as one of her lovers and historians afterwards described us, "men who, welcome as they were, were only accidental." Even Oxford found it impossible during the War to "sit apart from all the living pulses of the hour," and extended a welcome to a heterogeneous mass of soldiery who came to live in its "mossy piles of old munificence," and were taught the inhumanities often by transmogrified Dons assisted by regular N.C.O.s. Some of the Dons never achieved a militant ferocity, but the N.C.O.s were made of sterner stuff and, completely oblivious of their surroundings, made the haunts of ancient peace resound with martial bellowings.

To me, proud of my officer-type uniform, and wearing the white band of emancipation from the ranks, the whole thing was wonderful and a marvellous relief. Was not this the place of which I had dreamed while poring over problems in those distant days before the War? Could I not do most of the things I had read about? Read all the books in the world. Stroll down the Turl, flirt with a shop girl, buy straight-grained pipes, laze on the river in a punt, jump naked into Parson's Pleasure, or think idly of the Scholar Gipsy as our dusty, trudging route-marching column went swinging along close by where he used to wander.

It was refreshing to meet bright spirits of my own ex-world straight from the Public Schools instead of the excellent but, on the whole, boring soldiery among whom I had passed three years, and who seemed only occasionally capable of producing a wonderful example like Tom Green.

It was for me a strange period. At times I felt like an old soldier broken in the wars, and at others as if a sponge had obliterated all the immediate past and I was again the eager, pure, young patriot of 1914. And yet I felt much older than the Public School contingent. I felt that I knew their world and was really a part of it, but that also I knew such a lot more. I had lived in a hard, grim, ugly world of dirt and facts and sweat and blood, where the ordinary virtues, cleanliness and courage and self-sacrifice—more prized and valuable than brilliant wit or cultural patina—shone out like stars above the boiling seas. I knew something of men and how they thought and acted, the strength and weakness of the masses, the power of character and the dangerous swift onslaught of fear.

So—I was then twenty—I forgathered with the Wykehamists and others, who, for a difference of three years, were at school when I was on the desert, and renewed my youth. I began to study again. At first I thought my brain was atrophied, but gradually I found myself competing successfully with the brighter brains, which was a great relief.

I played tennis again, and cricket, and walked on an English lawn in flannels, and best of all, indulged in a propensity for friendships. The distant slaughter of the March offensives and the subsequent Allied advance did not unduly disturb my conscience, as I had done all I could to get out again.

Books again were at my disposal; in fact, for the six months I was there I read all I could outside my military studies. It was a time of *apaisement* and healing, and certainly a happy period.

I was quartered in Hertford College and afterwards at Keble. One day I hope that you will go with me, and we will look at its bridge and all the other things to see, and love the "memories taken root in stone," and though I cannot say with Newbolt:

> *"This is the Chapel: here, my son,*
> *Thy father dreamed the dreams of youth*
> *And heard the words, which, one by one*
> *The touch of life has turned to truth,"*

because, alas! my dreams were mostly elsewhere dreamed, yet it is my dearest hope that you will be able to study there unhampered by wars or rumours of wars, so as to be able to take a useful place in whatever English structure is vouchsafed to your generation.

Enough of Oxford. It made an indelible impression on me. I could hardly hope to describe it to you.

Training went on, and I had just passed my final examination—being second in my company—when suddenly the Armistice came.

It was a strange moment. After a wild dinner, in one of those moments of semi-intoxication when everything seems clear and sharp, when the brain is bright and the brilliant phrase comes trippingly, when inhibitions, self-distrust and lack of confidence roll away like swirling mists before the sun, and when the future seems but a bright prospect of triumphant achievement, I stood with Tony, my gay and brilliant friend, before Pembroke and heard Great Tom break his long silence. As I stood, Tony told me how for hundreds of years he had sounded every night at nine his 101 strokes till DORA silenced him for fear of Zeppelins. He told me of his dedication to St. Thomas of Canterbury, and how he sang *"In Thomae laude BIM BOM resono sin fraude."* So I heard the bells of victory, but I am not yet convinced that they pealed *sin fraude*.

Next morning brought a headache. After the joy of thinking that we had won, I felt rather lost without the stimulus of war. New ambitions had no time to rise. I wanted terribly to stay up as a student, but could not possibly see how this could be managed financially.

I had no career to which to return, no special training. I had no idea what I was going to do.

In a very short while I found myself commissioned and demobilized.

So ended the Great War for me. It was a horrid, impossible,

bloody business out of which I was lucky to escape so lightly. But, Ivan, for us who bore you with continual reference and warlike anecdote, who still cherish an experience of adventure and sacrifice which we hope you'll never share—while perversely retaining the right to criticize your generation for addiction to frivolity and lack of the martial virtues—it had its great and never-to-be-forgotten moments.

It is hard to analyse the atavistic appeal of such a stupidity, but it is foolish not to try to realize its force. The comradeship, the extremes of strain and effort, the rapid coping with crises, the sense of having to do with life and death issues: there is something in all this which is on a different plane from the ordinary events or even the "no less renowned victories" of peaceful days.

Also—for some people—the absence of luxury and soft living, the physical fitness and the endurance of hardship make for a spirituality and a negation of self which, by some exponents of Eastern and other religions, is attained as a result of conscious effort and self-denial, but which we most of us never attain unless it is forced on us by compelling outside forces.

If one is, at all moments and without hesitation, ready to sacrifice one's most valued possessions—life, friends and loved ones—for a non-material reason, even though it be foolish, unworthy or even vanity derived, then in this way one does arrive at a spiritual height which humble men hardly attain in dull self-seeking peace. For what will men endure discomfort and risk death? For gold, Ivan, for love, for power, for religion, for fame, for publicity its fallen sister, for sensation, for romance, and sometimes for knowledge. *Au fond* most of these are selfish reasons, but in a Great War there is a mass unselfishness—coupled with an immense proletarian sacrifice—

which is not so apparent in the trials of peace. It must be the business of your generation to prove that it is there and to give it its laurels and rewards.

Will you? Won't you? *Quién sabe?* At the moment you prefer playing pirates and smugglers in the garden to that tedious game called Producers, Consumers and Middlemen which I invented with so much labour, and from pirates to *Wehrsport* is but a step to youth.

I belonged to a generation that in 1914 felt like Corporal James Parr, who was killed twelve days after he wrote: "Don't tell me war does no good. . . . What do we gain? I think we gain the one thing that every man has wanted from his boyhood up—opportunity. Opportunity to show what he is made of. Opportunity to show that he can be the hero he's always wanted to be from the time when he first made up his mind to be a pirate when he grew up."

But to you I recommend the quiet common sense of Gilbert Murray, who says: "There is really a touch of something insane in the idea that civilization or the general level of human character can best be saved and improved by war. It is like looking to famines and pestilences to secure the improvement of public health. Of course, good can generally be extracted from it. It may by human strength of character be made to yield some good results among many bad, but wise education does not place its hopes in exceptional and crushing trials which only a few may overcome, or in rare and violent punishments which will terrify the wicked into virtue. It puts its hopes in a quiet and regular process of discipline and moral pressure which may form gradually the habit of intelligent interest and the enjoyment of right things. This is the sort of education our civilization ought to provide for us, not one built on blinding disasters and the hope of heroic reactions."

Both tendencies will probably attract you. I have indicated my preference. But, pacifist or paladin, whichever way you choose, remember the supreme counsel of Cleobulus of Lindos, the friend of Solon and one of the seven sages of Greece, and "avoid extremes."

PART II

SALADE RUSSE

"Any peace is better than Civil War."
Cicero, *Philippic* 2. 15.

CHAPTER VII

PEACE AND PLENTY

I LEFT Oxford to be demobilized, firmly decided somehow or other, by hook or crook, to make enough money to return and study. For three years that was my dominating ambition, and very nearly I achieved it, but at the last was disappointed.

The beginning was not auspicious. After a brief interval of enjoyment of the sweets of freedom, peace and civilian life, I began, as my gratuity disappeared like an ice before a greedy schoolboy, to turn my thoughts to the question of earning a living. Then I discovered that the Great War had left me, at the age of twenty-three, a rather more than usually helpless unit in the great army of job seekers who had nothing much to offer except the qualities which won the War—if won it was—and which were a drug on the markets of peace. I had no special training and, of course, no occupation to which to return. My people had been greatly hit by the War, and in any case I did not want to burden them with my support after having been independent.

It was a bad period. I spent hours and hours looking down the "Situations Vacant" advertisements in the newspapers and making out application forms in painful copperplate, stating my age next birthday, previous experience and age last birthday.

Heaven knows what I did not apply for. "Had I any previous experience?"

"No. Only riding camels, shooting at Turks and dodging fatigues, but no previous experience."

There were interviews with fat and prosperous directors.

"Very sorry for you, young fellow. Very difficult indeed, but we've nothing to offer you. All we can do to take back our pre-War staff."

One fat jolly Jew was kind and took an interest in my case, and through a cousin of his—such, my boy, are the solid links of consanguineous capital that bind the great class of directors together—I very nearly obtained a post in a tea-planting concern in Ceylon. But at the last, somebody with a stronger pull than mine—possibly a social position in Hampstead—got the job, and so destiny intervened and saved you being born in a hot damp bungalow.

It is a terrible thing, this unemployment: one which tries the courage and saps the morale of even the stoutest hearted. There is something in the continual waiting in ante-rooms, filled with the emanations of unsuccessful visits, which, coupled with the need for appearing at one's best when one feels at one's worst, fills the brightest and bravest spirit with black depression. How, thought I, can I hope to persuade these managers or directors of my superiority over the large number of Admirable Crichtons who are sitting eyeing me with dislike tempered with apprehension that I have a "special pull"? There we would sit, all of us dumb, glum and carefully dressed; then one would be chosen and, united by their common misfortune, the unsuccessful would gather their coats and start out again on some other fruitless quest.

There is no disease of the modern world which can be compared with it, except perhaps war, and what one might describe as machinization.

It began to look as though I should never get a job. At this time I was living in that—alas! too much taken for granted refuge, my home. My wound pension of eight shillings per week was made permanent, and I still had a little of my gratuity left. It seemed to me that I might as well learn something as do nothing. After working things out very carefully, I decided that I should just be able to manage a year's study under a Government course that was being arranged at London University for would-be journalists. I filled up forms, got second-hand books, and decided to give a perfect imitation of the poor Scotch student, although I had no bag of oatmeal, which was as well, as I have never been keen on that form of nourishment—a dislike which you appear to have inherited. However, I adopted a special system—a real one-year plan—worked out to the last halfpenny, which involved, amongst other things, my walking some ten miles a day to decrease bus fares. I dispensed with luncheon and gave up smoking. I was determined to show I could stick to it, and every day, for the first week or two, I got sadder and shabbier.

At the next desk to mine in these courses was an earnest blonde with beautiful eyes, corn-coloured hair and plenty of money. She was the daughter of a prosperous shopkeeper, and had just left her high school. She was the neatest and brightest thing I had ever seen; she had marvellous, clear, copperplate handwriting, always prepared her lessons, attended punctually to her lectures, was never late, never had colds, always had her stockings pulled up, and was, in fact, the perfect student. She had a well-lined neat luncheon basket, from which, in an unobtrusive and finished manner, she would produce a snowy napkin and then—her little white teeth sticking prettily from her firm red gums—she would bite neatly but decisively into the most appetizing sandwiches for which my mouth has ever watered, while I sat pretending to read a serious tome, but really trying to decide in my own mind whether I wanted her or her sandwiches more.

At times I would try to shock her nice well-ordered mind and serene assurance that everything was all right, by expounding extreme theories in which I myself did not believe. She was shocked, although anxious not to appear so, and I desisted from my malicious attempt to hurl red pebbles of sex or socialism into that clear pool of a contented bourgeois mind.

One day, shyly she offered me one of her sandwiches. There was a pink piece of ham peeping temptingly out of it: the crusts had been removed: it was square, symmetrical and toothsome. But how did this go with my rôle of the poor, proud student? I accepted it gravely, I am thankful to say. Gradually we made each other's better acquaintance, and she learned my circumstances. After accepting her sandwich I had a bad attack of soul. I pawned. . . . Oh, horrid moments of surreptitious removal from the family sideboard, of heading off maternal enquiry, of ineffectual untidy parcel making, of entry 'neath the arms of Palestine, of conjurer-like production, of contemptuous assessment, of reception of pieces of silver! I pawned one of my school sports prizes, namely, a silver cup received for running 440 yards faster—or with a better handicap—than my young fellow-barbarians, and invested the proceeds in a bunch of roses which I took round to her house with the utmost satisfaction. This, I thought, was splendid. The youthful, impoverished and war-scarred student pawns his athletic trophies to repay a delicate attention. It was, however, impossible to keep it up, as her stock of sandwiches was unfailing, whereas my reserve of negotiable rewards for athletic or intellectual excellences in the past was limited. Soon I gigo-lunched as it were, without a qualm, though I did make votive offerings whenever a windfall came my way.

I went to see her people, who lived in a warm Victorian interior full of antimacassars, aspidistras, wax flowers, lustres, the untouched *Chronicles of the Schönberg-Cotta Family* in leather bindings, and all that. She was the youngest daughter and, after having forced his earlier progeny into his business, the solid old Methodist shopkeeper had at last consented to give his youngest offspring a chance in something else, thinking, perhaps, that this product of his declining vigour might well be possessed of gifts which, though useless for commerce, might meet the inferior needs of journalism.

Hating my poverty for this and other reasons, I began to turn about in my mind some way of earning a little money to eke out my slender store. Perhaps, even, I thought, I could earn enough to fulfil my desire to return to Oxford. Had I not read of enterprising American students who paid for their university education by the sale of motor tires, by waiting in restaurants or even by arranging for the washing of the intimate garments of their fellow-students? It is true that I hardly saw myself strolling down the High with a large basket of dingy underclothes balanced on my head, but perhaps something might be done.

Then by chance I met Tony again, who had been my great friend as a Cadet. He had gone into business, and had various capitalistic aunts. He wished to try his newly acquired commercial experience on some sort of side line which would give him real intimate business experience. An aunt might be persuaded to provide a small sum as capital. All that was wanted was a good yarn. Tony was good at yarns.

After much pseudo-scientific examination of the sort of business that would suit our requirements, we hit upon an idea. Somebody had come into the advertising agency in which Tony was "learning," and tried to dispose of what was stated to be an infallible recipe for removing the wrinkles from women's faces. The firm's expert had stated that analysis had proved

that the mixture was harmless, but that he was not entirely convinced of its wrinkle-removing properties. The proprietor of
the article had left his address, but Tony was sure that his firm
would do nothing more in the matter. On the other hand, the
man had rather impressed Tony.

This seemed to be an opportunity. Every woman, we argued,
eventually became wrinkled. Though women might acquiesce
in grey hair, they could not tolerate wrinkles if there was a
reasonable way of getting rid of them. Our market was therefore unlimited. We had the chemist's assurance that the stuff
was harmless, and the inventor's assertion that continued applications brought a result.

Finally—Tony's aunt having come up to scratch and my
blonde having persuaded her father to invest—we made a bargain with the proud inventor, who was an ex-artillery captain
with a taste for chemistry and alcohol. He was to supply as
much of the stuff as we asked him for at a guaranteed price.
It was, if I remember rightly, two shillings a pint. He was
not to divulge the formula to anybody else, and the whole of
the manufacturing, selling and advertising ends—we loved to
use these phrases—were to be done as far as possible in our
spare time, mostly by myself, seeing that Tony's aunt had put
up the money.

We discussed all this far into the night with the pleasurable
feeling that we were assisting at the romantic birth of a future
world-famous business, and then stated our terms to the inventor at a conference lunch in an A.B.C. shop—a legitimate
charge we felt on auntie's capital investment. We were astonished to find that our collaborator proposed to sell us all the
rights for twenty pounds down. He was probably feeling
thirsty. We fell on him and beat him down, finally arranging
that he would supply us with the formula for five pounds and
ten pounds' worth of the stuff at a guaranteed price. We made

a mental reservation that, when we had made our fortunes we would seek out the poor man and pension him off somewhere in a small house with a large store of whisky. We insisted on delivery before payment, and finally compromised to the extent of a small advance. We also insisted that a guaranteed analysis should accompany the last few bottles. Thus, we thought, we were fairly well covered.

Our artilleryman agreed, and delivered his stuff in a couple of small barrels which we stored in a tiny room we had hired in Covent Garden.

We met in the evenings at Tony's and worked out what we called our "production and selling ends" and "advertising campaign," and we became frightfully technical about bottling and corking. We soon had a few attractive bottles made up, and then we began to tackle the problem of a name for the thing which we thought—perhaps rightly—would be the most important thing about it. I must also tell you—you may smile —that we made several copies of the formula, kept one each, and solemnly deposited the others in a heavily sealed envelope in Tony's safe, or rather in his mother's.

"This question of a name," said Tony, "is vital. Everybody knows how important it is. Look at the 'Uneeda' biscuit. The Americans are smart. They think about these things till they evolve something really snappy and suggestive. We must do the same."

We sat and looked at each other intensely, waiting for inspiration. Tony's mother looked in and said we ought to go to bed, as we both had to work next morning. We explained gently but firmly that we were at a critical stage in our business careers. She chuckled and sent us in some cold beer and chicken. This helped a lot. We thought intensely of things that were smooth.

"Roseleaf," said one of us.

"Too ordinary," we agreed.

"Velvetina?"

"Sounds too like a soap."

"Antiwrink? Smootholene?"

"Kill Wrinkle? Spelt Kyl-Ryn-Kyl."

That was it, and so it was.

Then we decided that we must have a romantic yarn to account for the discovery of this marvellous specific. We started off by trying to adapt the description of a similar specific which we had found in Jonson's *Volpone,* which goes: "I will only tell you: it is the powder that made Venus a Goddess (given her by Apollo), that kept her perpetually young, *cleared her wrinkles,* firmed her gums, filled her skin, coloured her hair" . . . but decided against it after grave argument. Eventually, we put the blame on a Sheikh from Al Yaman—I supplying the details—who made it out of the root of a thorn which grew in an inaccessible part of the desert, and the women of whose tribe, being famous for their magnificent complexions, were called by an Arab name—*Khuddud al durraq,* or something like it, which meant "Roses of Islam." All this, in spite, we added convincingly, of the notoriously hot sun of that part of the world.

We went into the possibilities of all sorts of striking advertisements, one of which, I remember, was called "How the Rhino Lost His Wrinkles," and which depicted an astonished-looking rhino gazing questioningly at his new smooth epidermis and then at the corrugated slough which lay on the ground beside him.

In short, we worked hard and had a lot of fun. I had an amusing time going round the various wholesale shops obtaining quotations for bottles and boxes for our "product." I found, of course, that the minimum wholesale figure was considerably in excess of our capacity, but eventually met people who would consent to supply smaller quantities. In the mornings and afternoons I went on with my studies, and in the evenings we worked in our tiny office-cum-factory.

At last we were ready, and we waited breathlessly for the response to the appearance of our first advertisement; this appeared in the back pages of a more or less reputable magazine which we were informed was the best medium for our "product." It was sandwiched in between a graphic illustration of a nose-stretching apparatus which apparently performed its beneficent function while the patient slept, and a dreadful woodcut portraying the miraculous action of a bunion remover.

We had, of course, been perturbed by the thought that our marvellous specific might be filched from us by some industrial pirate on the lookout for a good ramp, who would simply buy a bottle, analyse the contents, and then manufacture it on a vast scale, leaving us out in the cold. I had wonderful dreams —in intervals of bottling—of an interview with such a person, who, from his luxurious office in the city, would endeavour to dictate terms, only to be forced by our business acumen into an advantageous combine.

To cover this difficulty I paid a visit to an official in the Patent Office, for whom Tony had gotten a letter from a friend in the Board of Fisheries.

I interviewed this gentleman, who, with the true Civil Service outlook, took just as much trouble over my case—influenced perhaps by my war service—as he would have over a new weaving process, an invention for the utilization of banana skins or for perpetual motion. We went bravely into the question of patents. He was remarkably patient, but I suspect that he regarded me as his daily lunatic.

Eventually, we decided to put at the bottom of our advertisement the words, "Patent Applied for," which we thought would suffice.

After various worrying details were arranged, our advertisements appeared regularly in various magazines, the avuncular advance was nearly gone, and we settled down to wait for the harvest of postal orders which, we hoped, would put an almost unbearable strain on the post office authorities. But whilst we waited for postal orders, "we developed a campaign," and canvassed for small orders from the smaller perfumery and hairdressing establishments. This was a most instructive and amusing performance, and many were the conversations about Socialism, the War, religion and other weighty subjects which I had with the proprietors, who were in general, it seems to me, a most talkative class. Perhaps it was—maybe I flatter myself—that they recognized in Tony and myself something odd or unlike the ordinary canvasser. Be that as it may, they were usually fierce in argument, and the way to get a small order from them was to put up a dignified opposition to their thesis —in the rôle of the open-minded young man—and finally be squashed by the overwhelming fact or shattering statistic which they always produced for the *coup de grâce*.

Strange to relate, a number of misguided and corrugated individuals of the female sex did send for our specific, and the despatching end came into action. Our mail also included a testimonial from an ancient dame who stated that she had regained the schoolgirl complexion of her youth by its use. Beyond asking for another bottle, she seemed to have no *arrière pensée*, unless it was the desire to figure in print.

CHAPTER VIII

PRIVATE SECRETARY

JUST as Kyl-Ryn-Kyl made its first wavering uncertain steps, something happened which changed everything for me. The ramifications of causation soon become as untraceable as the vagaries of *routes d'intérêt commun* on a Michelin map when dusk is falling and the way is lost, but certain events in retrospect seem so noticeably to have been of portentous pregnancy that one wonders how on earth one did not remark their interesting position at the time. Anyhow, something clicked in the causal radius, and things began to happen.

As I was sallying from the front door of my people's house one fine morning in the early summer of 1919, prepared to do my usual six miles' walk *en route* to my studies and the vast Kyl-Ryn-Kyl plant, I met the postman, who gave me a letter. Some little time previously, as part of my job-getting campaign, which I still pursued intermittently, I had replied to an advertisement which had appeared in the papers, and which had advertised certain vacancies on a "specialist newspaper" for which I considered I might have a chance. At the time I had thought no more of it, but here to my surprise was a reply asking me to present myself at an address in the Strand any morning.

The next morning, arrayed in the smartest available raiment, I presented myself, and was received by a gentleman in a little office behind the glass door. I learned that the job in question was in connection with the propaganda being organized in favour of the anti-Bolshevik forces of General Denikin in South Russia which, at that time, were fighting against the Bolshevik armies and the corruption and stupidity of some of their own adherents.

Application had been made for ex-officers able to write good English and with a sound knowledge of French. Some two hundred had applied.

I was received kindly by a genial person with expensive clothes and a buttonhole, who complained that since he had advertised he had had to receive an unending procession of colonels and commanders.

"Well," said he to me when I had finished the tale of my modest exploits, "I dare say an experience of that sort may in the long run be more useful to you than if you had risen to be Bertie, the Boy Major."

With that he pushed the bell and said to the office-boy who entered, "Go and tell the queue outside not to wait, or they'll miss their dole. Tell 'em that the only job available is being hotly disputed by two ex-generals, a commodore and a field-marshal in the Siamese Defence Force."

Then he turned to me and said, "You go home and write me a 'middle' on Bolshevism."

"What's a middle?" I asked.

"Agreeable polished bunk," he replied tersely.

"Is that all?" I asked. "Isn't there a form to be filled up? Don't you want to know my age next birthday and Mother's Christian name?"

"No," he said. "Age is not important, and as I never had a Christian name myself, I don't care a damn about your mother's. Get out now and send me your stuff. No need for a stamped envelope, and if you don't hear, don't come again, for I am busy."

So I went home and wrote my essay. I remember that it began: "Bolshevism, which as an idea has much to commend it, has become the worst form of capitalism, because it consumes without replacing the stored wealth accumulated by millions of toilers."

Five days later I had been asked to call again.

I had very carefully considered whether or not I should pursue the matter. On the one hand it seemed weak-minded to deviate from the study course I had set myself, but on the other was the mysterious attractive unknown which beckoned me imperiously from what had become a dull and difficult period. I decided to go.

So, dressed for the part, I again went to the office in the Strand. I arrived extremely early in view of the possibility of queues of ex-generals, and after intimidating the office-boy, was allowed to wait in the office.

My interviewer came in, in great good spirits, chewing a large cigar.

"Well, young fellow," he greeted me, "you look very gay. Come into a fortune? Robbed the bank? Come on, say something," he went on. "I think I may have got a job for you."

"Well. Thank God for that," I replied. "I'd just decided to start becoming a self-made man."

Then I told him of my existing mode of life. He listened sympathetically and said, "I know all about that Scotch student and bag of oatmeal stuff. Only for the fact that I'm more Jew than Scotsman I'd be doing something like it in America now. Early on, however, I decided to ferment the oatmeal and, making a fierce spirit thereof, I sold it to thirsty fellow-students at a slight profit, and behold me to-day. The world is your oyster, my boy; you may get a pearl or peritonitis. But you won't get either unless you open it!

"Now to business," he went on. "As you know, I'm in touch with the Denikin people. There is a fellow called Asala who comes from them and who has just struck the town. He calls himself"—here he consulted a card—" 'The Representative of the Armed Forces of the Liberating Volunteer White Anti-Bolshevik Forces of the South for Commercial Diplomatic Purposes,' and all with capital letters. I'll give you a letter to him. He is staying at the Savoy. You'll be the first, but I'll have to send one or two others, so you'd better get a move on. He wants a secretary. Don't forget to call him 'Your Excellency.' "

I was duly grateful, took the letter, and, after a few supplementary questions, fled for the Savoy.

"Mr. Asala," said the hall porter, "Suite No. 82 at the Court."

I decided not to ask him to announce me, as I wanted to reconnoitre a little. I wished to spare no effort, and a preliminary survey is often useful in such cases. So as he was busy I sat down as if prepared to wait in the lounge, and when the porter was not looking I walked out and in again, and boldly went into the lift. We went up. I got out, and when it had disappeared, looked cautiously down the passage. "Nos. 80–92" said an illuminated notice, and a hand with spatulate fingers of impossible beauty pointed the way to fortune. "The hand of Fatma," said I to myself, remembering the Moslem superstition, "that means luck."

I went on cautiously till I came to No. 82. I listened outside for a moment, but all was quiet. I knocked gently, but there was no reply. It was still early. I tried the door and, opening it very cautiously, found myself in a sort of waiting-room. Into this three other doors opened. I gently shut the door of the corridor and, on tiptoe, peeped through each of the others in turn.

One belonged to the bathroom. It was empty. The second opened into a large sitting-room with a table in it, on which there were some papers. The third was the bedroom door. Sleeping peacefully, with one arm hanging over the side of the bed, was a man in brilliant pyjamas. His mouth was open, and he was snoring. I shut his door quietly and retired into the ante-room to think. I sat for about a minute. There was a telephone on the table opposite me. "What?" I thought, "should I do if it rang?" Then in a flash, a switch was pushed over on the causal switchboard, and I had a brilliant if immoral inspiration. I unhooked the phone gently, and ringing up the hall porter, I told him in a low official sort of voice that this was Mr. Asala's secretary speaking, and that if anybody at all came to ask for Mr. Asala, he was to ask if they came from the office in the Strand; if they did, he was to tell them to leave their address, that Mr. Asala could not see them that day, but that they would receive a summons from him in due course. The hall porter made no comment. Thus, I thought, I had an unsporting chance of eliminating the opposition candidates, should any arrive.

After accomplishing this, I felt slightly apprehensive, but rather pleased with myself. I waited and read *The Times*. Soon I heard stirrings and the bathroom door shut. Then more movement. Then a voice ordering coffee on the house-phone. After what seemed to be a reasonable interval, I knocked gently on the sitting-room door; it opened slightly, and a broad brown Slav face with little beady brown eyes and nose resembling a prune made of putty, peered out. There was a flamboyant dressing-gown, the carpet slippers were heel-trodden, and the general effect was unshaven and unappetizing. However, thought I, at least I have it to myself.

"Oo is eet?" said the face.

"Your Excellency," said I, slowly.

The face brightened. I went on.

"A friend of mine told me that I should come and see you with a view of entering Your Excellency's service as Private Secretary."

The gargoyle pulled itself together.

"Aar yers," he said. "The Propaganda 'e sent you round?"

"Yes," said I. "I have a letter."

"Secretary," said His Excellency, musingly.

"Yes," said I, "private."

His Excellency reflected, took the letter which I handed to him, read it, then looked up and said interrogatively, "Five sterlings per week."

"Of course," thought I, "I shall wake up soon"; but I did not blench, and said firmly, "With expenses if and while travelling."

"How so? What it mean, this *ifanwhile?*"

I explained that a lot depended on circumstances, and that five pounds per week would not keep me at the Savoy Hotel or cover travelling expenses.

"Ah!" said he, a light of comprehension breaking over his face like sunset on a field of stubble, "you mean out-of-pocket expenses. My Government he pay it all."

"Oh," thought I, "so we have a Government. That's something."

"All right," he went on. "I engage you on trial. Now come in, 'ave breakfast, and we will talk."

I went in full of joy and amazement.

"Last night," he began, speaking slowly and carefully, "I 'ave myself tried to engage a sthenodactyl. It is the first thing you must do."

I wondered if he was mad or a naturalist.

"A sthenodactyl, Your Excellency?" I said a little dubiously.

"Yes," said he, puzzled at my non-comprehension. "A sthenodactyl. You not know?"

He seemed taken aback at my not understanding.

"Heavens," said I to myself, "show some signs of intelligence."

"I have heard of a Pterodactyl, Your Excellency," I ventured.

"Wotzat?" said he.

"It's a sort of antediluvian . . . I mean a very old bird."

"*Boje moy!*" (My God!) was all the response this evoked. "Is he mad?"

Then he smiled.

" 'As it 'uge 'unger?"

"I believe they were very voracious. I mean . . . did eat a lot."

"It is ze same," he cried triumphantly. "Ah, yes. Last night I 'ave many letters. I must absolutely write. I go to find a sthenodactyl to write them. It is late. The offices are shut, the hotel can do nothing. I must write, 'aving inspiration. On the streets I find one, by Scott, a very old bird that eats a lot. Then she explain 'er life history, saying she is daughter of provincial pop with no money."

"Pop?"

"Wot you call priest. Pop in Russian. But also, think I, she may be Bolshevik spy or emissary of Polish or Georgian Government."

"I see," said I at last. "A typist you wanted."

"Yes," said he. "Sthenodactyl for confidential letters. Also, one of your duties is always most confidential to be. Do not talk of official affairs. It is most important. Do not wag the tongue about me. You smile. I not say him right? I see also you smile when I say pop. You 'ave English sense of humour. You must excuse my English."

"But, Your Excellency," said I, anxious to make amends, "you would laugh far more if I tried to speak Russian. You see, 'pop' in English denotes a small explosion, and is used in certain slang expressions. Your English is very good."

"It is not so good, but I approve that you should say so. One must be polite."

Breakfast appeared, and we talked on as we ate and drank. His Excellency then disappeared into his bedroom, and after a short interval, reappeared with his rather tubby form encased in the most beautiful fawn-grey suiting. He also wore a rainbow tie slightly cocked up towards a bloodshot brown eye, grey buckskin shoes, handkerchief of crimson silk dribbling studiedly from his breast pocket, eyeglass on black silk cord, an orchid in his buttonhole and he carried a gold-headed cane.

"Now," said he, "I go out. You are engaged. You go out to find good sthenodactyl, but better of commercial parents and not religious. Take a care. 'Ighly confidential will be some of the documents."

I said I would take great care.

"You will take lonch with me in grill?"

I accepted.

"Do not be late, and bring new sthenodactyl. At good lonch I 'ave sometime good idea I remember afterwards not. You wish money? Take advance for general expense. But keep ze account. Write the details down. And if you details forget, then invent them. But in inventions forget not I have political opponents. I mean, invention should be of a sort not unreasonable about small accounts. For the larger, I myself will all explain. Take care you of the pennies, and the pounds I will take care of myself. It is English proverb, no?"

"Yes," I said tactfully.

So saying, this genial person extracted a wad of five-pound notes from his breast pocket, shucked off two, as they so expressively say in America, gave them to me, held out his hand, which I shook, and departed down the corridor, stopping occasionally to admire himself in the mirrors with which the place abounded.

With my head in a whirl I was left with the two five-pound notes.

I returned to the sitting-room to think things out. Then I decided to go and get the sthenodactyl. As I went out the phone bell rang, and the hall porter told me that there was a gentleman to see Mr. Asala.

This person proved to be a persistent young man with a letter of introduction. I saw him, and regretfully informed him—using what I hoped he would think was a slight foreign accent—that the post had been filled.

Then I went out into the shining glorious Strand to an agency to get the most efficient sthenodactyl I could find.

CHAPTER IX

EN ROUTE FOR RUSSIA

I

So, Ivan, in this extraordinary way began a new and remarkable phase for me.

My new duties became so absorbing that I had to give up my course of studies and my interest in Kyl-Ryn-Kyl, which Tony finally disposed of somehow.

I debated considerably whether I should give up my studies, but finally decided that I must be quite free to exploit this new opportunity for whatever it might be worth.

I had long talks with Asala, whose English remained as incomprehensible as ever, but who was exceedingly kind and generous to me. His mission was to try to restore the economic life of that part of South Russia which was under the control of General Denikin, by arranging with responsible English firms a system of trade by barter, whereby the raw materials of South Russia would be exchanged for the manufactured goods needed by the population and for the military and naval supplies which Denikin's forces required. The barter arrangement was necessitated by the chaotic condition of the Volunteer Army currency, and by the fact that Denikin's Government had not been fully recognized.

I went to the War Office, and through various friends got in touch with the special sections that were dealing with that part of the world. They were very interested in Asala's mission, which was known to them, and hinted that they would like to be kept informed of anything of interest.

I also made a call on an unenthusiastic person in the Foreign Office, to whom I had been recommended by my cousin. This official thought the whole thing rather a disreputable adventure, and wondered why I could not get something more conventional to do, as if other opportunities were embarrassingly numerous. I explained at some length the difficulties. However, he also manifested some interest in what was going on, requested me to keep in touch with him, told me an amusing story about Lord Curzon, remained with great truth and regard my obedient Servant, and hurried off to Bill's wedding.

Asala was as kind, exotic and amusing as ever. He bought vast quantities of clothes from Savile Row, and each day more gloriously arrayed he got busier and busier with all sorts of merchants and emissaries who came to try to conclude contracts with the Government he represented. Financiers came and went, and the air was full of pre-loan conversations and rumours of concessions and monopolies. We lived in great style, had numberless heavy dinners and lunches with City experts, wrote memoranda, drafted contracts, sent telegrams to Russia, and generally behaved like the millionaires in popular fiction.

I used to arrive at the Savoy at about nine and dictate Asala's English letters to the appallingly beautiful and efficient sthenodactyl I had hired from an agency. She was far the most experienced business mind of us all, and her knowledge of commercial correspondence was only equalled by her "refained" manners and unshakable composure.

Then there was Samuel Finkelman. I was working at my Russian grammar one day in the sitting-room at the Savoy, waiting for the efficient Miss Brown to finish some letters. The door was flung open, and a large, fat man, expensively dressed, pushed in.

"What can I do for you?" I asked, as I rose to meet him.

He looked at me.

"You are the secretary of Mr. Asala?" he asked.

I said I was.

He extended a pudgy gleaming paw, and gave my hand a warm compress.

"Have a cigar," he said, drawing forth an outsize Corona.

I had noticed that it seemed to be a sort of rite amongst those who wished to establish business relations with Asala that they should incontinently give me cigars. Thus an expensive taste arose.

"Have another," he added, after I had accepted his offer, and produced a super-charged case.

I declined, gravely.

"I am Samuel Finkelman," went on my visitor, striking a Napoleonic pose. "First President and Founder of Samuel Finkelman, Inc. Pleased to have you meet me."

"Granted," said I, somewhat taken aback. "But I do not think we need any ink."

He stopped me with an unspeakably tragic gesture of both hands, which plainly indicated despair at my ignorance and/or my unspeakable levity in business.

"No. I do not sell ink, though I could get you all the ink in the world if you want. I am a corporation."

"Ah, yes," said I. "I understand. American."

"For two million sterling," said he, folding his hands on his stomach.

"You have practically an unlimited Corporation then," said I, looking at it. For I saw no reason to be over-polite in view of the way he had burst in.

His glittering hand advanced slowly and inexorably, and he seized my waistcoat button. His Semitic, powerful and unshaven face advanced slowly to within a short distance of my own. There seemed to irradiate from him an aura of power. There was also a blend of Havana, halitosis and eau-de-Cologne. I had the impression that, if he were opposed to me, no matter what I might do, one day he would get the better of me. I felt that, even if I got the better of him at first, he would watch and wait for a weak moment and exploit it ruthlessly. I felt that I was being hypnotized and slowly falling into the grip of an iron will and of a character unscrupulous and firm.

I came to myself and, backing out of reach, I lit the cigar hastily.

During the subsequent negotiations, whenever he came nearer, I swung round so that the lighted end was an inch or so from that part of his nose where the nursery slope became a ski-jump.

He went on.

"I come to offer your chief two million pounds' worth of goods."

He pronounced the figures reverently, as though they were part of an incantation.

"I will build my own ships. I will see to everything. Everything shall be first class. One fortune I have made in America. Another soon will be made in Europe. Those who help me now will make their fortune. Those who hinder——"

He snapped his coruscating fingers, and I instinctively looked for the opposition in the wastepaper basket.

Then he plunged into technical details.

This man Finkelman was one of the strangest characters I have ever met. He soon established a commanding position over my gay Asala, who was quite glad to let him form ambitious projects and generally get busy on his behalf.

In one of those moments of expansion which are often provoked in flamboyant personalities by an assumed lack of interest in them, he told me that he was the son of Jewish parents born in Kishinev. At the age of sixteen he had gone to New York to join an uncle. He had done everything. He had been a waiter, a musician, a porter and many other things until he had been able to get a position in a piece-goods business in New York. From this he had progressed and made money.

Thus Finkelman, a typical capitalist product.

So life went on in an unreal magazine-story sort of way which I enjoyed immensely. Often I contrasted my position with my former ascetic existence, and began to wonder whether my present affluent magnificence was or could be the result of that brief sacrifice.

At times, like the ancients in time of good fortune, I felt the need for making some voluntary sacrifice to restore the balance and to avert the crash. As I was unable to slay a cock in the Savoy, I used instead to increase my private charities. In spite of these atavistic precautions, I would be obsessed by the fear that the existing luxury was unsound, and that I should have done better not to have thrown up my studies, self-denial and austerities for all the rather dagoish and parvenu delights which made my daily life rather like a happy ending too long continued.

So, deliberately I introduced my skeletons to my mental feasts, but soon they were dispelled by the cheerful feeling of crackling five-pound notes in a new case, by soft, quiet, expensive comfortable clothes, and by the ability to revel in restaurants and theatres with that charming and agreeable hedonist, my employer.

If such a period comes to you, Ivan, enjoy it with both hands, while remembering that it will in all probability come to an end. This will help you to get the full savour out of it and hasten its finish, which may also be a good thing.

II

One fine morning Asala said to me, "Captain, I 'ave received a cable from the Government. I 'ave also received a letter from Harlampy Spiridonovitch, my confidential informer in the Ministry. The Government say I have enough contracts made and for more we could not pay; already perhaps we pay not for those we have. Harlampy Spiridonovitch tells me that the White Forces will advance in their mission of redemption and soon will enter into possession of all Russia. So I must return to be Johnny on the place. You come with me?"

I took the decision at once.

"Yes," I said, "certainly."

"All right," said Asala. "We go to Paris and Constantinople. The War Office have been asked to give us all facilities; you will arrange everything with them. Have you a revolver?"

"No," I replied.

"Take one of mine," he remarked. "I have three."

And so it was.

Everything was arranged. Tickets were taken and visas obtained. I said good-bye to my people, asked the War Office to warn the Military Mission of my arrival, and of the facilities they had promised me, enjoyed telling my friends with studied carelessness that I was going to Russia on Monday— one of the dearest vices of the restrained exhibitionist is the casual announcement of departure to Timbuctoo—and took a riotous farewell of London.

Officially, our stay at the Savoy closed in a blaze of splendour, and an enormous dinner by some of our principal contractors and financiers.

Finkelman sat next to me on this occasion, and on the impulse of the wine I leaned across and asked him what he really thought of our chances.

"Finkelman," said I, "would you go to Russia if you were in my place?"

"Yes," whispered Finkelman, through clouds of Corona fog. "I think I should. If your Asala is killed or shot there are always others. To me it seems recently you have the look of success. It is perhaps the excitement and novelty that gives you this. But I will give you fifty pounds per month and commission to enter my service, and you need not leave that of Asala. But what will you do in England? It is too old for young men. But what a place to come back to with money!"

He chuckled fatly and fingered his tie.

He was in high feather. He had made his contracts with Asala and sold and bought them back Heaven knows how many times. He was accompanying us to Paris. He leaned over again.

"I will give you five hundred pounds in notes if you will promise to tell me what F. [a rival Russian contractor] is doing."

I thought hard. I had already saved a little for my Oxford course, and this would bring it very near, whatever happened in Russia. It would be very easy. . . .

But somehow I could not.

"Sorry, Finkelman," I said. "I want five hundred badly. With it I could perhaps leave this orgy of finance and indigestion, go to Oxford, educate and English myself, and go on to solid security. But I can't do it, and I don't quite know why."

We discussed it a little more, but I held firm.

Next day, with headaches, we left for Paris.

I stood at the stern of the cross-Channel boat and took a last look at England, contrasting this departure with that other, five years before, when I had left in a troopship. I had that romantic feeling which makes journeys worth while. I felt that anything might happen and that surely something would. But what? Should I be killed after miraculously escaping in Arabia? Should I become a successful business man and make millions of roubles? Millions I made, all right, Ivan, but they were worth very little. Perhaps if Finkelman's luck held I might become a figure behind the scenes, and go in for thumping great loans and astronomical financial deals. Perhaps I might become an authority on Russia, make some brilliant reports to the brains in the F.O., and be admitted to become a gentle Brahmin myself. Then—perhaps with the roll of the ship—my mood changed to one of sadness and despondency. Why should I be driven to this strange expedient to earn a living and my coveted years at Oxford? Why be compelled to earn bread, butter and caviare by acting as private secretary to an extraordinary Muscovite who was obviously too charming to last and whose Government might disappear overnight? It seemed to me that we should all come to grief in Russia . . . perhaps a Bolshevik bullet or a bite from a typhus bug. Why could I not achieve some interesting haven of routine security?

I remembered my final conversation with the man in M.I.6 at the War Office, who had said to me, "Learn Russian as quickly as you can, and make sure you are paid in advance! Keep awake, and don't wait too long before beating a retreat! Everything melts much quicker than you would imagine possible when it comes to retreating in those parts."

This man was a remarkable individual who kept turning up in my life just before extraordinary events took place, so that afterwards when I met him I used to feel as if I had met the Wandering Jew. He had been one of that little band of officers of the guides who performed extraordinary feats during and immediately after the War. He had wandered off into Central Asia disguised as an Afghan woman; almost single-handed he had waged campaigns against Bolsheviks, Germans and hostile frontier tribes; he had annexed provinces, deposed kings and governors and issued new currencies. One of these magazine-story people whom one does occasionally meet in real life.

In a mood of black depression I retired to the bar, where I found Finkelman and Asala rivalling each other in surreptitious vomiting, both a horrible, unshaven green. I fled from the horrid sight and went forward to look at the seas tumbling against the bows.

There I saw a young Englishman bearing what the journalists call the indefinable stamp of the British naval officer. He greeted me cheerily, told me his name was Macarthy, and asked if I was going to the Peace Conference. As one often does with trustworthy-looking strangers on ships and trains, I took him into my confidence and told him my story.

"Well," said he, "that's queer. I'm going to that part of the world myself to rejoin my ship, a destroyer in the Black Sea. I spent all last year strafing the Bolo and rescuing first princesses and then myself. It's a great life. You keep your eyes open for the old *Montrose,* and if you come tearing down to the beach in your nightie one fine evening pursued by bearded Bolos and terrible Ivans, we'll take you off."

Curiously enough, this prophecy was to some extent fulfilled. With this companionship with one of my own kind I felt better, and after a drink with my new friend, life seemed rosy again.

Arrived in Paris, I gave Asala and Finkelman the slip and, after beating off the overtures of the "guides" and vendors of pornographic photographs, I strolled up to the Place de l'Opéra and drank an *apéritif* at the Café de la Paix, thinking that this was life indeed. It was curious, I thought, that I should have seen the Taj Mahal and the Arabian Desert before the Place Vendôme. But I can't attempt to describe Paris to you.

The next day the Peace Treaty was signed, and we had an amusing day with the crowds, ending up with a round of *boîtes de nuit*. Finkelman paid from the large exchange profits he had made on the strength of information from his friends to the effect that Germany would, after all, sign, which enabled him to make the right sort of gesture on the Bourse. I woke up where I had no business to be, was smilingly informed, "C'est la Paix," and went apprehensively to my hotel.

At that time Paris was infested by special missions and delegates of would-be nations, all with an axe to grind at the Peace Conference. Journalists were there by the thousand, and a new rumour was born every minute. As we had a vague official position as representatives of the South Russian Government, all sorts of people approached us on behalf of their forlorn hopes, pet lunacies or long-cherished political ambitions. I interviewed delegates of the distressed Yugoslavs in Fiume and of the disgruntled Italians languishing under Yugoslav oppression next door. There were loquacious Bulgarians, Macedonians, Albanians, Assyro-Chaldeans, dwellers in Mesopotamia, Parthians, Medes and Elamite minorities: they filled the hotels by day and the cabarets by night; they intrigued and borrowed money, tempted neutrals with invented decorations, and made maps of each other's coveted territories on clean white tablecloths and boldly nationalized whole provinces by daring *coups de crayon*.

III

We left Paris for Marseilles to board a transport on which I had been able to arrange passages through a pull with the Navy. I went out to see Marseilles at night, and got into a low haunt called Jack's Bar. I sat down, and after drinking beer, waited for something to happen. Two seamen began to quarrel noisily, and after a little there was a fight, knives appeared, and the lights went out. I took a chair, and holding it in front of me, both as a buffer and as a sign of neutrality—the tip may be useful to you if any of your young Communist or Fascist friends get fighting each other about girls or the general line of the party—I got to the door and fled for safety and the hotel.

We went ashore at Malta and eventually came to Constantinople. Many times after this did I arrive at Constantinople. I have come from Haidar Pasha, on the Simplon Orient Express and down from the Black Sea, but I shall always remember that first arrival in the early morning as the Bosphorus lay still and dreaming, with the minarets, the *caïques* and the cypresses.

This town was then in an extraordinary condition. It was full of Allied troops. There were British, French, Italian, Sikhs, Gurkhas, Turks, Jews, Armenians, Russians, Georgians and all the hodge-podge of the Levant. Through it all beat the slow rhythm of Moslem life, which had not then been torn up by Kemal. The old mosques and the venerable Turks made a pleasant contrast to the bustle of the military. They seemed to stare at the noisy moderns in their motor-cars, as though saying, "You will pass and we shall remain." The tranquil Golden Horn whispered, "Don't worry. There was greater activity than this before and it passed. What of the circuses, the siege and the massacres?"

. . . . .

Finkelman had stayed in Paris. Macarthy, greatly regretted, had gone up to the Black Sea after a convivial leave-taking at Tokatlian's, where Asala and I were staying, waiting for a sloop to take us to Novorossisk.

One day, as I was sitting in the lounge, I heard a voice behind me say, "Hullo, young fellow. How goes it? How's the one and only Asala? Still paying dividends?"

I looked round and saw it was the Major from M.I.6 who had befriended me at the War Office when I had gone to tell them all about Asala and to ask for facilities.

"Why," I said, "it's Major——"

"Jones—here," said he.

I remembered with a thrill that Jones had not been his name previously. I gave him my news, in which he was interested, and asked him what he was doing. He was somewhat vague and mysterious, which intrigued me still more.

I saw him on one or two occasions after this, and he gradually became friendly. One evening—we had met for a cocktail before dinner—to my great joy he proposed that I should go out with him and participate in a "stunt" which he had prepared. He said that he had reason to suspect that his regular assistant had become known to those whom he wished to gather in and that, if I wished, I might take his place. He was going to a little café in Stamboul, known to be the haunt of the Bolshevik organization which had linked up with certain extremists, Indian and Syrian nationalists, and was believed to be in receipt of subsidies from certain of our allies. They were out for the destruction of all European power in the East, and thought that this might best be attained by the propagation of Bolshevism amongst the native troops of the French and British forces.

As by this time I knew French fairly well, owing to practice with Asala's friends, it was finally decided that I should accompany him. It was agreed that we should pretend to be stewards from one of the boats in the harbour, and so into the rainy night I sallied through the back door of the hotel, clad in an old mackintosh, and with a soft hat pulled well down over my face, though I quite realized that this was an unnecessary precaution, as nobody was likely to recognize me. In my pocket was a small loaded automatic, and I was more excited than at any time since the War. We climbed into a cab with two fine black horses, drove in it to a spot near our destination in Stamboul, dismissed it, and assuming a semi-nautical gait, walked on. I was pleasurably exalted, for there is still something in intelligence work which appeals to the romantic in me—though actually from what I have seen it is often a sordid affair, involving contact with the sort of people that the French call sad individuals—and I was also having the pleasure of experiencing a previously imagined situation which, Ivan, as I may have told you before, is one of the joys of life that we owe to literature.

The place itself turned out to be a tumble-down sort of bar with dirty battered furniture. Some of the seats and tables were already occupied, but most were empty, as we had purposely arrived a little early, and, except for a few vague Oriental loungers smoking long pipes and drinking coffee, there seemed to be nobody of interest about.

We sat down at a table, and a waiter appeared to whom Jones said a few words in Russian. This man was in Jones's pay, and he whispered as he took our order that our quarry was not likely to arrive for a little. So we sat and drank some of the vilest Greek cognac I have ever been unfortunate enough to taste, whilst Jones entertained me with stories of his weird adventures.

Shortly after eleven o'clock, four men came in. They had a drink at the bar and then disappeared through a side door. Jones nudged me with his foot and tapped for the waiter. At this moment, a fifth man came in, and after looking round, took a table near us. Our waiter approached and, making one of those expressive Levantine signs which seem to render language unnecessary, informed us that, after taking the man's order, he would attend to us.

When he came he said something to Jones and hurried off to the bar. After a minute, Jones leaned over and said to me, quietly, "That's the chap, that's the fifth—sitting next but one to us. Look at your watch, pretend to discover it's late, shake hands with me, go straight up to your room in the hotel, ring up No. 55 at G.H.Q., and tell the man who answers from me to get on with it at once. He will know what is meant."

I repeated it all once to get it into my head—for I have never been able to understand how the characters in thrillers never forget their complicated and hastily given instructions— went through the pantomime and went out.

I remember now with some amusement that I carefully refrained from taking any of the cabs that were in the vicinity of the bar. I had read too many shockers in which the guileless champions of the right had, if females, fallen temporarily into the hands of their dark pursuer, and if males, awakened, bound hand and foot in a cellar underneath the Thames with the water rising every minute, through neglecting this obvious precaution, though for some occult reason the device is seldom used by the righteous to entrap the wicked. I suppose it is considered that no crook worthy of the name would fall into such a transparent error, or perhaps it is that heroes and detectives are too pure-minded to use such a trick, or maybe it costs too much to keep taxis ticking on in that way, so that only those with the resources of the opium trade or some other villainy can reasonably be supposed to be able to afford it. Be that as it may, my precaution gave me much pleasure. All went well. A mysterious person at G.H.Q. took the message, and although nothing appeared in the papers, the plotters were duly gathered in and Jones disappeared. I afterwards met him again in Russia and later on in the Balkans.

Feeling very full of myself, I went out again to an evil haunt named Bertha's Bar, which was run by a peroxide vice of uncertain old age, and there drank and danced with the local houris until the morning light showed them up. So ended a memorable day.

CHAPTER X

ICHABOD

I

SOON afterwards, Ivan, I got a message from G.H.Q.—everything was then still very military—to the effect that we could embark on H.M.S. *Hyacinth*, one of the Navy sloops which were used for the maintenance of liaison between the scattered units of the Allied forces in the Black Sea area.

One beautiful morning we boarded her, where she was lying "betwixt two seas," were received with bleak efficiency by her commander, and after stowing away our belongings, we paced the neat decks, feeling very incongruous and civilian as we went smartly out past Therapia and Büyükdere on our way to Varna. We had a pleasant voyage, and after touching at various ports we disembarked at Novorossisk in the summer time.

Asala saw the various authorities of the Volunteer Army Administration, and after some difficulty we managed to reserve a coupé in the night train that left for Ekaterinodar, the capital of the Kuban Cossack area, where were then located the H.Q. of General Denikin.

We waited for hours in the crowded station, which was teeming with people, many of whom had the air of having been there for one week, and of thinking it probable that they would have to stay for another.

At last the train puffed its way into the station from a siding and was promptly taken by assault by the crowd. Many of the carriages were already occupied by wise or crooked people, who had used either their intelligence or their money, or both, to grab seats whilst it was in formation on the siding. We eventually found our coupé, and got in with a military escort holding all sorts of people back. I stood and looked through the window at the crowd that surged about outside. It was varied and picturesque. Military uniforms prevailed, and one saw every type of the old Russian Army. There were generals with British Tommies' tunics covering their upper parts, whilst the lower were clothed in ceremonial scarlet riding-breeches. There were Georgians and Caucasians in huge shaggy sheepskin hats, leather riding-breeches, wasp-waisted uniform shirts decorated with revolver cartridge cases, riding-boots and gorgeous *kinjals*—Caucasian daggers worked in gold and ivory.

There were civilians and engineers from the railway in every sort of garb, and occasionally one saw British and Allied naval and military officers from the various missions, sailors, peasants in felt top-boots spitting sunflower seeds all over the place, and eating great chunks of red-fleshed watermelon. There were ladies dressed fashionably and others who wore khaki and blue Army socks. There were officials trying to look important and important officials trying at the last moment to get places for their legitimate and illegitimate families in the midst of a Russian exuberance of tears, last-minute embraces, cups of tea, expostulations, quarrels over seats, heel clickings, salutings, bowings from the waist and parcel distributions.

At last a bell clanged, and I thought that we were off at last. The groups broke up, there were wavings and farewell messages in the strange and musical Russian tongue. The engine snorted, shuffled along, and backed wheezily into a siding so as to give place to a military train with Cossacks in every carriage, on every footboard and on the roof. They were going to the Front, and as they steamed out they shouted songs with Slav energy and abandon. First there was a roaring, ranting melody, virile and even brutal at times, but always strangely stirring with that spiritual quality that Slav voices in unison seem to me to possess to a greater degree than any other.

> *"Nochka tiomnaia,*
> *Ya baioussia.*
> *Provodi menyah,*
> *Maroussia!"*

they sang, and then broke into another magnificent effort, a rah-rah-rah chorus which combined American vigour, negroid abandon, Wagnerian majesty and Welsh fervour. This was the first time I had ever heard such wonderful singing—even the Welsh and Highland Battalions had been nothing to it.

How shall I describe it to you, Ivan? First of all it was, if I may parallel a popular expression of to-day, extremely "soulful making." As I listened, I felt that I was willing to abandon everything, and that the only thing worth doing in the world was to join the shouting throng and march with them, all over the Russian steppe, fighting, sacking, drinking, swinking, sweating, loving, getting wounded, charging, dying. . . . A great emotion swept over me, and a feeling of extraordinary vigour; then suddenly I saw quite plainly the vision of a hearty strapping red-cheeked peasant girl, with her hands on her ample hips, her head tossed back, dancing merrily. On went the song, booming notes of organ music, rolling diapasons of melody sweeping over the great Russian land . . . churches with golden domes and golden bells . . . then the tune hinted of a vast futility . . . and through it all an undying affection for Holy Russia. . . .

The Cossacks steamed slowly out to fight their brothers, and our train puffed back into the station, where some hasty repairs were made to the engine. More bells rang, and at last we started. As we moved slowly out our coupé was invaded by a jolly Russian family, who apparently had only decided to start about five minutes before. They arrived piled up in an insufficient *izvoschik*, upon whose driver they declared war the moment they relieved him of their last parcel. For an instant I thought they would all fall upon him and tear him to pieces, so desperate was the dispute about the fare; eventually peace was made, the driver raised his whip and drove off, lashing his shaggy horses. The luggage of this family was hirsute and bizarre—they had every kind of parcel: they had pillows, feather beds, primus stoves, a samovar; they had trunks of exotic appearance; they had wicker baskets and gay chintz bags; they had all kinds of fruit, tins of bully beef and strange mosaic sausages wrapped in silver paper. They drifted vaguely along the packed train, making clucking noises of discontent. They seemed to have no tickets. "Little Mother, here is a splendid place," cried the daughter, a dark-haired girl with a magnificent figure, as she came to our compartment. "Thanks be to God, little pigeon," was the reply, and without more ado they surged in and began to bestow themselves and their belongings. Asala made a half-hearted protest, but was swamped in a torrent of expostulation and entreaty. So we talked and chatted till we reached Ekaterinodar, after a long and hot journey.

II

I should perhaps tell you something of what was happening in that part of Russia at that time. Korniloff's Volunteer Army had been formed, and had waged heroic war against the Bolsheviks. It may have been misguided and later riddled with corruption, but at the beginning it was certainly a most heroic affair. The early battles of the Volunteers against the Bolsheviks were extraordinary. They had no munitions and no supplies. The march of Korniloff and his Tekinese regiment from Turkestan over thousands of miles of frozen steppes inhabited by hostile peasants, the assembly at Novocherkassk, the training and munitioning of the Volunteer Army, really constitute an epic of heroism, endurance and improvisation. But they failed, Ivan, and their memory is in the limbo of lost causes, honoured only amongst a comparatively few refugee families living in misery in various parts of the world. But as they are dead, I suppose it matters not to them.

At that time Russia was the most extraordinary place the world can have seen. Red and White Forces swayed over the steppe in mortal combat; towns were taken and retaken. The most terrible cruelties and tortures were practised on both sides, atrocity begat atrocity.

Here is a description which I read somewhere and which I myself know not to be an overstatement of what happens when a town is captured and recaptured in a civil war: "Incessant rifle fire, the intermittent rattle of machine-guns, the crunch of skull-bones smashed by rifle butts, the groans and hoarse gasps of the dying, the howls of the frenzied mobs, cries for mercy from the tortured living, and blood, blood everywhere."

In a hospital in a town whose capture was imminent I have heard a wounded Russian boy drearily drag himself up from the pillow and ask whether it would shortly be time to kill himself.

Asala was optimistic about the chances of the Volunteer Army, but it soon became apparent to me that we were living in a fool's paradise, and that though things seemed to be going splendidly well with the Reds in full retreat, anything might happen at any moment. The money which was in circulation had no official rate of exchange, and foreign currencies were very hard to obtain; the White generals were divided, many were brave, gallant and able, others were not; but what struck me most at the time was the lack of "practicality," the unwillingness to give up personal jealousy for the common cause, the reluctance to come to a clear decision and, above all, the terrible amount of talk and discussion which took place on every possible and impossible occasion. Well might General Kaledin remark before he shot himself, that Russia was lost by too much talk. It was an extraordinary period, and every minute something cruel, bizarre, magnificent, amazing, comic, tragic or remarkable seemed to be happening. I have seldom lived at such a rate.

III

When we got to Ekaterinodar, capital of the Kuban, I installed myself at a hotel called the Kubanskoe Sobranye or the Kuban Club, and Asala rediscovered his long-lost family, who had arrived there to meet him.

This family consisted of a wife and two sisters, who all seemed to have had the most amazing adventures. Asala went every day to his Ministry, and every day he came back with a longer face. His friends were "out" and the "ins" would have nothing to do with him or his contracts. On the contrary, they denied his right to have made them. Things began to look blue, and the poor man, who remained as charming as ever, had great difficulty in paying my salary.

After a week or two of this I caught a severe attack of dysentery and became very ill. I got worse and worse, and was finally put into a Volunteer Army Hospital. This was a terrible business. The hospital had just been formed out of nothing very much, and was a struggling mass of patients and nurses. A trainload of casualties had just been received from the Front. Patients with gunshot wounds, typhus cases and people suffering from dysentery, pneumonia and every other sort of disease were all huddled together in a mess of misery. There were nothing like enough beds to go round, and at first I was deposited on a heap of straw on the floor. A little later on there was a conference in Russian about me. As far as I could gather, the question at issue was as to whether I was so ill that I ought to have a bed, or whether I was in such a parlous condition that it would not be worth while. Then somebody discovered that, though officially I was a Russian officer holding a Volunteer Commission, actually I was an Englishman. With magnificent politeness I was put into a bed at once and given special treatment. I wondered if that would happen in an English hospital were the rôles reversed.

I lay in my wooden bed and ate slops from a wooden spoon. I was very ill and wasted gradually away. My two neighbours died in the night and then two more after them. For three weeks I lay between life and death, in heat and pain and filth. It was far worse than anything I had experienced during the War. The worst of it all was the flies, which ran all over my face, for I felt too weak to brush them off. The best was the unvarying kindness and attention of the over-worked nurses and doctors. The Russians are capable of extremes. Here I saw the extreme of goodness and self-sacrifice, cheerfulness in the face of danger, and what is more difficult, the endurance of discomfort. I was frequently delirious, and my nurse used to tell me that I said the most extraordinary things in English and some other foreign language. Every day I thought I would surely die, and between the paroxysms of dysentery I thought of my approaching end with querulous self-pity. I would weep a little in my weakness and curse the day I met Asala. "Fool," I thought to myself, "this is how you pay for your brief spell of ostentation and luxury at the Savoy."

One day a doctor came with whom I could speak French. "Perhaps," said he, "from the English Mission I could get some emetine for you; if not——" He shrugged his shoulders.

Next day, instead of the nun-like features of my nurse, I woke up from a fitful sleep to see a red beefy soldier face looking at me—below it, the badges of the R.A.M.C.

"Who the hell are you?" it asked. "And what on earth are you doing here?"

Without waiting for a reply he bared my wasted arm, and with the utmost brutality and efficiency shot in a large dose of some drug, and then disappeared. He came the next day and did it again. In two weeks' time I staggered, a skeleton, away from that hospital with a discharge from the Russian Army in my pocket, which I still have.

When I got out I found that Asala was in prison under arrest for having exceeded his instructions. Through his wife I discovered that Akakey Akakeyvitch somebody or other, his particular enemy, had got control, and that his pal Harlampy Spiridonovitch, the ex-Minister, was in Constantinople with most of the cash, having left my poor Asala with the baby. I went to see him in his confinement camp, and found him supporting his misfortune with courage and humour. He said he would be released shortly for a civil trial, when his good faith would be established. Meanwhile, would I do what I could for his family? I had only thirty pounds left, as I had put what I had saved in London into a bank as a contribution towards my proposed Oxford studies.

Soon after this, to my great relief, the family of Asala disappeared in some mysterious way, and I was left to my own immediate problems. They were pressing enough. I had not yet learned Russian well enough to be of much use to anybody, and I had no friends. It seemed useless to try to get anything out of Asala's Ministry under the circumstances, and I shrank from exposing the decay of my hopes to some of the people in the Military Mission whom I had met on equal terms, and to whom I had exaggerated my status a little because they had seemed rather supercilious and inflated in their official security.

Luckily for me the exchange value of an English pound was enormous and the necessities of life were very cheap.

I decided to go up to Rostov, which had become the H.Q. of the then victorious and advancing Russian Volunteer Army, as I had heard that British firms were beginning to open up there in the hope of resuming their former profitable business with the Russian Empire. So to Rostov I went, and took a room in the best hotel. There I made the acquaintance of an English business man, on whom be peace. He had just concluded the outlines of a big deal with a group of Russians and was about to return to England to finance it. As the situation seemed—to say the least of it—liable to change while he was away, he wanted someone he could trust to keep him informed of developments during his absence in London. He decided he could trust me. He stayed a fortnight, introduced me to the Consul and the local mission as his representative, turned over his rooms and appurtenances, one of whom was very embarrassing to me, and offered me the choice of fifteen pounds a month or an enormous sum in roubles. I opted for the pounds, and in advance, for the probable period of his absence. He laughed and agreed. It was also settled that I need not neglect any other business opportunities that arrived, provided that they did not run counter to his.

So I again achieved a working basis.

CHAPTER XI

RUSSIAN RAMBLE

I

IN Rostov I began to meet the other business men and the people on the economic side of the British Mission. One individual I met had imported a large consignment of medicaments and medical instruments. He was a Yorkshireman, and had married a French wife, who had stayed in England to look after his children. He was not a particularly attractive individual, being surly, and as he knew no languages he did not make much progress. He used to come and use up my precious stores of pipe tobacco and alcohol, and I could never have the heart to say him nay or to turn him out, because I knew that he had been shell-shocked in the War and had an extraordinarily good record.

His experiences had undoubtedly rendered him abnormal, and I was not surprised when he came in one day and told me that his wife had gone off with somebody else—I personally wondered how she had been able to stand him so long—and that he wished to leave immediately. He asked me if I would take over the job of selling his consignment on a commission basis and for whatever I could get for it.

I agreed, and thereafter had a most amusing time going round with the samples and bills of lading to see the Customs people and various possible purchasers. I still remember the frightful correspondence that took place about a number of breast relievers, if you please, which had got broken in the Customs. It was a most amazing thing about which to have had to talk to bearded *Tchinovniks*. Eventually I sold my consignment to the railway organisation for an astronomical sum in roubles. My own commission amounted to about half a million, but in addition, I got a job with a British firm in a large way of business which had an official position and was working with the British Military Mission. Its functions consisted in arranging the supply of certain goods to civil departments of the Volunteer Army Administration against an exchange of raw materials, the whole operation being backed by a Government guarantee. My job was to go and arrange the transport of the raw materials from where they lay in sheds and villages up-country, and take charge of relations with the British Mission, to whom I was also to report on what I saw on my travels. As you can imagine, these journeys were neither safe nor comfortable, but they did improve my Russian.

I spent some time in the office of this company and obtained a little much-needed business training.

I had an amusing time trying to convert my melting roubles into something of permanent value, and I bought all sorts of things—subalterns' cheques, real and imitation jewellery, caviare, furs, carpets and all the foreign currency I could find. The problem was to get something portable and of permanent value which could be easily sold in a crisis.

If, Ivan, you should, in a revolution or the results of the present world economic policy, ever be faced with a similar problem, may I, as a result of much study and painful experience of the "flations de, re, and in," suggest that you put your assets in times of crisis into safety-razor blades? They are of small bulk and common demand. Jewels, at such times, can only be sold to the Commissar's wife, and when she is in the market there is often a glut, or the Commissar is in a position to get them for nothing. Also, their possession is fraught with some danger, seeing that the awakening proletariat seldom stops for explanations, and possession of such capitalist gew-gaws is usually considered as all the evidence that is needed. On the other hand, I fancy that shaving would in England, at any rate, survive the shock of revolution. Furthermore, dia-monds are very difficult in cases of small payments. It is annoy-ing to have to give one away for a loaf or a tin of sardines or a railway ticket, as I have seen occur when the people "got control of the means of exchange," and as may happen if some Chief Shirt or other starts putting his economic theory into practice. The same is true of fur coats and carpets. I could not bear to see you cut my Shirvan in half so as to get a privilege milk ticket for my grandson. Another good line is the little flints that go in cigarette lighters, for smoking is also likely to sur-vive, and they are very easy to smuggle. I once made a lot of depreciated currency by taking quantities of them across a cer-tain frontier in my sponge-bag.

So life went on, and I went all over the south of Russia and had many experiences.

On one occasion I met an enthusiastic youth in the Armoured Train Detachment of the Volunteer Army. We had a tremen-dous dinner, and in a moment of youthful and alcoholic abandon I accepted his offer to go up to the Front forthwith, and woke up next morning to find myself in a bunk in a carriage of the Volunteer Army Armoured Train Service on an unreliable railway line, with a machine-gun firing away at no visible target from the next window, whilst we beat a hurried retreat, having apparently penetrated the Bolshevik line more or less unawares. It was all too unreal for me to worry much about it. We were away two days, and I remember that I lived mostly on vodka and marmalade. But my most vivid memory was the effect of machine-gun fire on a morning-after head!

It was about then that I first met your mother. I had been invited to what, with more euphemism than accuracy, was called a "cup of tea" at a local hotel. The proceeds were in aid of the Volunteer Army. It began as a cup of tea, but ended, as one might say, in a kettle of fish about three in the morning. As I happened to be the only Englishman present, I was asked to make a reply in response to the toast that had been drunk to the British Mission. This I did with the precise articulation of one doubting the enduring stability of the universe. I got through the speech with credit, however, and did even better with the formidable toast that followed. When, however, I came to sit down, my chair collapsed under me, and I looked up from the floor to see your mother's face registering school-girlish glee at my discomfiture. So for the rest of the evening we danced together, until she was removed by her parents at a decorous hour. Much later, I went out of the hotel room into the clear cold night, in which, owing to frost and alcohol, everything was sharp and bright as in a fairy-tale, and dreamed great dreams as I rode home on a sleigh with a fast horse and the bells tinkling.

II

The Volunteer Army began to get demoralized and corrupt. In the main street of Rostov, on one of the principal shop fronts, there was displayed a large map showing the position of the rival armies. In order to get an idea of the situation, it is necessary to imagine that Messrs. Harrods, instead of displaying in their shop windows the latest styles in "beach modes" or "slumber wear," were to show a map of England on a large scale, that across it was pinned a piece of blue wool stretching from Yarmouth to Birmingham, and that in the centre of the line there was an ominous arrow-shaped sag pointing towards London. Imagine also that on the other side of the line was an army so hostile that if it reached London a large proportion of the inhabitants would have to flee in order to escape death and despoliation, and that on the day of occupation money would have no value.

Every day the dent in the line became more and more pronounced, and it soon became obvious that Rostov would have to be evacuated.

Then there began a scurry of Headquarters officials and the less easily movable portions of families towards Ekaterinodar and Novorossisk. Every day the atmosphere became more and more menacing and local Bolshevism began to rear its head. The night life of the city grew gayer and more hectic every night, for none knew where he next would drink or flirt or whether, indeed, he would ever do so again.

The exchanges fell and fell as foreign money came more and more in demand. I went around trying to convert my roubles into something solid and helping the office people to try to get transport for our stocks.

The weather grew colder and colder, and the crowds at the station larger and more miserable.

My English business man had returned to liquidate his affairs, but had not stayed long, after coming back to his favourite hotel to dine to find its façade decorated by three corpses of men who had been hanged, to discourage the agitators.

I met my friend the Intelligence Major, who appeared in a new incarnation, and told me that everything was cracking and that I should prepare to leave at any moment.

At last, one wintry morning I was told by the Mission that

all British subjects would have to leave that same night. I saw the authorities, who told me that I was to be in charge of a waggon on a certain train reserved for the members of the British colony. The R.T.O. said that I ought to report to him at 4.30, and that a British sentry would be at my disposal to guard the waggon.

I went down in good time, and fighting my way through the surging crowds, I got to the R.T.O.'s office, which was besieged by all sorts of people who were endeavouring to get accommodation on the train. I was told where the waggon was, and found it in a siding, guarded by a corporal and a file of men, who were stonily resisting the pleas for places of aged persons, nobles, officers, friends of the general and attractive females. Members of the British colony, looking irrevocably Victorian in that *galère,* began to arrive, passes were inspected, and all sorts of arguments and disputes about the accommodation of family retainers, friends and relatives took place. One grim woman required a whole coupé for herself, dogs, pets, samovar, cushions and impedimenta, and when I explained to her that people's lives were in question, she only replied that the general had promised her a coupé and that if she did not get one she would complain in person. I told her with some glee that I hoped she would, as the general in question was some fifty miles up the front line. Finally, I relaxed the iron rule, let in as many women, children and old persons as could be squashed in, stowed my own impedimenta, and leaving the corporal in charge with strict orders to turn everyone away, went off to report to the R.T.O. that all was ready.

Then we waited while everything grew colder and more miserable than before, though that had seemed hardly possible. The scene in the station yards was terrible. Ladies in fur coats and dainty shoes were paddling about in the slushy snow, pushing luggage on perambulators, wheelbarrows and sleighs, trying to get information and places; officers were wandering about disconsolately; people were drinking tea in all sorts of unexpected places and the restaurant of the station was crammed with humanity, much of which must have been there several days. Anywhere under cover the atmosphere was fœtid, whilst outside there was a bone-chilling thaw.

The railway employees were doing their best, but many of the men were in sympathy with the Bolsheviks, and others, who had no intention of leaving their homes, soon realized that, whatever their opinions, as they would very soon have to pretend to be Reds, the safest policy was to sit at home and keep quiet, avoiding contacts with either side until the issue should be clearer.

Later on, a military train arrived with much fuss, and with my R.T.O. friend I strolled along to see what was happening. It was General Wrangel arriving from the Front after his dispute with the Commander-in-Chief, General Denikin. Wrangel was a remarkable man, of whom I saw a good deal afterwards, and who, if he had succeeded to the supreme command a little earlier, might very likely have altered the course of events. At that moment, however, all I saw was a tall barbaric figure in Cossack uniform, who swept out of the train in company with his staff for a conference with the G.O.C. In about half an hour he jingled back again, looking stern and determined. In five minutes his train was under way, and he steamed out of the station. His advice had not been taken, and he retired to the south. Everyone was sorry to see him go, for his reputation was great, and above all, in that confusion, his forces were disciplined and sure.

Under the impression that I had witnessed an event of importance I strolled dejectedly along to my waggon, where I found my faithful corporal resisting the blandishments of a beautiful and heavily laden countess. Feeling a despicable cad and coward, I gave her instead of a seat a note to the R.T.O., though I had the gravest doubts as to whether she would ever be able to get within appealing distance of him. This, Ivan, was an action I have often regretted. Even now, at this distance of time, I can clearly recall the pathetic look in her large appealing eyes and see the quiver in her upper lip as she summoned her reserves of strength to appeal in desperate need to someone she did not know. She asked just once and took what was, as she knew, tantamount to a cowardly refusal to help, with such a brave resignation and absence of fuss that I felt bitterly ashamed. There was of course no room, Ivan; my orders were absolutely unchangeable; I was to take nobody who had not a pass and who was not either a British subject or closely related to one. Still, she might have been squeezed in. The waggon was already crammed, there were other trains for Russian civilians—though Heaven alone knew where and whether they would go—I had already refused less attractive ladies without appealing eyes, delicately formed features and a soul wavelength which concurred with mine; indeed, there were fifteen or twenty ordinary middle-aged unattractive females waiting eagerly a few yards away for any sign of weakness to renew their applications. Were not their claims as good as those of this seductive creature? Had they not lives to lose? Could they not suffer as she? Of course they had and could. But as she turned and picked her despairing way through the slush, yet dainty in her desperation, I wished . . . and have never stopped wishing, that I had broken the rules, and by an affirmative word caused *her* face to light up in gratitude to *me*. I hope, sentimentally, that she got away without repugnant sacrifice, or that if she stayed, she became an idealist Communist and married somebody high up in the Party who could give her an interest in life, a warm room, export caviare, superior rations, silk stockings and take her to the ballet.

At last an engine came and shunted us, and we thought we should soon start. And then we were left for an hour on a wind-swept siding, and rumours flew thick and fast. The Bolsheviks had surrounded the town; all the engine-drivers had gone over to them. There was fighting in the station. The local Reds had got control. Two British officers had been killed. The Chief of the Mission had been captured. Then the engine puffed back again and took us to the rest of the train. This was fuller than any train I have ever seen. There were soldiers on the roof. Our roof was soon covered with them.

"Why is there such a noise of thunder?" asked a rabbit-toothed governess of her toad-like mistress.

"It is the soldiers stamping on the roof," was the reply.

Then she asked me: "Can't you stop them?"

"No," I said. "They do it to keep their feet warm."

"They are knocking thousands of bugs down," she complained disgustedly.

They were.

"Well," I said consolingly, "they will soon be all down now."

A curious conversation, Ivan, and one which has often caused me to smile reminiscently when I should have been listening to a lucid *exposé* by the Delegate of Neopomponia on the economic policy of that almost great State.

At last we started; then we stopped for five minutes for no known reason. Finally, with the soldiers stamping and singing, we drew out of the station and proceeded on our way to the south and comparative safety.

The train jolted itself along in a more determined manner:

we progressed rapidly along the frozen fields outside Rostov, came to a junction which had the curious name of Tikhoretskaia, stopped, changed our engine, and rattled along over the snow-covered Kuban steppe on the way to Ekaterinodar.

Most of the time the soldiers stamped, the bugs bit, the British colony fidgeted, talked scandal, discussed rumours, made tea, made friends and quarrelled.

I sat on my heaped-up luggage, which consisted of two valises and three kitbags. One of the kitbags had in it various objects of value which I had bought with the roubles I had gained in various deals resulting from the sale of the firm's imports and of small consignments received from panic-stricken merchants for liquidation, while they, seeing the crash coming, bolted for the comparative security of Novorossisk and the Black Sea ports; the second contained a million roubles in notes. Of this last I made a pillow, and stretching myself out as well as I could, I slept soundly till I was told that we were coming into Ekaterinodar, the headquarters of the Kuban Cossacks, the town where I had arrived with Asala, full of hope as the White Armies advanced to Moscow, where I had had dysentery, and where poor Asala had been imprisoned and still was, for all I knew.

Actually, my dear Ivan, I heard that he had been released in time and had made good his escape from the Whites and Reds and Greens and all the rest of them; but I have never seen him again, though I am always expecting him to arrive in my office and ask for my assistance in the floating of a Turkestan seven per cent. loan for old times' sake.

Arrived safely at Ekaterinodar, everyone felt a little more secure as we had put several hundred versts between us and the approaching Bolsheviks, and, shifting as fronts were in those days, it hardly seemed possible that there could be any immediate danger. Actually, the White forces retook Rostov a few days after this, and your uncle—who is now dead, poor fellow —was able to go and inspect the rooms in the hotel where your mother and her people had lived a few days before, and even to retrieve some of the things that had been left.

I got out of the train at Ekaterinodar, and walking down the station yards in search of some water to wash with, I suddenly came upon your mother looking indescribably cute with a large kettle of hot water which she was holding with some difficulty over the wavering flame of a spirit lamp. All around were rails, engines, soldiers, refugees, Cossacks, peasants, sidings, derelict waggons, bits of old iron and a mixture of slush and coal-dust. We met and shook hands, and I was given a little water. She told me she was going with her family to Novorossisk. For five minutes we exchanged experiences. Owing to your grand-father's influence with the White Ministry of Communications, he had been able to secure a special waggon for himself and his friends, but it had broken down a good many times, owing, it was thought, to Bolshevik sabotage, and this had caused a good deal of excitement. She was facing the situation with the calm of one who, at a tender age, had seen her father and brother arrested, had set off alone in revolutionary Moscow at night to warn her brother's friend, and having got to his flat had learnt that it was he who had given the plans of the abortive coup to the Red authorities. Later, at the age of sixteen, she poured brandy into the gangrenous wounds of civil war casualties because in the ship in which she was fleeing from Odessa no other disinfectant was available.

For a brief space we stood and talked, and then we parted, both of us, I think, with a presentiment of future association. I have before, I believe, indicated the futility of studies of causation—of saying, for example, "If your mother had not looked so fascinating with her furs and her kettle and all, there would have been no *coup de foudre,* I should not have asked for her address in Novorossisk, and then you might never have been born." Futile perhaps, but futility is sometimes amusing, and I find the combination of a kettle, a young girl, a White Army evacuation, a railway station, myself in flight with a million roubles and a bag of objects of art and virtu an excellent reminiscence liqueur.

The train went slowly out of the station, and I recomposed myself on my million roubles, and wondered how far I really was towards the realization of my ambition to collect the six or seven hundred pounds I needed for Oxford. At that time I had scraped together about two hundred and fifty pounds in sterling, the result of the various commercial operations I had succeeded in arranging, plus what I had been able to save from the salary I was paid by the firm. Living was cheap, and for the moment I was being reasonably well paid in English money. If, I thought, as the train bumped along, the situation could hold together for another year, I might just manage, seeing that, in addition to the sums already obtained, I had invested about fifty pounds in bargains, curios, jewellery and the like, some of which I had obviously been able to get at much less than their value. There was also the possibility that I might be able to pull off a deal for the firm and make a good sum in special bonus or commission. On the other hand, some of the cheques and drafts I had bought with my roubles might be valueless; the front was obviously broken, the Reds were in full cry for the coast, and if I was not careful I might end up in a Red prison or with my throat cut.

Next morning we arrived at Novorossisk and the coast. The British Mission was strongly encamped near the port; there were comforting-looking grey British warships in the harbour, and I was thoroughly pleased at having got successfully out of the panicky and miserable atmosphere of Rostov.

I took a room in the overcrowded hotel, deposited my roubles and papers with the firm—I remember that the safe, guarded by a stalwart Ukrainian peasant, was a large room containing masses of roubles, carpets, tins of caviare, silver bars and bottles of cognac, perfume and the like, whilst in the middle was a tin box full of officers' cheques, contracts, bonds, and documents—and after a thorough cleansing and de-lousing, I sallied out to celebrate my successful arrival.

After dinner, with all sorts of *zakouski* and some vodka, I went round the cabarets. Then tiring of sweet champagne and Caucasian dances, and somewhat exalted, I walked along the road which skirts the harbour, thinking high sparkling thoughts, while the cold sea breeze impacted on my heated face and the firmly grasped handle of the revolver in my coat pocket prevented the evanescence of the Dutch courageous attitude in which I found myself.

I thought it all great fun, Ivan, to be by myself with just the right amount taken, an automatic, a sense of a certain achievement, a clear sparkling night and a feeling that I really was in rather a peculiar position, surrounded as I was by Russians, Caucasians, generals, officers, merchants and cabaret vamps. I felt that I need not really go to bed at all that night, as I had got two days' leave. I shouted with laughter, Ivan, on that windy street in Novorossisk, and thought what a fine boy was I. I took out my revolver and fired two shots at the pavement just for the fun of hearing the crack of the report and the clean smack and whir of the bullets as they ricocheted off into the sea. Then, fearing that I should alarm the patrol, I strolled on, while frantic mirth bubbled up and was suppressed, and I endeavoured to look as if I had had nothing whatever to do with the recent fusillade.

In this mood I approached a large house, from which came gay sounds. I approached cautiously, and found that I had come to a British N.C.O.s' mess, where a sergeants' and corporals' dance was going on, attended by all sorts of people who had apparently drifted in from anywhere in the same way as myself. I was recognized by the corporal who had escorted our waggon from Rostov, and induced into the festivity. I drank, and made friends with an enormous sergeant from the S. and T. Corps. Soon I found myself whirling round the floor in an imitation of the Caucasian dance known as *Lezginka*. This, Ivan, is a picturesque performance that will probably survive till you are of an age to go to a cabaret. With an enormous shaggy fur cap on my head and gripping a *Kinjal*, or Caucasian dagger, in my teeth, I whirled round the room while the band—which was more or less inebriated—played faster and faster and the audience clapped their hands. Suddenly, for no known reason that I can remember, the affair changed from the wild rush of the *Lezginka* to a variety of Sir Roger de Coverley, and I found myself with one arm linked with that of my elephantine S. and T. sergeant, while the two of us gyrated solemnly. He was so tremendous that he whirled me off my feet, and I flew off from him at a tangent through the door out into the garden, and came to a standstill in an unfriendly bush. I remember seeing the enormous red face and ginger moustache of the sergeant peering at me, and then I knew no more. Actually, the sergeant-major threw me into a box car and drove me to his railway waggon, held me upside down whilst exhorting me to use the time-honoured method of two fingers on the back of the tongue, and put me to bed.

I awoke next morning to see and smell him enjoying a hearty breakfast of Army bacon and sardines, and turning round I avoided the horrid sight, while every throb of my head hammered home the realization of retribution.

I stayed for a day or two with my sergeant, and lived on Army rations again, supplemented by caviare. It was not in this mission that the troops, when supplied with caviare for a ration, complained that "this 'ere blanky potted meat is too fishy, sir," but my sergeant did remark, as he drank a couple of bottles at that revolting breakfast, that "this 'ere local champagne is all blinkin' bubbles and no ruddy guts," and I felt that the description might easily have applied to my own morning-after condition.

This existence proved somewhat too Gargantuan, and although pressed to stay, I departed laden with cheese, jam, leather coats—fur-collared, one (Russian issue, aviators, for the use of)—boots, shirts and all sorts of other illicitly obtained stores which I had purchased with my depreciated roubles.

I then transferred myself and my belongings to an even more splendid railway waggon than the converted *teplushka* which was the sergeant's home. This was the special waggon allotted to the U. S. Consul, a friend of mine, who was also a worshipper from afar of your mother.

His waggon was very splendidly fitted. In it was "Willie, the War Correspondent." He was quite the toughest individual I had so far met, but with it all he was extremely kind and unselfish. He always carried an enormous revolver, or, as he called it, "packed a gat." But the bulge in his outline caused by this armament was as nothing to that caused by his flask of what he called "hard liquor." As he put it, he was "always willing to hand out a shot from either!"

I made an excursion or two with Willie, and I particularly

remember going with him to inspect a small town on the outskirts of Novorossisk, which had recently suffered from the attentions of the Greens. The Greens were inhabitants of Russia, who objected equally to the depredations of Reds and Whites. They were mostly outraged peasants with a sprinkling of deserters from either side, and their method of trying to ensure the peaceful exploitation of their farms was to shoot at all strangers and raid the lines of communication of any army that appeared in the vicinity. Willie sympathized with these ideas, and wanted to get in touch for the delectation of the great American public. I wanted, for a certain reason, to get an idea of their real situation. So we got off the train and knocked at the door of the first house we saw that had a light showing. As soon as the bell began to jangle, a fusillade of shots was fired at us and we flopped down into the mud, profane but unhurt.

Willie was furious, and drawing his gun, started to fire back, with the result that the fusillade stopped.

"Oh, boy," said Willie from the floor, "those sons of bitches jus' doan wannus."

So we withdrew, and found that, in the meanwhile, our waggon had been moved down some unknown siding. After tramping about in the rain for several hours, we at last found it, and I can still remember how hospitable and bright it looked with the lights shining through the window and a smell of roast chicken coming through the door to meet us.

Soon after this Willie went to Armenia to "feature the massacres," and the Consul showed me a letter from him, in which he complained of being very ill of "pernicious Armenia," a remark for which I owe him many thanks, as I fear I have often adopted it without due acknowledgment. He was a good fellow, in spite of the yellow Gods he served and the amazing language which he used.

Soon after William left, my Consul lost his waggon, and I went to live in the funny little house of an Esthonian widow who suffered from religious mania. I do not know exactly to what sect she belonged, but she was convinced that the end of the world was imminent, and that this was rather a matter for rejoicing than otherwise. She had a son of fourteen years whom she had driven almost half-witted with her devotions, and whom she used to terrorize every night with apocalyptic visions, with the result that the poor boy used to pray far into the night in a loud voice that kept me awake; all my banging on the wall could do was to make him relapse into a whining mumble that was just as bad as the more full-throated petition.

On one occasion, when I had regrettably gay company, the widow appeared and began to pray for us with such vigour that perforce we were ashamed, and went out to a cabaret to try to forget her, which even the protagonist of a different philosophy had difficulty in doing, such was the extraordinary impression of fanatical doom which emanated from our denouncer. Whenever I see that gloomy old gentleman in chains that comes in and curses everybody in *Rigoletto* I am reminded of that old woman, whereas I have no such clear recollection of the other.

III

At about this time, after returning from a trip inland in search of some sunflower-seed oil which we wished to obtain and export against a consignment of mixed chemicals, the chief of the firm had the happy idea of sending me on a tour in the Crimea. This area then seemed fairly strongly held by the Whites, and it was hoped we might find some exportable goods which we could buy with the large sum in local currency with which the firm had got landed, and which was melting, as regarded its real value, as the exchange went down, like a snow-ball in an oven, whilst retaining to a certain extent its local purchasing power. I was given a vast sum in roubles and a credit, and then told to go and buy what I could, get it out, and come back. I was to pay particular attention to the possibilities of exporting some of the Crimean wines, as in view of offers received from a man to whom I had letters of introduction and who had been in charge of the Tsar's cellars and vineyards in Yalta. Altogether a mission to gladden the heart of any young man, and one which pleased me immensely.

Anyway, after bidding good-bye to your mother, whom I used to visit most evenings, propitiating your grandparents with frequent gifts as an excuse for constantly being about—gifts which I purchased from my pleasant sergeant in the S. and T. —I left Novorossisk in a small cabotage boat which was going to Anarpa and to Theodosia. It was about the size of a tugboat, and was full, as only a Russian boat can be in times of stress and revolution. Through commercial influence, I had obtained a half-share of the captain's cabin.

We sailed out in magnificent weather, and soon arrived at Anarpa, where I went ashore to lunch.

After dinner I boarded my small steamer again, and found that it had become even more crowded than before, though that had hardly seemed possible. The sea was calm and cold when we started, and there were thousands of sea-birds brought in, I imagine, by the cold, wheeling about in the air or squatting disconsolately on the icy waves. There were icicles hanging from the old posts that adorned the harbour, and I felt thoroughly indisposed to go anywhere on that small craft. Just after we had left the comparative shelter of the harbour a tremendous *nordost* arose. The *nordost* is a local wind of extraordinary velocity, like the *bise* at Geneva or the *bora* at Trieste, and like them it is almost entirely local, being savage and ferocious in certain localities, whilst at a distance of from ten or fifteen miles a flat calm may prevail.

This had been my first experience of a really strong gale in a small boat, and I must say I disliked it. The strength displayed by sea and wind seemed to me altogether unfair. How could anything stand against it? I felt like that Etocles about whom I had been reading in the Greek Anthology which I had taken on board with price lists, rates of exchange and general instructions, and who complained, as he sailed the Tyrrhene Sea in a gale, of the difference between the wind which filled his sail and "that which fans the threshing-floor."

The *nordost* thrust and thrust at the little tug until it lay over on its side almost in despair. It hardly seemed possible that it could ever recover, but slowly it did, and luckily for us the wind had slewed the bows round, so that they were now pointing towards the harbour, which we had left some three-quarters of an hour before, and towards this, the wind almost straight behind us, we raced through the flying scud. There seemed to be no waves, as the sea was blown out flat.

On the deck close to where I was standing, holding on to a stay, were a number of heavy barrels full of sunflower oil. These had been only lightly secured by an end of rope. When the wind struck us they had cast loose, and were rolling and bumping about the deck in a terrifying manner. In the middle of all this I perceived a small girl of about eight or nine years of age, who, presumably being sick or desirous of watching the sea go by, or moved by some unknown small-girl motive, had been standing in the scuppers looking over the deck rail. It seemed to me that she could hardly avoid being crushed to death by the heavy barrels which were thumping and thudding and swishing and rolling all about her. She herself was apparently oblivious of her danger, for the wind had blown her skirts around her head, and I had a vision of long black-stockinged legs surmounted by a pitiful and split-panted posterior. I had no wish to leave the security of my stay and, indeed, I thought that we should all soon be in the water together, and, with this in mind and a sick feeling at the pit of my stomach, I was looking about for something that might conceivably float, and to which I could attach myself for the few shivering seconds I might hope to survive in that cold black sea.

Slowly on all fours I crept down the sloping deck, waited for a second while a hideous black barrel swooshed by, ended up with a rush against the deck rail, bruised my knees, swore, and grabbed the girl. Twice we started back to my stay, and twice fell back to the rail, mercifully avoiding the barrels, but the third time we made it and regained the stay. In a minute or two the parents of the child appeared, and as the ship was by this time a little steadier as she fled before the gale, they were able to remove their offspring into the horrible depths of a cabin below. I stayed on deck and watched the sailors trying to deal with the barrels. In about twenty minutes we had been blown into the small harbour, the captain reversed his engines, and we fetched up with a most fearful bump against the landing-stage which, luckily for us, gave to the shock somewhat, so that we remained wedged against it. Ropes were thrown over and the embrace made more secure.

I departed hastily, and went again to the hotel where I had dined. There I was sought out by the parents of the child, who thanked me heartily, saying that I had saved her life.

So far it has fallen to my lot to be somewhat directly instrumental in the saving of two lives, and I have often amused myself by contrasting the difference between the Cornish soldier whom I once fished out of the Red Sea and the little White

Russian girl whom I prevented from being crushed to death by barrels of sunflower oil on the Black. One gave me a penknife and much beer, and the other a damp kiss.

Next morning we set off again in comparative calm. I landed at Theodosia, followed by the waving handkerchief of my small friend. From there I went inland towards the Front, and drove many kilometres in a petrol-driven car that went along the railway lines. I met various hard-drinking officers, but there was obviously no wine exporting to be done, so I came back to Theodosia to catch a boat for Yalta.

At Theodosia the Russian General in charge of the White Army was a dashing individual called Slascheff. He wore an all-white uniform with a great flowing coat, white fur hat, white boots, white gloves and white-handled dagger. He had two female A.D.C.s also dressed in white, and was a dope fiend. He was a man of great personal bravery, always willing to expose himself, and for this reason had a great following among the Russians. After the evacuation from the Crimea by the White troops, he decided to go back to Russia to join the Bolsheviks.

I was sitting in the hotel at Theodosia having a vodka previous to dining in solitary state—I remember with some amusement that I had felt it necessary as being the only Englishman in the hotel to put on my dinner-jacket in order to preserve the prestige of our imperial race, and not let down the feuilleton writer—when there was a tremendous commotion, and the General arrived in his white uniform and with his female A.D.C. and his G.H.Q.

They sat down to dine, and I occupied a table not far from them. The vodka flew, and things got noisier and noisier. Soon an officer detached himself from the group, came over to my table, clicked his heels, saluted and asked if I was English. I replied that I was; whereat he presented the general's compliments, and asked if I would come over to their table to join them. This with suitable gravity and stiffness I did, and was presented all round and given a seat next the general. The dinner was a whirlwind one, but afterwards it became far too fast for me. The general had just come back from a minor success at the Front, and everyone was out to celebrate. The officers did Caucasian dances, and then we went in for *charachkas*. This, Ivan, is a custom whereby you are brought a large cup filled with wine or vodka or whisky, or some other spirit, which you are supposed to drink off at a draught, whilst the other guests sing a Russian song to your health which has a splendid chorus: "Peetita, peetita," meaning simply drink, drink; which they howl while you endeavour to drain the contents of the cup without blenching or heel taps. When you have finished creditably you turn up the glass with a dramatic gesture, which you will have no difficulty in making, for you will feel just in the mood. I did my share, got remarkably intoxicated, was encouraged to dance the *Lezginka,* fell over, recovered, passed out and was cleared away by the hotel people and put to bed whilst the others went on till morning.

When I awoke next morning the ceiling of my bedroom seemed to be like the angels; it kept ascending and descending. When finally I got down, except for broken glasses and smashed chairs I found no traces of my general or his bodyguard, who had all gone back to the Front in their train. I was profoundly thankful that they had not taken me with them, as had happened on another occasion.

CHAPTER XII

WINE FOR ROUBLES

On the quay at Yalta I was met by Vadarsky, the Russian who had been in communication with our office with regard to the possibilities of the export of Crimean wine. He was an excitable person, dressed in yellow leather boots, black-and-white striped trousers, a leather coat and a cloth cap; he wore a beard, which varied between the spade and the bird's-nest. He was excitable, voluble, extremely persuasive and for a man who had lost nearly his last kopeck in the Revolution, extremely optimistic.

Whenever, during the discussion concerning the possibility of wine export, I talked about difficulties and dangers, his mind flew over the obstacles like a seagull over the waves, and descended with unerring accuracy on the comfortable topic of the fine price we should get for Crimean wine when we got it into Constantinople. He had been in charge of the Tsar's wine-growing estates and cellars, and had recently formed a group for the exploitation of Crimean wines abroad. He and his group were very glad to get into touch with the representative of an English firm, as they had been isolated for some time, and had been unable to establish touch with any possible sources of foreign money, which, quite naturally, was what they wanted before they parted with their wine.

On arrival at Yalta, and on transferring myself and belongings to the shore, I saw that we had come alongside H.M.S.

Montrose, a neat flotilla-leader whose trim grey appearance was very heartening, as she represented a sure get-away if any trouble arose, and trouble—if rumours were right—was waiting round the corner.

On going to pay my respects, I found that fortune had favoured me. For the No. 1 of the *Montrose* was none other than my friend Macarthy. He greeted me warmly, and as for me, Ivan, I was overjoyed to have found a jovial comforting person of my own kind in a position where he could be extremely useful.

I was taken on unofficially as assistant interpreter and intelligence officer, and given a cabin, so that I lived in the *Montrose,* and went ashore every day to do what Mac called my funny business ashore. Whilst ashore I was to gather what information I could as to the state of affairs, and retail it to Mac every evening. This was an excellent arrangement, as I was able to get opinions and "contacts" which the "official" intelligence officer could not get. This man, by the way, was an extraordinary individual called Timasheef, who always referred to himself as the White Devil of the Black Sea. He belonged to a Cossack regiment, wore an enormous white fur hat and bristled with revolvers and daggers. He laid claim to most extraordinary exploits, and afterwards wrote a book about them. Even if only half were true, which is improbable, he had had a most extraordinary career.

This was my first experience of the Navy, so to speak, at home, and extraordinarily fine people I found them. They one and all seemed to sympathize with my efforts to carve an education for myself out of the Russian Revolution, and were out to help me as much as they could. Mac was a host in himself, and the commander was extremely kind. I remember that he invited me to dine in his cabin, where he lived, so it seemed to me, in awful and lonely state. For the rest, I lived in the wardroom of a thoroughly happy ship, and that, my son, is a very fine experience, and I hope that one day you will have a similar privilege.

It was very curious to leave this secure base and go out into the troubled town, which seethed with rumours and boiled with refugee tragedies, frantic night-life, and frenetic currencies; every time I heard the good honest Cockney of the marine who looked after me and greeted me when I returned from my shore expeditions, I felt that I had wakened from a dream.

My negotiations with the Vadarsky group progressed apace, despite the necessity under which I found myself to make frequent visits to the *caves* in order to sample the goods. These visits were rather amusing, and it was a sight well worth seeing when Vadarsky reverently sampled a barrel and smacked his lips loudly both for advertisement and because of a real satisfaction.

I, poor uncivilized individual, knowing nothing of wine, could only make appreciatory noises of confirmation, and do my best to have watertight safeguarding clauses in the contract. Now, I flatter myself, quite wrongly perhaps, that I should make a better show.

In the neighbourhood of Yalta there sprang up a new movement which, as far as one could gather, was neither White, Green nor Red, but merely lunatic. Everybody was anxious to know what it meant and what exactly were the designs of the young adventurer who was at the head of it. His name was Orloff and his main idea was, it appeared, to protest against the inefficient way in which the Whites were carrying on the anti-Bolshevik campaign. He had no difficulty in gathering together a regiment of the disgruntled, and in spite of the protests of the White leaders, advanced in force on Yalta with every intention of taking it.

The Vadarsky group had asked me to a large dinner which they were giving with the intention of putting the finishing touches on the contract on which we had been working. It is really a splendid thing at the age of twenty-four to have an enormous and magnificent dinner given to you by a group of experienced business men who know how to eat, and who don't mind what they spend, as they hope to get it all back, and more, as the result of the deal. The dinner was duly given, and a poem it was, the *zakouski* alone being worthy of several verses. With the soup there came a sound of insistent cannonading. When I asked what it was about, my neighbour with a shrug of his shoulders told me that it was the usual Russian accompaniment to a meal, and that I must not let it divert my attention from the masterpieces before me. Somebody else explained that the operations were against Orloff, and that the gallant Count Whatisit was directing the operations for our side, and that with his magnificent battery, superb cavalry and unbeatable foot soldiers he had gone to a point some five miles away, and that doubtless the ridiculous Orloff was even then running like a hare hotly pursued by the unconquerable Count. So we went on with our dinner.

Soon, however, a message was handed in to Vadarsky, who told us that with incredible stupidity the egregious Count had been lured out of the town by a ruse, and had found nobody to fight, whilst the cunning and sinister Orloff had cut him off from his base by appearing from an entirely unexpected quarter, and might be expected in the town at any minute. So we swallowed our coffee hurriedly, and I dashed in an *izvoschik* to my secure *Montrose,* and very glad I was to get across her gangway again. There I made my report; there was a hurried conference, and it was decided that we should stand by, ready for anything, whilst taking no initiative against Orloff till we knew what sort of line he would take. Next morning he entered the town with his motley crew. I had been sent ashore to see what I could, and somewhat apprehensively I mingled with the throng, and noted, amongst other things, that he had two machine-guns, one mounted on a bullock-waggon and the other on a perambulator chassis.

He sent the *Montrose* a message to inform us that he proposed to take no hostile measures against us, but would be glad if we could see our way to recognize him as the supreme Government of Russia. Our old man thought this going too far, and so a sort of vague neutrality supervened. Meanwhile, Count Whatisit had wired for reinforcements, which arrived, and he then surrounded the town. Orloff levied a substantial contribution on the local banks, gave them official receipts, and marched out to pastures new, whereupon Count Whatisit marched in, and was greeted with rousing cheers by everyone, including my group, who had made a pressing appeal to me to have our guns trained on their wine dump, to which Macarthy and myself had replied that we would guard it with our last drop of blood if they would transport it aboard.

Finally, I completed all my business, arranged for the transport of the wine and could find no further excuse for staying on. Much as I regretted it, it was time to leave my secure retreat aboard the flotilla-leader and go back to adventuring without a base. I did not like this, but there it was.

I hoped to make some money on the wine-export contracts, and I began to think that I had had enough adventures. Oxford and security beckoned me. But how to get back to Novorossisk was a problem, for, Ivan, in those days journeys were difficult and not lightly to be undertaken. My experience with the *nordost* outside Anarpa had prejudiced me against small local boats, and there seemed to be no large ones available.

However, Mac was equal to the occasion, talked to the wireless man and discovered a Greek destroyer, of all things, which was going to Novorossisk, and asked for a lift for me. Sure enough, the *Ierax* appeared, Mac took a look at her dingy decks, and with superb scorn christened her the "Gimcrax," but I gladly accepted the offer made by the kindly and conversational captain.

Mac in his negotiations had somewhat exaggerated my importance, and consequently, to my great delight, when I came aboard with my baggage I was piped over the side, a thing which has never happened to me since. Mac must have told them that I was some sort of High Commissioner.

The *Ierax,* though her decks were covered in coal to the depth of at least an inch, made nothing of the journey to Novorossisk, and the next day I landed full of souvenirs and bottles of sample vintages from the Vadarsky group, with which I improved my relations with your mother and her family and with the head of the firm, who received me kindly.

CHAPTER XIII

ONCE ABOARD THE LUGGER

I

During my absence, the general situation had gone from bad to worse: the Volunteer Armies were almost completely demoralized and the Bolsheviks were rapidly closing in on Novorossisk. Every day more refugees poured in, and Denikin's officers were having the greatest difficulty in keeping the regiments in any sort of military formation, as the general and very natural tendency was to make a dash for the ports, in order, at least, to be able to assure the evacuation of families and dependents.

Winter had set in, and it was fearfully cold. Fires were lighted on the main streets, so that people could warm themselves and avoid being frozen to death. Typhus was rampant, and many people died of exposure and misery. The rouble rocketed about in jumps of thousands at a time. The British Military Mission was encamped in a cement works outside the town, warships were arriving, and transports were being collected in case of need. There were anxious conferences at G.H.Q., and nobody knew how long things would last. There was a feeling that the end could not long be delayed, and a horrible feeling that is, I can assure you, when everything is melting and nothing can be depended on.

My firm had drawn in all its staff, and we had only a small office in the town. Most of the personnel had already departed, and every day saw somebody pull out for Constantinople and safety.

Very soon, an English director, the local Russian representative named Tchaikowsky, a Pole called Bucharski and myself were all that were left. The situation was serious, as we had some thirty thousand pounds' worth of goods in sheds at Novorossisk, and there seemed to be no possibility of getting them out; first, because there was a general embargo on all export; and secondly, because there was no tonnage available, as everything was requisitioned by the military and naval authorities for purposes of the general evacuation. The English director very decently offered to pay my fare to Constantinople and give me a month's wages. At the time I had scraped together about three hundred pounds of my own, besides what I had been able to send home, but the total was still well below what I needed for my Oxford scheme. During a conversation he proposed, as a purely voluntary alternative, that I should stay on with Tchaikowsky and Bucharski, and that we should try to clear the most valuable part of the goods as best we could. He was negotiating for the purchase of a small Russian schooner, on which he hoped to get some of our goods away. He said that if I was game to stay on and watch the firm's interests during the evacuation and subsequent voyage, he would continue my salary, pay all my expenses and, in the event of our being able to salve anything, would see that I got a good percentage. He went on to say that he himself would have to leave with the British Mission to look after the firm's interests in Constantinople, whither a number of cargoes had been consigned *en route* for Russia, and which had to be stopped and disposed of there.

At this juncture my Intelligence Major again appeared in a new guise, and from him I learned that the end could not be long delayed. I had a talk with a friend at the Military Mission, who advised me to go in something more reliable than a doubtful schooner while the going was good, but said he would do the best he could, while there was anything to be done, if I did decide to try to escape with the schooner. He added that things, once they started, would go very fast.

Then I had a talk with Bucharski, who was a tower of strength and an excellent fellow in every way. The plan seemed very vague, but there was a chance, and if we got away with anything we should be handsomely rewarded.

It seemed to me that here was a chance of making more than enough money for Oxford at one swoop, together with a most romantic adventure thrown in. So I accepted, with some hesitation, as the reverse of the medal might well be death in a Red prison or in the Black Sea, of whose unpleasant moods I had already had experience.

Once the decision was taken, I threw myself into the thing wholeheartedly. I went with Bucharski, with whom I had made a sort of offensive and defensive alliance, to look at the schooner. Bucharski was of stalwart appearance, an expert racing motorist, an amateur yachtsman of the first class, as strong as a horse and true as steel. One of the best, Ivan, and one of whom I shall always think gratefully.

Tchaikowsky, the Russian director, who held a power of attorney for the firm, was a different proposition: clever, polite and exquisitely unreliable. However, Bucharski and myself were determined to stand no nonsense from him, although he was officially senior to us.

The firm had a large and powerful motor-car, a Benz of weather-beaten appearance and multitudinous horse-power, which had belonged to the German General of Division during the period of the German occupation of Kiev, whence Bucharski had removed it by means only known to himself. He could make it do anything he liked except sit up and beg, and it was the apple of his eye.

We drove down to the harbour and inspected the craft which was to carry ourselves and all our hopes. She was a three-masted Black Sea schooner with a 90-h.p. marine Bollender engine as auxiliary. She was called the *Lucy and Zoya*, was of 150-200 tons, or thereabouts, and was completely filthy. She had a deck cabin, a small kitchen and lavatory forward and a large, roomy and capacious hold into which we thought we could stow ourselves, all our belongings and merchandise. She was usually employed in the Black Sea port-to-port trade and was extremely solidly built. Not a beauty, but a good sea boat with tremendous beam, thick stumpy masts and everything solid enough to last for ever. She was finally bought by the firm under all sorts of queer conditions, and I managed to get a Navy tug to get her into a position where we could load her.

One evening, after being fearfully busy all day with questions of ship's papers, for which we had to bribe all sorts of people who knew they could not possibly remain in office over the week-end and who were doing business with their trunks packed all ready to leave, I went round to see your mother and her family, and found that they had already gone on board a ship which was lying in the harbour. It was a British ship, and I had been able to arrange for them to be taken on board. This was a great relief, as I had always wondered how they would get away. Of their adventures, of how they lived on bully beef and cheese and jam, of how they slept on the gangway, of how typhus broke out, of how they managed at last to get off at Constantinople instead of being sent on to Egypt and a concentration camp, I will leave your mother to tell you, but it was an extraordinary affair, though after all no more extraordinary than many of their previous vicissitudes.

When the negotiations were finally completed for the purchase of the *Lucy and Zoya* and we had got her with her papers to where we could load her up, we began to make preparations for the voyage. Time was obviously short, the Bolsheviks were getting nearer and nearer, and the state of the port was becoming more and more anarchist and disorganized. The motor was put in order. It worked perfectly under tests until, as you shall hear, it later, with the innate perversity of all marine motors, chose the most precisely undesirable moment to break down completely and never go again. The sails and rigging were overhauled, and the whole ship cleaned and disinfected with cresol, which I got from my old friend the S. and T. sergeant, who besought me not to go in for what he regarded as a damfool scheme. With the boat we took over a boatswain, a stalwart Old Bill of a fellow, who had spent all his life on the Black Sea, and who would do anything at all provided there was vodka about, and nothing at all if there was not. He could never get over my not knowing as much Russian as he did. "Such a clever *barin*," he would say, "so small, so clean, and yet he can hardly speak properly, and as for drinking, why, I could take more in my left pap than he in his whole stomach." Whereat he would roar with laughter, and ask me to help pull up the anchor.

With the boatswain there was a vague sort of crew of four or five, who seemed to be his property.

Then I had Anton Gladky, who was joint servant to Bucharski and myself. He was a huge bearded Ukrainian who had been with Bucharski in his regiment. He was particularly attached to me, and gave me faithful service. He had one embarrassing habit. Whenever I dined out at an officers' mess in the

Mission he seemed to take it for granted that I should drink too much and require to be carried home and undressed, and for this reason he always appeared wherever I went to dine and stood by to help me as soon I came out. I could never break him of this habit, nor could I prevent him from eating garlic in chunks. A good fellow.

For captain and navigator we had a man called Maximoff, who had been in command of destroyers and submarines, but who had never succeeded in getting command of himself. Poor fellow, during the Revolution he had on two occasions just escaped being thrown into the furnaces of his own ship by his sailors, so that I suppose he had every excuse for having no nerve left. The boatswain took no notice at all of him.

This was our nucleus, but it soon became apparent that we should be lucky to get away without a hundred or so people climbing on at the last moment, for we received applications for passage from every sort of person, including the wife of the Russian Captain of the Port, whose husband had deserted her, and to whom we promised a passage provided she brought us a set of official rubber stamps which we needed for our deficient ship's papers. She was a baroness, and she came across with the stamps, but at the last moment deserted us in favour of a Naval lieutenant, who promised to evacuate her in a submarine. I met her afterwards in Batoum, and she told me of her adventures.

I spent a hectic time tearing about with Bucharski getting exportation permits and additional papers for the *Lucy and Zoya*. The English director was already on board his ship, and we saw him off in a flood of champagne.

In our shed we had all sorts of things. There were great bales of textiles, there were boots, there were tins of guts for making fiddle strings and fishing lines which smelt abominably;

there were barrels of caustic soda, chemicals, gentlemen's suits
—one of which I commandeered and wore for many a long day
though it really did not fit me; there were ladies' shoes, some
of which I gave away, but that is another story; there were forty
cases of the Tsar's special brandy—a tangible result of my expedition to Yalta. It was forty years old, and tasted like some
sort of celestial milk; and every sort of extraordinary bale and
package. There were bags of roubles, cases of cheap jewellery
and caviare. In addition to this, we had two motor-cars—our
own Benz and one belonging to the general in charge of part
of the British Mission, though how he had got it Heaven and
his staff alone knew. I advocated taking this, as I knew that
there is nothing a general will not do for his own, particularly
when it is the result of a peculiarly ingenious ramp, and my
advice was more than justified. If I had asked him to stretch a
point in favour of saving the firm's official archives, he would
have raised all sorts of difficulties, whilst reams of red tape
would have coiled and coiled around our dubious expedition.
But for his hard-earned motor-car, his staff, whom I entertained, could make the general do almost anything.

At last we got our papers more or less in order. When this
was accomplished, I had what afterwards proved to be a stroke
of luck. I met a naval officer who knew and liked my friend
Macarthy. As I had our car, I took him for a ride round the
town, gave him dinner and a bottle of the Tsar's cognac. He
was supposed to be doing an Intelligence ride, so as to be able
to inform the admiral personally of the state of affairs, for the
admiral, like all admirals, did not want to be dependent for his
information on the Army, and I wished to repay the Navy for
the hospitality I had enjoyed on the *Montrose*. I have forgotten his name, but he was on the admiral's staff, and a good
fellow as you shall learn.

When I came back after depositing him at the landing-stage, I was told confidentially that, in the opinion of the Navy, we could only count on one more day, and that after that anything might happen.

We had a conference, and next morning we began to load our stuff. Labour was scarce and Bolshevik. Nobody would work for roubles which had ceased to be of value, and most of the ordinary dockers, with natural prudence, thought that with the Bolsheviks arriving the next day it was hardly the wise course to be seen working for foreign capitalists who were trying to remove what remained of the resources of the proletariat from the country.

The military were rushing about in all directions, all busy with their own stores, and though the general was willing to send us a working-party of British soldiers to load his car—and, at a pinch, being a reasonable man, our own—he drew the line at guts, brandy, caustic soda and the rest of our stuff. It was Bucharski who solved the problem. He found a group of White officers whose regiment had left them, or *vice versa,* and in view of the fact that money had no value, he arranged to pay them in kind. So we split open some bales of boots and suits, and set them to work after having arranged a rough-and-ready scale of payment. I shall never forget seeing the line of men in ragged uniforms humping the heavy bundles from the gloomy railway shed, down the quay, along a plank, and pitching them with gusto into the hold of our absurd lugger, while Bucharski and I patrolled anxiously up and down trying to maintain a rough sort of check on which to construct a bill of lading and prevent pilfering. Every now and then some official or officer would come along and try to stop us, ask to see our permit or demand a bribe. We cajoled, bluffed, bribed, threatened and used the name of the British Mission for all it was worth, and more. One agitator who tried to Bolshevize the working-party we drove away with revolvers, and then when he came back, locked him up for an hour in an empty shed, the while he threatened us with horrible menaces as to what would happen to us if the Bolsheviks caught us next day. All sorts of people came and begged us for passages and had to be refused. Halfway through the job the working-party grinned good-humouredly, and went on strike for double pay. They got it and a tot of brandy each.

As evening fell, and the pile of stuff to be loaded began to assume more reasonable proportions, we began to get very excited; we were nearly through our task, and grimy and exhausted we feared that something would happen. It did. The working-party went on strike again, and this time stipulated for passages on the lugger. This we refused to agree to, but I compromised by giving them a personal note to the officer in charge of the Mission evacuation proceedings, who very kindly guaranteed them places. At last we had finished. Night had fallen, and we had lit a bonfire for light to work by, as the electric light had been cut by the local Reds.

When the last of the workmen had gone, Bucharski and I opened a bottle of the Tsar's brandy, and decided to get the *Lucy and Zoya* under way. The crew were not there. Luckily, somebody knew where they were drinking. Like good sailors, they had absolutely refused to have anything to do with the loading arrangements. Bucharski went and dragged them by force and threats from the café where they were. Then the motor refused to start. We sweated and strained and cursed. Nothing happened. We made a bargain with a motor-launch which appeared from nowhere and which tugged us out from the land. The price was five pairs of topboots. We chuffed slowly away from the gloomy docks. Once under way we cheered and had a muster. There were forty persons on board, and it was only next morning that I discovered what an extraordinary gang they were. We found out that the volatile Tchaikowsky and the equally unreliable Maximoff had been authorizing passages right and left.

First there were three respectable merchants who, by some extraordinary feat of wangling, had got themselves and a small but select cargo of Heaven knew what on board before we had finished loading. These we charged an exorbitant sum for passage. There was a male heterosexual dancer who powdered his face. There was another male dancer who afterwards became quite well known. There were three girls from the chief cabaret of Novorossisk, who did a dancing turn, and who were professionally known as the "Glittering Soap Bubbles," some of them with pet dogs, and for the rest, an odd collection of poor unfortunates who had just got on board somehow. All these emerged from nooks and crannies made by the baggage in the hold. We had a hasty inspection to see that nobody was suffering from typhus, threw out about ten individuals who were obviously suffering from something, disembarked them forcibly in the dinghy, and slowly made our way to where the warships were anchored off the quay of the British Mission. We were hailed and challenged, but I shouted "British Mission" to all and sundry, and we were allowed to proceed.

We dropped anchor at about ten o'clock, and I went ashore, while Anton Gladky, my orderly, roped off a space in the hold for Bucharski and myself, and threatened all and sundry with sudden death should they dare to intrude.

Once ashore I went in search of stores, for we had only reckoned on a ship's company of ten, and there were already over twenty all told.

I found the Mission quay bustling with well-ordered activity.

Stores were being loaded by Tommies under arc-lamps, and everything was in welcome contrast to our own recent affair. A friend told me that all was nearly over, and that in about an hour everything would be evacuated except a company or so of infantry with machine-guns who were to hold the base till dawn, when they would be taken off by the *Stuart,* a destroyer leader, sister ship to my friend the *Montrose.* I got some stores and sent them off, and went on board the *Stuart.* There I made myself known and was promised reasonable assistance without any guarantee by the No. 1, who, by a stroke of luck, was a friend of Macarthy's, and had heard of me. I spent most of the night ashore, and at about five in the morning rowed out to the *Lucy and Zoya* with more stores.

There I found they had given the motor up in despair. We hoisted the anchor and the sails, and with a slight breeze we managed to get a little farther from the dangerous proximity of the shore. I was completely exhausted, and went to sleep for an hour or two.

II

When I awoke it was full daylight. Anton brought me some tea and bread and bully beef. I felt pretty sure that a harassing day was in front of us, so I decided to shave and have my boots cleaned.

It was a cold bitter day. If you could have seen me then you would have seen a slight wiry figure somewhat stooped. I wore a huge Cossack fur hat, riding-breeches, trench boots, a sports coat, a furred mackintosh with an immense fox collar, big gauntlets on my hands, attached to my wrist a *nagaika,* or Caucasian riding-crop, with a stiletto concealed in the handle, field glasses slung around my shoulder, large revolver in my pocket and a small one on my hip. I had passports, money and some valuables on me; in my pockets and all down my trench boots were notes in all sorts of currency. I had all my other valuables in three kitbags and a Wolseley valise which served as a bed; I had a hammock and a despatch-case full of office and ship's papers.

I felt stirred and keen. So far, things had gone well. We were out of the town. We had thirty thousand pounds' worth of goods stowed on board, and if we could only get them to Batoum, which was our destination, I felt that I should get a good slice of commission, a reputation for dash and probably a job until I was ready to go to Oxford. I thought that, what with savings, commission and continued salary, a thousand pounds at the end was not beyond the bounds of legitimate optimism.

Then I went on deck. It was a flat calm. Bucharski was putting things in order, aided by the boatswain. He drew my attention to the extraordinary scene around us. We were about two miles from the quay where we had loaded, and behind which was the waterside front of the town, and one mile from the Mission quay, which was on our port side. The town was already on fire, and a pall of smoke, pierced occasionally by shooting flames, hung over it. Through my glasses I could see that the quays and piers were black with people, soldiers and civilians waiting to be taken off. In the harbour, not far from us, were the Allied warships, the British flagship, one or two cruisers, some destroyers, a seaplane, and, close to the Mission quay, the destroyer which was taking off the last detachments of the British infantry which had acted as a screen for the evacuation. There was a crackle of firing from the port and quays, and the tapping of machine-guns was insistent, irritating and menacing. Through my glasses I could see troops hurrying about in all directions, whilst slowly every sort of boat, ship and raft was leaving the port. Their decks were swarming with people.

As I stood and looked, there was a tremendous explosion. It was the *Emperor of India,* which had begun to bombard the approaching Bolsheviks with a view to covering the evacuation of the refugees. The French battleship, with five funnels, that the Tommies in the Mission used to call the *Packet of Woodbines,* took up the tale, and very soon the bombardment became general.

However, it seemed to me that it behoved us to do something, and I made enquiries of Bucharski as to the last report on the engine. People were still working in a despairing and desultory manner on this, but it remained obdurate and refused to emit even an encouraging chuff. So after a brief conference we decided to try to sail away. Our destination was Batoum, about 240 miles away down the coast in Georgia. Batoum was then under British occupation, and provided the nearest sure haven.

We hoisted our patched sails amidst cursing and heaving, but there was not much wind, and what there was seemed to be in the wrong direction. For an hour we tacked about the harbour entrance seeking vainly to get out to sea, but without success. Meanwhile, all round us the most tragic scenes were being enacted. Shrieks and groans came from the shore when we drifted near it, and all the time the fires in the town grew more terrible.

We tacked to and fro, but we could make no real progress. It soon became apparent that the Bolsheviks were advancing along the coastline and evacuation activities became more and more frenzied. Destroyers were dashing to and fro, and even the huge and austere *Emperor of India* began to take off the infantry detachments that had held the town during the evacuation. There were terrible tragedies. Companies were left on the quay and shot down. Men cast themselves into the sea and endeavoured to swim out to the boats. Small tugs and rowing-boats sank under the weight of men who had climbed into them. Strings of barges were floating helplessly, loaded to the waterline with civilians, children and women. It was a scene for one of those old-fashioned wall paintings one sees on the walls of the Escorial, Ivan, and I sincerely hope that you will never have to participate in an affair like that. I must admit that all that went on around me did not move me much at the time, as I was far too busy with my own affairs. The day wore on, and the various craft began to make good their escape from the harbour and stood out to sea, all except ours, which continued to roll about in a disgustingly inefficient manner. Soon it became obvious that something would have to be done, as we could see the Bolshevik infantry through our glasses, advancing along the coast, and already stray bullets were dropping around us.

The beginnings of panic seized our ship's company. The Glittering Soap Bubbles were walking about the deck or reclining in graceful attitudes of hopelessness, like so many dying swans; the crew was standing about in groups talking to itself about joining the Bolsheviks; the doleful swearing of Bucharski came from the engine-room; the three commercial gentlemen were smoking gloomy cigarettes, and the rest of the ship's company were lying about talking or drinking tea in a resigned sort of manner. The only person who was doing anything useful was Anton Gladky, who, spitting into the blacking tin with undisturbed cheerfulness, was cleaning my boots with great energy.

I took a sudden decision. I clambered down the rope ladder into the dinghy, and shouted to Bucharski that I was going to see if any help could be obtained from the *Emperor of India*. He came up from the hold, and wiping his hands on a piece of waste, agreed that this was probably the only thing to be done.

A large and grimy sailor, after some persuasion by the boatswain, came and rowed, and I took the tiller, and slowly we came to the flagship. She had been opened up specially to facilitate the embarkation of refugees and troops, and getting aboard her was comparatively easy, and for this I was grateful, as I did not fancy clambering up what, from my cockleshell, looked like the side of a skyscraper, on a rope ladder in full view of everyone. The *Emperor of India* had finished loading troops, and was apparently standing by and waiting for the harbour to be cleared, so as to be able to depart. There was a sentry on the gangway, who was so astonished when I spoke to him in English that, after a moment's hesitation, he decided to let me through, when I asked to see the officer on duty or the admiral, or anybody who would see me.

I shall never forget the extraordinary contrast presented by the *Lucy and Zoya,* which I had just left, and this vast steel bulk full of ordered activity, so solid, powerful and secure. I was conducted by all sorts of companion-ways to an upper-deck level, and asked to wait outside an office while an orderly went in to explain.

I have often wondered how he described me, but in any case, he must have done it so as to arouse curiosity, for hardly a minute elapsed before the door was opened and I was asked to go in.

There was an officer seated at a table and, standing in front of him with a notebook, a writer who was taking down instructions. Then I realized that my luck was in, for the officer was none other than the one I had met the day before and whom I had dined and wined.

"Hullo," said he. "What on earth are you doing here?"

"Nothing on earth and very little at sea," I replied with a grin, at once confident and overjoyed to be dealing with somebody I knew, instead of a possibly unsympathetic stickler for things as they ought to be done.

He listened while I unfolded my tale of misfortune, hesitated for a moment, and then, while my heart stood still, said, "Well, we'd better go and see the admiral. He was asking me a moment ago what the hell that crazy schooner of yours thought she was trying to do."

"Hold on," said I; "before we go in, tell me what sort of an admiral he is. Does he like people to speak up and be bold and say their piece with aplomb, or does he like to swear a little before he does anything for anybody?"

"The latter, usually," said my friend. "But he's worked off his liver already, and done all the swearing he needs to do to-day, as you may imagine."

We went in to an inner office. The admiral was there; smallish and bearded, with a cold blue eye. He looked at me for a moment, and asked me what he could do for me. I explained the position.

"Well," he said, "I don't think much of the people who are handling that craft of yours."

I endeavoured to explain that she was heavily laden and that the breeze was light. He asked a few questions, and I answered them as best I could. He was interested at first; then amused. The battle was nearly won, I thought. Then he shot at me, "Well, what do you want me to do about it?"

I hesitated, and thought of our poor disreputable *Lucy and Zoya* upsetting all this magnificence and ordered precision. I dared not formulate too definite a request to be extricated, so I said, "Well, I should like your advice, sir, please."

"Advice be damned," said the admiral. "What you want is a tug."

I smiled respectfully. The admiral felt better and went on, "But why should I? What's the reason? I cannot tow every rascally lugger that's broken down."

Then I remembered the general's motor-car.

"I've got some Government property aboard, sir," said I. "The others are different."

"Yes, only human beings on board them!" snapped the admiral.

I said that, in addition to the general's car and the Tsar's brandy, I also had the Glittering Soap Bubbles and some valuable War Office stores.

"All right," he said at last.

Then he turned and said to my friend, "Make a signal to *Steadfast*. I authorize it. She can tow her out of danger, and then she can shift for herself."

I began to thank him, but he made a sign of dismissal, and out I went with my shaggy hat in my hand.

Admiral Sir Michael Culme Seymour, Ivan. He's dead now. May he rest in peace.

So we went down to the wardroom, and I had a wonderful cocktail, and was an object of interest to the people there. Which, Ivan, was very agreeable. It was a strange day in my life, and I often summon it from the dead past when I am supposed to be reading the answer of the Latvian Government to the questionnaire regarding social insurance.

I left the wardroom on air and alcohol. Various people presented me with whisky, cigars and English magazines. Laden, I went down the gangway. Feeling theatrical in my rig, I saluted the place where I thought the admiral was, and various people waved in return. The *Lucy and Zoya* had drifted nearer, and soon I was clambering up her rope ladder, while eager faces peered over the side.

"Well," I said in Russian, "we are saved. They are going to tow us out."

All faces brightened. Valentina Feodorovna, the temporary wife of the firm's local representative, gave me a theatrical embrace, and the Glittering Soap Bubbles indulged in a few of those complicated, twinkling and joy-denoting leaps which are technically known as *entrechats*. The boatswain, seeing them, made an obscene gesture and spat over the side. The crew had another drink, and the general opinion was that all would be well. Sure enough, in about ten minutes up came *Steadfast*, smart and grey, at a great pace. Then it was a question of hawsers. I took the dinghy and saw the officer. He was full of efficiency. After various attempts we were all roped up. Bucharski said to me, "Tell 'em not to go too fast, as we are very heavy and our ropes are rotten." I did so, and soon we were under way. Shots from the shore fell astern.

"Hurrah, hurrah," shouted everybody. Then the rope broke. Groaning, swearing and activity replaced contented calm as the way went off the old tub and she relapsed to her former static wallow. But the *Steadfast* men were worthy of her name, and got another rope made fast, and for a little we progressed again. Then they became ambitious, and tried to bustle our bluff and buxom old lady through the leaden sea at too fast a rate. She jerked and rolled, and again snapped the rope. After further lamentations they bent another one, and we set off again full of confidence.

By this time we were quite close to the *Emperor of India*. As the *Steadfast* passed with us in tow, I saw her men fall in on the after deck and stand to attention, whilst an officer saluted the admiral's flag.

"Ah," said I to myself, "this is obviously the thing to do, and one must not be guilty of neglect." So I hastily mobilized Valentina Feodorovna, the motley crew, the Soap Bubbles and the cigarette-smoking merchants, and fell them in, in a ragged line on our littered deck. Standing theatrically in front of them, I saluted professionally, and then made a deep bow and fired three shots from my revolver. The ballet girls curtsied gracefully, the crew looked inexpressibly sheepish, the merchants merely uncomfortable and a tremendous roar went up from the masses of people on the flagship's deck who were watching us go by. It was a marvellous moment. I have never seen anything more amusing or so beautifully apropos, because at the psychological moment the rope broke, and a second and louder yell went up from the *Steadfast* and the *Emperor of India*.

We wallowed on for a little, and again relapsed into rolling inaction, whilst the laughter went on and the faces of the refugees on board the flagship registered every degree of amazement.

However, *Steadfast* again came to the rescue, gave us a brand-new British hemp rope, which would have sufficed to hang an elephant, and on we went. At last we were clear of the harbour. *Steadfast* cast loose, roared good wishes at us through a megaphone, and went off to carry on her other duties.

We hoisted more sail, and following the curve of the coast we crawled at last away from that scene of misery, fire and tragedy.

And that, Ivan, is exactly how it all transpired that winter's day in the Black Sea off Kabardinka and Zilonyi Mis.

CHAPTER XIV

CAUCASIAN CRUISE

WHEN I awoke the next morning we were sailing slowly south-east along the Caucasian coast. All was quiet and peaceful, and, after the stirring happenings of the day before, I had slept long and sweetly in the bed that Anton had made for me in the hold.

It was a beautiful morning, and I got out a packet of books and made myself snug beside the deck-house while we floated lazily on.

I had been able to secure some literature from the library of the Military Mission, and most of it I had chosen with a view to finding out a little about the country on my route to Constantinople. On the way out to Russia, on arriving in Turkey I had gone north-east from Constantinople in the sloop past the mouths of the Danube and Odessa, to arrive eventually at Novorossisk, and this therefore was the first time I should see the Caucasus proper.

I was really excited at the prospect, for, added to the natural interest that all must have in seeing what to the ancients was the very boundary of civilization, the cockpit of the ancient world where Alexander, Mithridates, Genghis Khan and Timur Leng had fought, the manner of my seeing it was to my mind right and proper. Just so must these waters and the coast have appeared to sailors, merchants, soldiers and travellers of all

187

ages. I had only to close my eyes and imagine myself in a Greek ship on a minor mission for Alexander to see approaching the hostile Persians whom, rightly or wrongly, I pictured in Phrygian caps, dark, swarthy and hook-nosed.

I sat on the deck and read of the history of the Caucasus, and there can be no part of the world where more stirring events have happened. In the beginning, close to where I sailed in the *Lucy and Zoya,* was the land of Gog and Magog. Then, in the ancient world, came the great struggles of the Greeks, Persians, Romans, Seljuks, Mongols and Turks. Thither had come the first Christian missionaries, Justinian, Chosroes Nushirvan and the Genoese traders. It had always been regarded by the ancients as the home of wonders. Herodotus, Strabo and Ptolemy had filled it with man-hating Amazons, and in its mystic confines "gold-guarding griffins and one-eyed Arimaspians" fought eternally. Even to the Muslims it had been the uttermost limit, for they believed that there was Mount Qaf, whither the jinns would sometimes transport unlucky mortals and, after deluding them with carnal delights, turn them into stones or suffering beasts.

In the mountains that lay behind the dimly seen coasts, on Elbruz and on Kazbek, had been born the myths. On Kazbek, Prometheus hung in chains, and the ocean nymphs came to pity and console him, whilst to the north wandered Io, driven by the gadfly. Dreaming between past and present, I imagined the wreck of the *Lucy and Zoya,* the arrival of the Soap Bubbles and their climb up to the heights to find a Prometheus to console. I laughed aloud and went on with my reading.

I read of Colchis—the very coast along which we were drifting—and one morning, when we suddenly caught a glimpse from our lugger of a snowcapped height, I recalled that passage from Kingsley's *Heroes,* where he described the arrival of the

Argonauts: "And at day-dawn they looked eastward [just as we did], and midway between the sea and sky they saw white snow-peaks hanging, glittering sharp and bright above the clouds. And they knew that they were come to Caucasus, at the end of all the earth: Caucasus the highest of all mountains, the father of the rivers of the East. On his peak lies chained the Titan, while a vulture tears his heart; and at his feet are piled dark forests round the magic Colchian land." This was splendid, for I was feeling rather like Jason myself, and evidently the boatswain had much in common with Tiphys, Bucharski was our Heracles and there was a witch-like Russian woman aboard who was like a faded Medea. Though the *Lucy and Zoya* was no *Argo* to leap the breakers like a horse, yet after all she was a stout ship, and probably much nearer what the *Argo* was really like than any other craft I could have chosen.

Then my books told me of later events. I read of Marco Polo, who described the country and the peoples I was going to visit: "The people are very handsome, capital archers and most valiant soldiers. They have a practice of wearing their hair cropped like Churchmen."

Followed Jehoshophat Barbaro—marvellous name—who visited the Caucasus about 1450 and who was terse and less complimentary than Marco: "They are a beastly people," said he.

The names of the Caucasian tribes enthralled me. There are Cherkess, Kabards, Ossets, Chechens, Lesghians, Hessurs, Ingushes and Tcheremiss.

The Cherkess are the nearest to what we call Circassians; the Lesghians are Sunni Mohammedans. They produced the famous Sheikh Shamyl, who defied the Russians for so long, and about whom we must read, about him and Hadji Murad and the Murid sect, for it is a most romantic story and well worthy of its magnificent setting.

Of the Ingushes, Ivan, I like to think in these degenerate days, when the Oriental conception of hospitality has been driven almost everywhere into the most complete desuetude owing, I suppose, to the fearful frequency with which we visit each other. For I read that they have this charming custom: "At entertainment the host always waits upon his guest and eats only what the latter throws him."

The Hessurs, of whom I saw no trace—though I made a special effort to find some of them and nearly got captured, car and all, by another tribe, the Ajars, whilst doing so—were alleged, as late in time as 1877, to "array themselves in helmets and chain armour, carry shields and spears and declare themselves descended from the Crusaders"; as for the Tcheremiss, they were described as being in the habit of sacrificing foals to the Virgin Mary.

Slowly we sailed along the coast, and at about the same speed the Bolshevik Army drove back the forces of one Shkouro and his "Army of Wolves" who was trying to stop them. Shkouro was a picturesque White bandit who plundered everybody, and whose "wolves" printed his own money on his special train. The officers used to cut off great wads of it with scissors when they approached a town, as I had seen with my own eyes in Russia.

We never dared to put into the shore and enquire where we were, because we never knew who might receive us. In fact, we were completely isolated from the world. We had no wireless, and the King of England might have died and all London been stricken with the plague and we should never have known anything at all. It was a very strange feeling, and I often used to wonder what, if anything, was happening in the world as I sat of an evening with the tiller in my hand keeping her gently on her course whilst the crew played cards, the Soap Bubbles practised their steps or knitted, and the restless Bucharski monkeyed around with the deceased engine.

One day we were blown in nearer the shore, and we saw a boat coming out to us. We had a hurried consultation and hoisted a British flag—to which, of course, we had no right—which I had secured from the wife of the captain of the port in Novorossisk, who had presumably obtained it from some amorous sailor. Up it went upside down and floated languidly from the mast. Meanwhile, the boat drew nearer, and soon became visible as a sort of superior launch with about seven or eight people aboard. The boatswain swore that this was already the free and independent Social Democratic Republic of Georgia, and that we were out of Bolshevik clutches. But none believed him, as he had already made several obviously unfortunate guesses as to our position, and even if he were right, nobody had the least confidence in the good offices of the aforementioned Republic, which would probably have been only too glad to sequester, arrest or embargo us and generally annoy us for money.

The launch drew nearer. We had a hasty council of war. It was arranged that I should, as the *bona fide* Englishman, conduct the negotiations through an interpreter, so as to give an air of official correctness to the proceedings. On the other hand, should diplomacy and the prestige of the Union Jack prove unavailing, it was agreed that we should hoist the water-butt up on a sling, so that at any moment if things went badly we could precipitate it into the launch and capsize it. This enterprising idea was Bucharski's, who had a great dislike for Georgians, at whose hands he had suffered during a previous voyage. So up went the water-butt, and we waited. There were two senior officers in the boat, covered with epaulettes, daggers and revolvers, and at first they were inclined to be difficult, but the

Union Jack and my English—or perhaps they saw the water-butt poised, the uncompromising face of Bucharski, the terrifying mug of the fierce-moustached boatswain and the scowls of Anton Gladky—convinced them, for after brief *pourparlers,* during which I threatened the withdrawal of all Allied support to Georgia, they drew off, having told us where we were, which we were very glad to know.

We were not far from Poti, and within measurable distance of our destination. Mention of the water-butt reminds me that, very soon after we had started, we discovered that unless it was strictly rationed we should soon have no water. So Anton Gladky and a reliable sailor, who looked as if he never drank it, were told off to guard the supply, and see that everybody had no more than his ration. This was a difficult task with people like the Soap Bubbles, who were discovered to be actually refusing to wash in anything but fresh water. An alarming disturbance took place, and we threatened to put them in irons if anything of the sort occurred again. What they did not do to get more than their ration hardly bears repeating, but one morning, when I inspected the water level and found it alarmingly sunk, there was a hang-dog look in Anton's eye, and when I reproached him bitterly he said, "Well, what can a man do, and I never did care much for water, *Barin.*"

I am sorry I missed the opportunity of witnessing the seduction of the bluff and burly Anton by the water-seeking Soap Bubbles, for it would have been a marvellous ballet scene.

In order to deal with this emergency the inventive Bucharski constructed an apparatus for the evaporation of salt water, which actually gave us a bucketful of fresh water a day. It was made of kerosene tins, the petrol pipes of the two cars, an oil stove and much ingenuity. The salt water was boiled, the steam went through the petrol pipes, which were cooled in a salt-water bath, the steam condensed, and a thin dropping of saltless water eventually appeared.

For all the voyage we had had calm weather, with light and variable airs, but one night, the twelfth of our journey, the wind freshened, and soon became something that the ordinary individual would call a howling gale, but which I was assured was really only half a one, a strong breeze perhaps on the Beaufort scale. Anyway, it shrieked unpleasantly in the rigging, and the spray from the waves came over the deck and frightened the Soap Bubbles away. Luckily I was not ill, as I had got my sea legs by then. The old boatswain took command, and we started to sail rapidly, nobody quite knew whither.

All night we sailed on, and most of the next morning. Our jib blew adrift, and remained flapping dismally in the wind. Nobody seemed to want to take it in, and the boatswain said that it did not matter, the *Lucy and Zoya* not being the Tsar's yacht. I disliked it very much, for the flapping and thrashing added to the confusion. We reefed our sails, and the old lady wallowed sturdily through the seas. I was afraid that the mast would come out of her, for it was straining and groaning and had a big crack in it. However, it was tremendously thick and did not let itself and us down. The wind abated a little, things grew calmer, and the Soap Bubbles returned from the hold with a little more life in their white faces.

I was just going to have lunch when Anton told me that the boatswain knew where he was, and that he had just sighted a bit of land which he was sure was near Batoum, our destination. I went forward, and the boatswain became even more confident. In about an hour we saw shipping, and it became fairly evident that we were really approaching Batoum. We broached a bottle of the Tsar's brandy, the sick came from their holes in the cargo, the ladies began to powder their faces and I to shave.

I may inform you, Ivan, that Bucharski and myself had seriously considered landing in Georgia, selling the cargo for our own account, and making off with the proceeds through Resht and Enzeli to Teheran. We felt fairly certain that we could get away with it all right, and that we should have had no difficulty in freezing out the others. We thought that we should be able to clear five thousand sterling each, and that if we got through to India nobody would know of our crime, seeing that, in any case, as we were so long overdue we had probably been written off as drowned or captured by the Bolsheviks. The plan appealed to us, and we had thought of taking the boatswain into our confidence and landing in Georgia, at Poti, which we thought must be the nearest suitable spot. However, we decided against it, not so much for reasons, I regret to say, of honesty, but largely because there were too many people on board who wanted to get to Batoum, and whose lives might have been endangered if we had put them ashore at Poti or elsewhere. I have often wondered what would have happened if we had yielded to the temptation. We should certainly have had a weird time and we might have been successful. However, even though we might have made six or seven thousand each, I feel sure that at that time I should not have been able to keep my share. But it would have been fun to go through Persia and, being in reality a pirate, dine with the Legation at Teheran in the guise of a respectable business man.

Batoum grew nearer and nearer, and we could make out the port and the buoys. Our journey was nearly over. As we sailed slowly in I was watching through a telescope, and I saw signal after signal being flown on the flagstaffs. Sirens hooted and howled as we came nearer and picket-boats dashed about in various directions. All this agitation struck me at the time as being rather abnormal, and I thought it odd that people should be so apparently concerned about us. I thought that they imagined that we must be a Bolshevik craft.

I conferred with Bucharski as to whether we ought not to wait for a pilot, but he said that the boatswain knew the harbour very well and that we might as well save the money. So we sailed slowly in while the agitation grew more intense and then calmed down suddenly. On we went with our jib flapping over the stay, looking, I should think, very odd. The boatswain sailed her in very competently, and about fifty yards from where some other sailing craft were lying he gave the order to let down the anchor. Down it went with a rattle. The Soap Bubbles pirouetted about and kissed everybody within reach; the boatswain received our congratulations, and I went down the rope ladder into the dinghy. A motor-boat dashed up, and an excited officer stood up and said to some one next to him in good naval English, "Now find out who these blank, blank, blanks are, where they come from, what the blank they mean by coming right in across the minefield and tell them that they are under arrest."

This annoyed me, and before the interpreter could get going I stood up in the dinghy in my fur hat and said, "Arrest be damned. What for?"

The officer was very astonished at being addressed in English. I asked him on board, and told him our story, while everybody crowded round and chattered in Russian. He explained that nobody thought we could have come from Novorossisk, as all other craft from the evacuation had arrived long ago. He seemed particularly sore about his precious minefield, and I learned afterwards that we had really been lucky to have gone through it unscathed.

Probably our shallow draught had saved us from hitting anything, and anyhow, the minefield had been laid some time ago. We were, however, a nine days' wonder.

Within an hour of our arrival a working party came for the general's motor-car. I was sorry to see it go, for having it had certainly saved our lives.

CHAPTER XV

TIFLIS TO TILBURY

THE next few days I filled in being very busy with papers and formalities connected with the *Lucy and Zoya* and the preliminaries of the sale of her cargo.

Our original plan had been to go on in her from Batoum to Constantinople, but there was a consensus of opinion that there was no point in trying Providence too hard. So we decided to liquidate all that we could in Batoum, and let the boatswain sail the *Lucy and Zoya* to Constantinople if he could, but without us.

I went and stayed in the Officers' Rest House, and never shall I forget the first civilized bath and dinner I had after the fortnight on the lugger. Life was very pleasant. There were one or two battleships in the harbour, and I went to dine aboard. My story had become known, and the resulting interest was very gratifying, and I thoroughly enjoyed telling the professional sailors all about it. I discovered that *Steadfast*, the destroyer that had towed us out, was expected to arrive in a day or two, and when she came I sent Anton Gladky round in the dinghy with a bit of the broken tow-rope attached to the ends of two bottles of the Tsar's brandy and a polite note to the commander recalling the circumstances.

I was asked to dinner, and we had a wonderful time. It was great fun being rowed out by my two sailors in our dinghy and dining in a dinner jacket with the commander and then going to the wardroom and hearing the complimentary remarks of the N.O.s as they looked at the *Lucy and Zoya* lying sleepily at anchor. We organized return hospitality aboard, and it helped us greatly with our relations with the military, who were inclined to be very suspicious of us, for which indeed they had some justification.

The Soap Bubbles got an engagement and so did the male dancers at the local cabaret, which was called the Empire. I used to go behind every night with my naval friends, and many were the bottles of Napareouly—the local Caucasian wine— we drank in celebration of our voyage. Altogether, a good time, but one way and another I wasted a good deal of the money I had saved.

The sale of the cargo went on slowly, amidst various difficulties, and at last I thought I would like to go up to Tiflis to see if I could not hasten matters by selling something there. Tiflis was then the capital of the Georgian Social Democratic Republic, which for a little time managed to preserve its independence against the Bolsheviks, but was swallowed up at the last. From Tiflis I wanted to go on to Baku and then across to Persia. The Republics of Armenia, Georgia and Azerbaidjan were still holding out against the Bolsheviks, but were fairly tottery. So I planned a flying visit, intending to get back as soon as possible to Batoum, which was the only safe spot in the neighbourhood, though even there nobody knew how long the British forces would stay.

I went to see the Georgian Minister of Finance and got a visa. Tiflis was a place I had always wanted to visit. For in my young days, Ivan, places like Tiflis, Bokhara and Samarkand were the goal of every right-minded youth. I wonder if they still are, in spite of the Communist experiment and all that. Perhaps we will go together one day.

I suppose I shall never forget starting for Tiflis from
Batoum. I had had dinner with Bucharski at a Russian restaurant, and we had as our guest one of the officers from the *Royal
Sovereign*. It was a good dinner, with just the right amount of
vodka and caviare, and then a rather bad champagne. Elated I
was and in fine fettle. Was I not the man who had played a
great rôle in saving thirty thousand pounds' worth of the most
romantic cargo—including caustic soda and the Tsar's brandy
—from the very claws of the Bolsheviks? Was I not going to
Tiflis, city of Tamerlane and romance, and then on to Persia
through Baku and Azerbaidjan? Should I not have, when I
returned to England—O rank exhibitionist—many opportunities of making casual references to these things before honest
suburban girls and local untravelled bucks? Had I not had an
excellent dinner? Were not my plans all going well? Had I
not almost within my grasp the money necessary for my stay
at Oxford?

Oh, Ivan, how I enjoyed it! Outside, the powerful Benz lay
waiting to snort me along to the station, where my reserved
coupé lay. I should not wait in any vulgar queue. My tickets
were ready, and a special safe conduct—obtained, Heaven
knows how, by Bucharski from the Finance Minister of Azerbaidjan, and written in romantic Arabic characters with a tremendous seal—in my pocketbook gave me a sense of privilege
and importance. I had my Caucasian riding-whip and my revolver. Would I not stride up and down the platform waiting
for lesser individuals to buy their hard-fought tickets? Oh, dear,
oh, dear, how exalted I was as we drove at a dashing pace to
the station, while the alcoholic fumes lent brightness to the
air and brilliance to the occasion!

At last I got in, waved good-bye to my escort, and gave a
hundred Caucasian roubles—about threepence—to the faithful
Anton, and then settled in my coupé and lit a cigar. Only one

thing was missing, and my luck was in, for even that was vouchsafed me by a benevolent imp.

Walking along the corridor looking for a seat was a plump and toothsome Georgian girl with a beautiful face and a roving eye. She had no place, and spoke a little English. I had a whole coupé to myself. *Noblesse oblige.* She was a widow. She laughed at my impetuous advance, relented, and then mocked my inexperience. And then at Tiflis next morning made a rendezvous which she never kept.

It is strange that my most clear-cut memory of that romantic town was my meeting with an extraordinary American in the bazaar. He was in the U. S. Navy as a shorthand writer, and had gone up for a holiday from Constantinople. Whilst in Tiflis he had made the acquaintance of a beautiful girl—and, Ivan, there they are beautiful though stupid—and had married her at the American Consulate the day after he met her, though she spoke nothing but Russian and he nothing but slang, so that, except in the language of love, they were unable to communicate with each other at all. When I asked him how he was getting on he replied: "Oh, boy! I may be dumb, and she sure is, but stripped she looks like a million dollars." I mention this as an absurdity of memory. Why I should be incapable of remembering my visit to the Taj Mahal and have to go through life with that as a memory, Heaven alone knows, though I have no doubt that it is my own fault that I am so unlike the poet who wrote:

> *"My mind lets go a thousand things*
> *Like dates of wars and deaths of kings,*
> *And yet recalls the very hour—*
> *'Twas noon by yonder village tower—*
> *And on the last blue moon in May*
> *The wind came briskly up this way,*

Then pausing here, set down its load
Of pine scents and shook listlessly
Two petals from that wild-rose tree."

.   .   .   .   .

I went about my business, and got involved in complicated commercial negotiations with the Minister of Finance. Finally, I finished the draft proposals and sent them off to the firm in London, with the Minister's initials on them, an achievement, my Ivan, which in other and only slightly luckier circumstances might have had a very marked effect on my fortunes. However, my friends and Mr. Wardrop, who was the world's greatest expert in Georgian poetry and also the British High Commissioner in Tiflis, told me that everything was very insecure, and that the infant Republic was endeavouring to take Batoum from the British with one hand and with the other trying to ward off the rapidly approaching Bolshevik menace. Things, it seemed, might not last long, and the Bolsheviks would probably endeavour to swallow them all up fairly soon. This was annoying. I decided to try to get through to Baku while the going was possible. I had my kit packed and a place reserved in the train for Baku, when I heard, through some American relief workers, that things would probably blow up there at any minute. I decided to wait. And then to go. Finally, caution won, and I waited. The next day brought the news of the Bolshevik capture of Baku, and that all Azerbaidjan had gone red as blood. If I had gone I should certainly have undergone the horrors of a Bolshevik prison, as did certain of our people who had the misfortune to be captured there. Naval ratings they were, and they sat in a foul prison for seven whole months before they could be released.

Things even in Tiflis were by no means quiet. There were local riots, the exchange fell, and to my experienced eye all the symptoms were evident that I had seen in Russia proper before the collapse of the White Armies. I decided to get out. I delayed a day, and my friend the Finance Minister fell from power. Then came the news that relations with the British forces at Batoum were strained to the breaking-point, and that hostilities might break out at any moment. I gathered that Jordania, the President, was insisting on the evacuation of Batoum, whilst Cooke-Collis, the British General, would not agree to go.

I packed up and took counsel with my American friends. Charming people they were, and extremely kind to a Britisher. They thought I might go on their relief train. This I decided to do.

My return from Tiflis was very unlike my departure from Batoum. I drove up to the station in an old cab and got into a carriage full of cheerful Americans, who fed me Camel cigarettes and various forms of cereals.

The latest news was to the effect that the Georgian Government had broken off all diplomatic relations with the British on the question of Batoum, and might be expected to start hostilities at any minute if an ultimatum they had presented was not accepted. All Englishmen were to be arrested at the frontiers.

At length we neared the frontier of the area occupied by the British. It was rumoured that nobody but Americans would be allowed through, and that the carriages would be searched. The Chief Lady Help, or whatever she was called, was equal to the occasion. Rejecting a high-spirited attempt to disguise me as a nurse on the ground that I had not shaved sufficiently recently, she took me to the baggage waggon, where there were two motor-bicycles belonging to the Mission. She gave me a sort of khaki coat and a forage cap, which she took off a protesting despatch-rider who was as wax in her capable hands. She told me to busy myself with the engine of one of the motor-bicycles. This I did. Covering myself with oil, grabbing a spanner and chewing gum as expertly as I could, I waited with my heart in my mouth for the inspection at the Frontier.

It was a nasty moment, Ivan, for if any questions had been asked, or had my papers been required of me, the whole business would have been shown up, and I should certainly have been arrested for espionage and probably left in prison till the Bolsheviks came in. I sat and fiddled with the motor-bicycles, and presently in came a comic-opera Georgian with a fierce moustache and a frogged uniform. Fortunately, I was experienced enough to pretend that I had no knowledge of French or Russian or any other tongue than English, and as for passports, I said slowly and repeatedly that they were with the chief of the train. Luckily, the man was in a hurry and left me, threatening to return and investigate further. Thereupon I went back to my carriageful of relief workers, who played up splendidly, and scolded the unfortunate Georgian in American when he returned. Soon, to my unspeakable relief, I saw him turn disgustedly away from the chief of the train and give the order to proceed.

We crossed a neutral zone, and theatrical Georgians gave way to British Indian troops. I resumed my glasses, thanked my comrades, and heaved a sigh of relief.

Arrived at Batoum, I was surprised not to see Bucharski on the station. I took a Ford and drove down to the quay, where I had left the *Lucy and Zoya* ten days before. There she was, but, when I started to go over the gang-plank, I saw that she was guarded by Indian soldiers, who showed threatening bayonets and refused to let me on board.

I paused, and remembered suddenly some Hindustani.

"Hukm hai," said I, and waved the first piece of paper I found in my pocket.

The sentry hesitated, and finally did not protest as I brushed by and went over the gang-plank.

In the deckhouse I found the disconsolate Bucharski, whose face lit up when he saw me, as if my mere presence would be enough to lift the ban of authority. I was told that a sudden visitation had been made and that from the G.O.C. had come orders that the *Lucy and Zoya* was to be put under arrest. No further explanations had been vouchsafed.

Early next morning I went to see the General's A.D.C. I was told that the usual intelligence report had been received to the effect that we had stolen the ship and the cargo, and were actually Bolshevik agents who were trying to dispose of stolen British property under the very eyes of the outraged Lion. I explained the circumstances, and luckily for me the A.D.C. had some knowledge of the arrangement entered into between the War Office and our firm. A telegram was sent to G.H.Q. in Constantinople, an affirmative reply came through, and I was again restored to a position of respectable heroism. I was told that the G.O.C. never apologized, but would I come to dinner with the A.D.C.?

This incident was amusing, but ultimately it worked out to our advantage. The misleading report was traced to somebody who was trying to buy our cargo cheap, and wished therefore to discredit us, and I asked the authorities to tread on him, which they did, so that eventually he was glad to agree to our price.

I was told privately that I ought to try to liquidate our affairs as soon as possible, for the probable term of our military occupation was fast drawing to a close, and after that nobody would guarantee anything.

So we pushed on the arrangements. I, too, was keen to get

home and reap the reward of my efforts, which I still thought would come to a few hundred pounds in view of the prices which we had realized on some of the stuff, although we had had—in spite of Tchaikowsky's business experience—great difficulty in obtaining reliable cheques and drafts for what we sold.

I amused myself with the exploration of the surrounding country in search of my strange tribes. We drove out with Bucharski, who was a superb driver—he now dashes round Montlhéry, Brooklands and the rest of the autodromes at phenomenal speeds in supercharged sports models—all over the surrounding country, which was beautiful and interesting. On one occasion we nearly got cut off by the Ajars, a local and ferocious tribe, who would probably have held us to ransom, but we managed to retreat at 100 kilometres an hour over a crazy bridge on which the Ajars were advancing and which was being fired at by them.

We still had some cargo, of which we could not get rid. Finally, we found one night on the waterfront an American sea captain who had a fine steamer which had just come in. She was of the Bull Line of steamships, and had been at Poti loading manganese. We made friends with this man, who was a good sort, but a queer character. Finally, it was arranged that we should ship the guts, some of the textiles, the caustic soda and the Benz car to Constantinople and England. At the last moment, the captain—he was a New Englander, who read his Bible every night and used the most awful language all day —asked me whether I would go with him as supercargo. He confided in me that, though he feared no mortal man in a scrap, he stood in a blue funk of any little whippersnapper of an official in the ports to which he went. He had had several rows through not treating them diplomatically, and that had cost his owners money. He was sure that he would have trouble with his papers at the various ports of call, and told me pathetically that in those days any local authority who saw a sizable American ship on the horizon decided at once that the right thing to do was to make difficulties and hold her up for a large quantity of dollars. He thought that I, knowing the languages and having experience in the ways of port officers and Allied Commissions, might be of the greatest assistance to him in dealing with what he described as "frogs, wops and ornery bastards." He offered to take me on as supercargo, give me half his cabin and the services of his negro steward, take me to Liverpool free, and give me a "donation" if, at the end of the voyage, we had had no trouble. I jumped at this offer, which suited my romantic requirements and my pocket.

So I became a supercargo. The captain was a fine fellow, and I never ceased to wonder at the fear and trembling which any sort of official formality caused him who could easily knock down any member of the crew. I saw him knock a drunken Swedish sailor into the water at Constantinople, and then pull him out and carry him aboard over his shoulder. The man's Consul made trouble next day, and my captain's heart was completely won over, and he nearly died of laughter when, after consulting with me, we gravely informed the Consul that we had had to arrest the man for "attempted suicide." This *solution élégante* so appealed to him that he never forgot it, and I am sure that if I were to meet him now on the Quai Wilson, Bible in pocket, and pipe in mouth, he would at once offer to take me with him to the Port of Iquique, or wherever he happened to be going.

So our stuff was loaded on his steamer, and after a dinner of great festivity I bid farewell to Bucharski and Tchaikowsky and the faithful Anton, and with several thousand tons of modern steel under my feet, set out for Constantinople. We had a fine voyage along the Black Sea coast. We stopped at Samsoun, Ineboli and Trebizond, and I had parleys with Consuls and missionaries and port officers. An excellent voyage, and one I would like to do again.

As we came through the Straits, Kemal's troops were firing at the Greeks, and a shell or two passed harmlessly over us. For the rest, it was a pleasant journey.

When we got to London I was received with surprise and astonishment by the heads of the firm, who had only had very vague news about the whole matter, as Tchaikowsky's letters had gone astray. Alas for my dreams of new jobs and fat commissions! They had sustained such severe losses in the affair with Russia that they had gone into liquidation. Furthermore, what I had sweated to save for them was not even an asset, but actually a possible liability. For the head of the firm, who had left Novorossisk before me, had been told in Constantinople that all our stores had been burned and that we had been captured. He was, in fact, claiming from the insurance company somewhat more than we had been able to realize on what we had got out. The members of the firm were very kind, and told me I was all sorts of a hero, and that to show their appreciation of my conduct they would subscribe personally to give me fifty pounds and a splendid testimonial.

I understood their position. They had no money and owed large sums. There was nothing to be done. I took their fifty pounds, thanked them, and in a fit of furious disappointment plunged into a wild jag over London and Paris, which lasted two months, after which I pulled myself together.

I had given up Oxford and resolved never to think of it again, which was very silly of me, Ivan. But what would you? I was young and foolish.

PART III

NEAR EAST

"I saw the Ottoman's fortress—austere and darkly impending, high over the vale of the Danube—historic Belgrade. I
had come, as it were, to the end of this wheel-going Europe,
and now my eyes would see the Splendour and Havoc of the
East."—EOTHEN.

CHAPTER XVI

BALKAN TANGLE

I

WHEN I came to the surface, it was borne in on me that I had not really gained much except experience, and that I must again begin the wearisome job of hunting for employment.

This time, however, I resolved to try to get into something permanent and respectable, for, thought I, adventures were all very well, but they were very difficult to transmute into an assured livelihood.

There was a Government Department which was dealing with the problem of placing demobilized officers, and I went up to this continually. The result of these *démarches* was that at last I received a letter, and was told to see a high official in that privileged fastness, the Foreign Office, where I was given the general background and the facts which had led up to the production of that rare and precious thing, a vacancy.

Whilst I was in Novorossisk a guarantee had been given by the British High Commissioner in South Russia to General Denikin to the effect that the British Government would guarantee the evacuation of those of the civil dependants of Denikin's forces who were in danger on account of the presence at the Front of the male members of their family. This guarantee had been given and had had to be carried out. This was done with a thoroughness that everyone must admire, though the unfortunate taxpayer may be excused for having grumbled about the strain imposed on him. Most of the refugees whom I saw piling on to any sort of boat in the harbour of Novorossisk, that fateful day when I left in the *Lucy and Zoya*, had been transported to Egypt, Lemnos, Cyprus and Constantinople. There they were being maintained by the British Army, and were costing many thousands of pounds per month. There seemed to be nothing to do with them except keep them where they were. The administration of the camps was being performed by the Army, but as the author of the guarantee had been under the instructions of the Foreign Office, the bill was being sent in to that institution.

The Army grinned happily, found jobs for a number of its officers, gave the refugees as good a time as they could, and sent the "beautifully in order vouchers," as an Armenian accountant I once had, used to describe them, in to the Foreign Office, who had to find the money to pay them.

Justly alarmed at this, for it, unhappy situation, the Foreign Office stirred itself to some purpose, and having vainly written rude letters to the War Office about the appalling cost of its administration, had then tried to find a radical solution, and failing that, a less expensive one. It was quite impossible to go on paying for them for ever. Under these circumstances they had had the correct general idea that the place to put the refugees was in the Balkan Slav countries, where they would find a sympathetic atmosphere and an environment in which, owing to its similarity to Russian conditions, they would have some chance of finding employment.

The solution was elegant, but the great difficulty was that Yugoslavia and Bulgaria were sovereign countries, and as they already were sheltering a large number of refugees who had arrived unexpectedly, they saw no reason why they should accept fresh batches of Russians who had already a rich and powerful protector and one, moreover, who could not afford, for reasons of prestige, to leave its protégés to starve, even if it had wished to, which they were not prepared to believe.

The subsequent negotiations were long and difficult.

However, the Foreign Office eventually secured a partial victory and an agreement was signed between Dr. Trumbitch, the Yugoslav Foreign Minister, and Sir Alban Young, the British Minister at Belgrade, by which it was agreed that the White Russian refugees under British control were to be transferred to Yugoslavia, where the Yugoslav Refugee Service would look after them, *provided* the British Government paid a certain sum per head for their maintenance.

The British liability was unlimited as to time, but the Yugoslavs had agreed to try to settle as many of the refugees as possible, so that they should no longer be a charge on anybody but themselves or their relations. The British Government was to have a representative on the special organization which looked after the Russian refugees in Yugoslavia. This was called the Serbo-Russ State Commission for Russian Refugees, and it was to this body that the Yugoslav Government handed over all the official funds which it had allocated for the relief of the unfortunate Russians who had escaped to Yugoslavia. The duties of the British representative were officially limited to controlling and approving the calculation on the basis of which the monthly payment to the Yugoslavs should be made, to seeing that the money was used for the maintenance of the refugees and to endeavouring to obtain accounts.

Unofficially but efficaciously, however, added the high official, he was to see that the refugees were told who was really paying for them, but above all he was to try to plant as many of them out as possible, so that they should become self-supporting. It was hoped, he added, with a twinkle, that they would take such good root that in the fairly near future they would cease to become a charge on His Majesty's Government. Anything the man who went out could do to achieve these objects would be well seen. On the other hand, he would be under the orders of the British Minister, to whose Legation he would be specially attached, whilst retaining the right to report direct on refugee matters to the Secretary of State.

The high official outlined these matters benignly, and asked me whether I thought I was suitable, adding that the official requirements for the post were a knowledge of Russian and accounting, but that in his opinion what was wanted was somebody who could exercise tact and firmness. He then asked me to go and see the person who in his Department was dealing with this question. I went to see this person, who was kind to me, and who explained a little more in detail.

The curious features of the negotiations in connection with this job which, as explained to me, seemed rather important and alarming, were the speed with which things happened, the comparative ease of obtaining it, the lack of serious rivals, though at that time there must have been many people who would have jumped at it, and whose qualifications were more than equal to mine, and most astonishing of all, the rather diffident way in which people asked me whether I would do them the favour of telling them whether I thought I should fill the bill. I thought at the time that the testimonial from my recent firm, which was a very good one, coupled perhaps with the fact that the Foreign Office were more likely to believe one intelligent if one had done one's military service in the ranks instead of as an officer, might have supplied the solution, and perhaps it was so, but, be that as it may, I soon found myself a temporary official of the Foreign Office under orders for Belgrade.

II

In 1921, then, for the third time, I left England in search of fortune and fame. As I boarded the train at Victoria and bought myself *Punch* and the latest book by Mr. Wodehouse, I was feeling pleased with myself and pleasurably expectant. I was perhaps neither so elated nor so anxious as when I had left for Russia in company with the then magnificent Asala, but, on the other hand, I felt that I was more experienced, and that this time the possibilities, although perhaps not so exciting, were more solid. Whatever might happen could hardly be so extraordinary as what had passed with the Volunteer Army, and I felt with a tinge of regret that it was up to me to eschew the more flamboyant adventures, and endeavour to attain that high degree of respectable and prosaic ability which is the backbone of the Civil Service, and which receives its due reward in security of tenure, reasonable emolument, power and honours.

Instead of wandering about in topboots and a furry hat, with a revolver and all that, I must try, thought I, to emulate the bored, well-informed but apparently uninterested gentlemen who, behind largish spectacles and a barrage of Christian names, conduct Great Britain's foreign policy to their own satisfaction. I comforted myself for some time, however, with the reflection that, after all, anything might happen in the Balkans, and indeed, Ivan, I think their adventurous charm may persist to your day; at any rate I hope so.

So the train slid out of Victoria as I dreamed of Balkan princesses, Macedonian brigands, the Kutzo Vlachs, Seton-Watson, old bearded Pashitch, Serajevo, Venetian Ragusa, King's Messengers, British Ministers, lost despatches, Albanian tribes, stolen ciphers, amorous queens and Mirko, the faithful old retainer who always stabs the pursuing boarhounds.

In due course I passed through sunny Italy, Slovenia, the Croatian Plain and came to Belgrade. I was met by the Legation porter, and after getting settled in the Hôtel Bristol, I rattled in a cab over the bumpy road to see the British Legation.

I was received by the First Secretary. He was called Hope Vere. He is dead now, poor fellow, but during his lifetime he must have been quite the queerest member of a Service that does not exactly specialize in the normal. When he received me he had been poring over his washing bill, which, he complained, in addition to being inaccurate as regards the number of handkerchiefs, was even worse as regards his pants. How much, he plaintively asked, did I think he ought to pay for the purification of his vests, and how should he resist the amorous advances of his uncomforted landlady? When I was not helpful on these points he giggled, and suggested that I should see the Minister.

The Minister received me kindly, and indeed during all my stay he and his charming wife were uniformly kind to me, even though we did not always see eye to eye. For I was in a hurry to get results, being young, whereas he was at a stage of life when it hardly seemed possible that any good could come from action into which one was not absolutely forced after having registered the usual pessimistic reserves.

I settled down and plunged into the strange and attractive atmosphere of Belgrade at that time. Everything was rather disorganized, every sort of Allied Mission or Commission was wandering about—the Minister, who hated them all, killed them off at about the rate of two a month, but many persisted—the exchange was tottery, life was cheap, the people friendly, the ravages of the War were still evident, and Yugoslavia as an uneasy whole was engaged in trying to weld itself together under the ill-starred Alexander.

Quite close to the Legation was the Kalmegdan, or the "Field of the Princess." From it one has, I think, one of the most romantic views in Europe. From the old citadel which saw the struggles of Christian and Turk and where many a poor wretch has been impaled for the faith, one can see the peak of Avala, which is celebrated in the Serbian songs which one day you must hear if still the *gusla,* melancholy and plaintive of years of oppression, survives. Below are the great rivers flooding on, with islands in the main dark stream. Beyond stretch the great flat Hungarian plains, behind which the sun sets gloriously, till out come the twinkling lights of Zemoun, once Austrian Semlin.

I soon found that living in the inevitable Hôtel Bristol was not so satisfactory, as it cost too much, and so I looked about for rooms where I could live and have an office to receive my refugees. After much search I eventually found accommodation with a Serbian family who lived in a little one-storied house set about with a garden and cherry trees in a street just off the Slavia, which is at the other end of the Kralj Milan Street. The head of this family was a fierce-looking and diminutive Serb, who had been the bandmaster of the Royal band. Apparently, before the War, the Serbian Royal band used to travel abroad a great deal to play—though I thought it was only the Blue Hungarians who did this. In one of their *randonnées* they had gone as far as Australia, and there my little man had married a buxom Australian wench, who had come back to Serbia, where she had lived with him for many years and borne him two daughters. She had almost forgotten how to speak English, but was not unhappy, except that she wished to go back just once to Australia to see how it had got on.

In this little house I had three rooms. I used to lie awake

in my bedroom in the morning and listen to the hum of con
versation which came through the windows from the Russia
refugees who were waiting outside to see that man of all powe
the *Anglisky Prætstavitel*, or British representative. Hurried
I would dress and have my breakfast, usually a cup of Turkis
coffee and a roll, and perhaps some home-made cherry brand
if it was a cold morning, and then hold my court.

By the time I had arrived, the refugees had been transporte
from the Isle of Lemnos and planted out in colonies all ove
old Serbia. They lived fairly well on their monthly allowanc
and whatever they had saved from the wreck or could earn.

I had arranged to meet the heads of the colonies once
month. These were usually old admirals, generals or judge
and it was their job to present any petition or complaints fro
the members of their colonies.

It was an amusing experience for a young man, and I learne
a good deal about human nature therefrom. Very soon, i
pursuance of the instructions given me by the Foreign Office,
began to devise schemes for trying to put them on a self-sup
porting basis, and even then the problem of the means tes
with all its difficulties, exercised me.

One day the president of my best-behaved colony came t
see me with a petition for an advance of twenty thousan
dinars, which he said was necessary to put some of the mem
bers of his colony on a self-supporting basis. He was a pe
suasive old gentleman, with long Tirpitz weepers and a chestfu
of decorations. He said that, imbued with modern ideas an
spurred on by the necessities of the moment, he had decided t
permit in his colony the formation of a Co-operative Societ
Contrary, however, to the usual idea of a co-operative, whic
is to sell goods cheaply, the aim of this co-operative was to pr
vide opportunities of work for as large a number as possibl

thereby, in the not too distant future, saving the British Government a considerable sum of money, and enabling the refugees to become, as he put it, "standing on themselves."

The sum that he required as an advance from the British fund was considerable.

"And what," said I, "do you propose to do with the money, general?"

"Ah, Your Excellency . . ."

Here I pause and say quite frankly that, though I knew that he didn't mean it and that I wasn't entitled to it, and that he only used the term to get me into a good frame of mind, yet I could not avoid being pleased and flattered by this form of address and more ready to persuade myself into a favourable attitude.

"The members of our group," he went on, "may be subdivided additionally, to the already division of the sexes, into three chief lots, as in the case of Gaul."

Here he looked anxiously to see whether this "unaccountable, uncomfortable work of God that may have been sent for some good purpose to be revealed hereafter," had seized his classical allusion, and continued:

"The first lot are of two sexes, and wish to open a restaurant, which I feel sure will be a success, seeing that there is no reasonably cheap and respectable dining-room in the whole of Vrniatchka Banya, such is the extraordinary character of the inhabitants.

"The second group, also of both sexes, have decided that they should open a cinema. The third group are unmarried, and think that a taxi service would pay, so that with one Ford and two *izvoschiks*, one of which will be driven by a Kalmuck officer who is almost a horse himself, I think that we shall really be successful.

"I shall be the president of these groups, so that unity of control is assured. Professor Bogdanoff, the Vice-President of the colony, is drawing up the statutes, which will be translated and sent to you for transmission to King George."

Here he drew himself up and saluted, whilst I bowed from the waist in response.

"This will be in the form of an illuminated document specially illustrated by the talented daughters of the *Batiushka*, himself a priest of magnificent reputation."

Well, Ivan, I wanted terribly to help and do some good, so I fought the grant through the local Finance Commission, and made an eloquent speech in French to my Serbian colleagues, who wanted to do something else with the money themselves, and I even hinted that no less a person that Lord Curzon himself was interested in the success of this plan, as he had personal friends amongst the aristocratic refugees.

"In that case," said old Lyuba Jovanovitch, the President—after Nikola Pashitch, the wiliest and toughest politician in Serbia—"we can only agree and trust that Lord Curzon will take a more reasonable view as to the undoubted excellence of our claim to Fiume, based as it is on an ethnographical majority of crushing proportions, promised solemnly as it was to me, personally, by a certain colonel of the English Mission at Salonika in 1918, and earned by the clamant blood of thousands of massacred Serbians who died to save the Allies."

It was a good speech.

They got their money, and after a week or so I received encouraging reports and photographs. However, one morning the president, assisted this time by the vice-president, arrived again, and said that there was urgent need for another ten thousand dinars to keep the co-operative going.

"But," I said, "I thought from your reports that all was going well, and that everything was working to capacity."

"It is," replied the general, "and if the British Government will once again be patient and generous, all will be well."

"But what about the cinema? Isn't it going?" I asked.

"Yes. It has never been better," was the reply.

"I think," broke in the vice-president, "I had better explain. All goes well, and the simple Serbian villagers are amazed at the success and civilizing influence of our enterprises. Already the town of Vrniatchka Banya bids fair to surpass in culture and attraction the other towns of Serbia, and deputations from other refugee colonies arrive almost daily in order to learn our secret. Doubtless you will soon receive their delegations."

Here I groaned, and said that I would receive them only when the first grant was repaid. Nothing daunted, the professor continued his statement.

There was, it appeared, a fatal weakness in their statutes for which he took full and complete responsibility. It was that clause by which all members of the co-operative had granted each other reasonable credit as regarded any enterprises conducted by the group. This had at first seemed only reasonable. But in practice it had not given satisfaction, for what had happened was this. The days had opened fairly, and each member of the co-operative had decided to work hard so as to repay as soon as possible to the generous British Government the loan it had received. At about lunch-time, however, feelings of hunger had supervened. So all the members, except those actually engaged in running the restaurant, had thither repaired and, served graciously by their colleagues, had enjoyed a hearty meal. Being members of the co-operative they had not, of course, paid cash, but had merely signed chits. It would not have been right for the members of the restaurant group to have served their colleagues without some sort of recompense, so, exhausted by their labours, they had decided to go to the well-earned relaxation of the cinema. But the cinema was some way off, and so they decided to give a little employment to the taxi and *izvoschik* group. So they had hired them, and paid them with promissory notes. Arrived at the cinema, the taxi drivers, unnerved by the bumpy Serbian roads, had decided that they too needed relaxation, and all had entered the cinema. Everyone paid in notes of hand drawn on their share of the future profits of the co-operative enterprises.

"Now," said the professor, "the paper position of all the enterprises is excellent, and all that is needed is a little cash advance to restore the liquid assets, for the rustic Serbians have suddenly refused to honour any more of the Society's drafts."

After this I refused to finance any more co-operatives, and instead, elaborated a system of individual grants for the setting up of small businesses which had some success.

One may joke about this, and, indeed, some of the experiences I had were most amusing, such as the case of the man to whom I gave an advance for the establishment of a soda-water factory, and who was arrested as a Bolshevik by the Serb police owing to the continual explosions caused in his rooms by the worn-out siphons. There was also the man who claimed that he had discovered the West Pole. But I was compelled to admire the resource and fortitude with which these unfortunates set themselves to earn a living in strange and difficult circumstances.

Some of the individual cases with which I had to deal were most curious.

There was General Djounkovsky, who, amongst other exploits, had once—as he claimed—blown up a bridge against the oncoming Bolsheviks, and thereby saved from extermination the whole of a British Military Mission. Unfortunately, either the fuse had been too quick or the general had been too slow, for in the resulting explosion he had, as he said in his petition, received a piece of bridge in his thigh. He claimed compensation from the British War Office, who had, of course, regarded the incident as closed. The resulting confusion was enormous, and the Minister finally put an end to a desultory correspondence by writing a devastating minute, in which he said that the general should be penalized for playing bridge without contract, and added that, from his personal experience of British Military Missions, he thought that their capture would probably have hastened the Allied victory.

Next there was Colonel Hong. Colonel Hong was a Korean who had taken service with the Russians because he disliked the Japanese. He had lost an arm, but said that if we would only send him to Korea he would be able, as he put it, "to support himself on his father." So, after endless negotiations, I arranged matters, and off he went one fine morning. On the way to Korea he appealed to every British Consulate and Legation he could find *en route* for further funds, and despairing telegrams reached us from all parts of the world containing requests for the verification of his incredible story. He finally reached Korea. I hope he is flourishing.

There was my colony of Kalmucks from the Crimea—another subject of unfailing interest. These, as you ought to know, Ivan, are Buddhists, and extremely clever with horses; indeed, rumour had it that one of them could hold long conversations with sick horses and cure them by the Coué method. With my help they had established a little Buddhist *Khram,* or temple, in a small house outside Belgrade. The Minister whose permission I had obtained before making the grant which had rendered this possible had remarked, "Well, if the vagaries of His Majesty's foreign policy as at present conducted require the establishment in the suburbs of Belgrade of a temple for Kalmucks owing allegiance to Buddha, I have nothing to say, except that I refuse to accept any responsibility regarding possible difficulties with the Archbishop of Nish."

In their temple they had a picture of the Dalai Lama, a little wizened priest, a temple bell and many interesting appurtenances of their gentle faith that I have now forgotten, but which made a great impression on me when I went as their guest of honour, which seemed to me to be a really unique experience. In view of my support I was a welcome visitor, and used to watch the little Kalmuck babies and the sturdy children being taught how to look after horses and drink mares' milk or koumiss. Once, too, I lunched with them, ate of a fearful stew, and drank greasy tea. The Kalmucks were, when I left them, fairly prosperous, as their knowledge of horses had stood them in good stead, and they had obtained jobs as grooms and contractors. Later on, most of them went back to the Crimea.

III

After I began to find my way about, understand the position and establish my influence in the Serbo-Russian Commission and amongst the refugee organizations, I decided to make a special report. I worked hard at the preparation of this, and still remember the thrill I had as I burned the midnight oil in the bandmaster's house, and finally produced my first important report and recommendations addressed to the Lord Curzon. I had studied the diplomatic jargon, and had great fun in adapting that delightful style in which ambassadors recount their stewardship. I interlarded it with phrases such as: "I was received by the Minister for Foreign Affairs with great cordiality, and Dr. Nintchitch intimated . . ." "I did not fail to point out to his Excellency," and several other of those pompous and consequential clichés which I then regarded as obligatory for diplomats.

It seemed to me that I must not confine my report to a mere exposition of the situation, but that I must put forward constructive proposals leading to economy. This, Ivan, usually forms a good *tremplin* for an *arriviste*. I had momentary qualms about making a reputation for myself at the expense of the unfortunate refugees, but I soon persuaded myself that, after all, the situation could not last, being generally untenable, and that the best way of avoiding a sudden brutal cessation of the help that they were getting from His Majesty's Government when the burden became too much for the taxpayer, was to string things out and give way gradually to the screams for economy and dole suppression that, quite naturally, were already alarmingly insistent. In any case, it seemed impossible to say that no solution at all could be hoped for.

I sat and worked and thought and revised till I had got the thing stated just as I wanted it. In order to prepare this report I had asked for and obtained permission to visit all the refugee colonies in which we had an interest. These were nearly all in old Serbia and grouped around Nish. So I made an official tour. This was a memorable experience. I went by train and carriage, and sometimes on horseback, to villages and towns in Serbia. Jagodina, Vranja, Vrniatchka Banya, Nish, Zaitchar and many other Serbian towns. I was always received in great state and ceremony, and usually had an official dinner given me, at which I had the greatest difficulty in keeping sober and cautious under the wave of Slav hospitality that threatened to engulf me on arrival.

At each colony I held a sort of court and settled all sorts of questions, some of which even involved alimony grants in cases of divorce. I was not more than twenty-five or so at the time, and enjoyed it thoroughly.

I still have some of the letters, written in the queerest English, sent to me by the refugees in those colonies after my visits. I remember one which was an answer to one of mine refusing in the kindest and politest terms to grant a man a sum of money for which he had asked so as to be able to divorce his wife, and which began,

"DEAR SIR LAWFORD,—Your beautiful letter has plunged me in despair. As for my wife, she is horrible to me, having read it while I was in a café. I hoped that as an old ally of your King I should find you more good looking."

The author of this letter afterwards became a chauffeur, and on the strength of his knowledge of English I was often enabled to get him jobs as driver to visiting Englishmen. One day the Minister asked me to produce him for a fussy and pompous business baronet, who was plaguing the Legation regarding certain concessions he had been unwise enough to obtain and finance. So I warned Ivanoff to be ready in the morning. The Baronet arrived, demanded his car in a hurry, and was greeted by Ivanoff who, bowing low, said to him these pregnant words, "Knight, I sorrow. But my automobile to-day is completely debatterized. To-morrow only it will be rebatterified."

Later on I went to Serajevo. There I had to inspect a Russian Cadet Corps which was very well organized on a military basis. It was curious, with a bewhiskered general beside me, to receive the salute of Russian Refugee cadets, victims of one war and in training for another in this town where the whole business started. It was strange to see the Town Hall on the way to which that fatal day of June 28th, 1914, the first bomb had exploded, and where the unfortunate Archduke had received his last welcome address; then Franz Josef Street, where the fatal deed was done, and where Princip was seized by the crowd.

I met the queer old British Consul, who had been in Serajevo when it all happened, and who invariably began his recital of events with the same formula: "As soon as I heard the noise of the explosion I at once *realized what had happened,* and sent a telegram to Maurice de Bunsen at Vienna and a copy to the Foreign Office." It was an interesting experience to dine with this nice ineffectual old man who had "at once realized what had happened," and hear him dilate on the promptness of his puny counter-measure. As I stood there and paused for a moment to think of the fearful consequences of that moment for the world, the Consul's sister said that tea was ready, and that we should go back, which we did.

So I incorporated the results of my travels in my report, finished it at last, sent it off and relaxed in the local society. My point of view was accepted, and I received a commendatory reply. Much encouraged I went from strength to strength, and managed to get a number of refugees satisfactorily settled and no longer a charge on His Majesty's Government. My salary was increased by £200 a year. In a word, I found my feet, and though I took a good many risks one way or another, I was lucky and managed to maintain the small reputation I had established.

For the rest, I frequented embassies, legations and the ministries, and played a small rôle in the diplomatic life of the capital. I travelled extensively, met all the Balkan celebrities, and even began to know something about the Macedonian problem. My office grew, and I thoroughly enjoyed myself in the queer unstable interesting atmosphere of the time.

Diplomatic circles amused me. When my work was over—and often when it wasn't—I found it agreeable to stray into their narrow important little world, which then seemed so huge, and converse amiably with well-mannered chargés d'affaires and smooth secretaries in quest of information. It was amusing and useful to a young man to make a fourth at bridge with Balkan ambassadors, worldly Excellencies and their hard-playing powdered corseted consorts, and note their social technique.

Life went on agreeably in Belgrade, and I worked hard and amused myself harder. I went all over the country and met many interesting people. I saw and talked with old Nikola Pashitch, and most of the then eminent politicians in Yugoslavia. I met the ill-fated King, frequented strange Balkan cabarets, played tennis, and went bathing, shooting and ski-ing. On the whole, Belgrade was a most interesting phase.

CHAPTER XVII

LEAGUE MISSION

AT about this time the League of Nations had just started a High Commission for Refugees under the leadership of Fridtjof Nansen. This organization was destined to play a great part in my life—though I must say my first contact with it was not exciting, as it consisted in filling up a voluminous questionnaire about refugee affairs which had been sent out to me by an official at the Foreign Office, who, with a sigh of relief, had sent it off to me, and told me to answer it as and how I liked.

Some time later I was greeted by the Archivist, a cheery soul, who told me that I was "for Geneva," and showed me a telegram instructing me to go there. The Council of the League had asked Sir Samuel Hoare to make a tour of the Balkans and Constantinople in order to report on what might be done about the refugee problem: the Foreign Office had been asked to place me at his disposal and had agreed.

The Minister sent for me, very kindly gave me his blessing and said that if all my schemes came to pieces in my absence and caused him unceasing worry, it would only be what he expected.

So in the autumn of 1921 I packed up, said my good-byes, was given an uproarious send-off by the members of the colony and friends, and set off for Geneva.

My first acquaintance with the League of Nations was auspicious, and everything went well until the question of the sinews of peace arose. Sir Samuel was in London, and it was decided that we should meet in Prague. From there we were to go to Constantinople, visiting Rumania and Bulgaria either on the outward or on the return journey.

I flatly refused to start without the advance of a sum sufficient to cover the major expenses of the trip. The then Acting High Commissioner for Refugees agreed that this was only reasonable, and then ensued a very good example of an administrative battle.

First I gathered there was no money available, and then there was no authority to give me any, and in any case it would take two days, whereas I wanted to leave that night, as I had to go to Berne to get a Czech visa. The Acting High Commissioner was equal to the occasion. He achieved heights of eloquence and vituperation in about seven languages on the 'phone. He was of the same nationality as Captain Bluntschli, and reminded me very much of him. He was superb, and eventually he won. Money was produced, and I was given an idea of what it was all about. The Acting High Commissioner told me that the Refugee Commissariat had just started, and that it wanted to do something to help the situation at Constantinople, where very large numbers of Russian refugees from Wrangel's and Denikin's armies and civil organizations were in a terrible condition. They had to be fed by charitable organizations; the Allied Forces occupying the town felt that they were in danger of epidemics and other grave possibilities; something had to be done to relieve the pressure. Sir Samuel had been asked to report, as it was felt that the opinion of a level-headed and influential person might focus the situation and produce plans and help. The report was to be made to the Council of the League.

At Prague the Mission separated. Sir Samuel and party went to Athens and Rumania and I to Belgrade and Constantinople.

I arrived in Constantinople, and taking up my residence at the Pera Palace, proceeded to get busy.

Your mother will tell you in what guise I reappeared with a hired and shiny League motor-car, and how I used to carry her off from her office where she had a job working in the Royal Army Ordnance Corps. It was an excellent period for me. I met all the celebrities and the somewhat terrifying relief workers and the representatives of the American Relief Administration and all the enthusiastic amateurs who came with marvellous schemes which they wanted the League to sponsor.

I had long busy days, and in the evenings there were blissful interviews with your mother, who had then just recovered from typhus. Sir Samuel arrived and things got busier.

It was plain that the only thing to do was to try to get as many as possible of the refugees out of Turkey, as the situation was obviously untenable, and so we laid our plans to this end.

Then I went off to Bulgaria, where I had long interviews with the Cabinet, then back through Prague and to London to help Sir Samuel with his report.

Afterwards I went back to Belgrade.

Sir Samuel had been kind enough to include in his report to the Council of the League a flattering reference to your father, which in good time was destined to bear fruit.

During my visit to London a plan had been laid for the transfer of the Russian refugees in the charge of the British Government to the newly formed High Commissariat of the League. There was a period of negotiation, I was summoned to London and Geneva, and after a while the whole matter, with the details of which I will not bore you, though at the time they were of absorbing interest to me, was signed, sealed and delivered.

I was to become a temporary official of the Secretariat and one of Dr. Nansen's assistants. I had some doubts about the wisdom of the step I was taking, and profiting by my hard-earned experience I made the best bargain I could for myself. At last all was arranged. For two months I was to serve two masters and arrange the details of the transfer of the Russians in Cyprus and Egypt from the Foreign Office to the League, and then I was to be appointed to the League.

The essence of the affair was to find somewhere to put the refugees at once so that they should not go on costing the large sums which were necessitated by their presence in British Army camps.

I dashed off to Constantinople to consult with the League Commissioner for Refugees, a certain Colonel Procter, who was a very high official of the important institution known as the Imperial Ottoman Bank, concerning the solution of the problem of where to put the new League refugees. It was arranged that we should approach the Bulgarian Government.

Off I went to Sofia, and interviewed everybody, ably assisted by our local representative. I saw the King and Stambulisky and all the Council of Ministers, and we arranged a bargain, by which we were allowed to import the refugees immediately, having agreed to pay for them after their arrival.

It was a hectic business and most interesting. I kicked my heels for hours in waiting-rooms and interviewed every sort of person and official. At last the thing went through the Council of Ministers, and I was hurrying back to Constantinople on the Simplon Express, feeling that a great triumph had been won. And so it was, and if it had been achieved in other fields it might have made my fortune, for in one month we had solved a problem which had baffled everybody for a year or more. From

Constantihople, feeling extremely important, I was taken on an American destroyer to Egypt.

If you want to feel the joy of travel you should when young, and by way of being successful, arrive in Cairo by the night train from Alexandria on a warm evening with money in your pocket and a difficult job before you. Go straight out to Mena House and look at the Pyramids in the moonlight and then drive back, and sit on the terrace at Shepheard's or the Continental Savoy drinking a cold drink in the Egyptian night with the garden in front of you and Islam, tourists and officialdom mingling uneasily under the stars.

Things were going well with me. I had a credit of one thousand pounds at my personal disposal, and that always gives one a feeling of prosperity, even though it has to be accounted for. I had called on the Resident, Lord Allenby, had lunched at the Residency, and seen a little of proconsular state from the right angle—formerly it had been all saluting and presenting arms—and had been more than kindly received by that splendid soldier. I was also in personal contact with the G.O.C., the gallant General Congreve, now alas! dead, and in constant negotiation with hard-faced majors in G.H.Q., who became amenable when they discovered that the representative of the League neither wished to ask them impossibilities nor was prepared to agree to any obvious ramps at its expense.

With the Russian refugees there were many troubles. They were very well off where they were, and the idea of going to Bulgaria and the practical solution which I had prepared for them did not seduce them at all. The distinguished Russian G.O.C. of the Don Cadet Corps, which had been established on the banks of the canal at Ismailia and petted by the whole of Ismailia society for social reasons—and humanitarian ones too, perhaps—was the hardest nut of all to crack. He was a general, and rejoiced in the name of Tcherriochoukine. He was an obstinate old die-hard. He put forth three hundred odd reasons why he should not move to Bulgaria, but I overruled them all. When he saw that I was adamant, he sent personal telegrams appealing against the decision to the Crowned Heads of Great Britain, Italy, Scandinavia and Holland, to Winston Churchill, the Pope, Lord Curzon and every conceivable great man and authority. The telegrams, of course—such is the kindly custom of the Foreign Office—were referred back to the Residency, where the alarmed Secretaries hastily pressed them into my hand and asked me to deal with them as I thought fit. I communicated the answer verbally to the astonished general, who was used to different methods. At last he gave in, and subject to my agreeing to his retaining the command of the Cadet Corps in Bulgaria, turned from an attitude of immovable opposition to one of much helpfulness varied by occasional relapses, when I insisted on the demobilization of his military organization.

I had an amusing time chartering with G.H.Q. a ship to take my odd cargo, and finally we fixed on the *City of Oxford,* a steamer of five thousand tons, which had come to Palestine with a draft of men for the Palestine constabulary. As she had been fitted out for trooping she served admirably.

During this operation, I saw something of the business methods of the Levantine, for I was approached by the most unscrupulous owners of the most unseaworthy boats and had the greatest difficulty in keeping clear of their machinations.

This was an anxious time, for, as the arrangements began to near completion and plans ceased to be theoretically interesting and became subject to the acid test of action, I began to sit up at night going over things to make sure that everything was all right. Of course the detailed arrangements had to be made by

G.H.Q., but I was personally responsible for the reception arrangements in Bulgaria and for the general co-ordination. It was a big job, and I was heartily glad when at last I started on the *City of Oxford,* the chief personage on that noble craft, always excepting the Master, a dour individual who expected plagues, epidemics and revolutions to break out at any moment and who often vacillated between scriptural and alcoholic consolation. As assistants I had two officers and a doctor lent by the Army.

I organized the refugees into groups, and I must say they entered into the spirit of the thing very well. I had a reception tour every morning and listened to complaints and answered innumerable questions about the future in Bulgaria.

One day, as I was doing the rounds, I heard a small Russian child being shushed by its parents as, pointing at me, it exclaimed, poor mite, in a piping treble: "Is that the League of Nations? I thought it would be bigger." This, I felt, was fame as it should be, accompanied by a corrective.

We had to call at Cyprus to collect another batch of refugees, and here again I had been nervous about the arrangements. All went well, however, and I was able to see something of the island. It was a fine sight as we cast anchor early on a fine morning and I saw the first signs of bustle caused by our arrival.

On we steamed with our cargo of refugees to Constantinople, whence, after interviews with the G.O.C., we set out for Varna. At Varna I was met by our local representative, his charming wife and your mother, who had come down to meet us. We successfully disembarked the refugees and organized a big camp, where they were soon more or less properly installed.

When the arrangements had been completed and it was time for the *City of Oxford* to return to Egypt via Constantinople for the second convoy, it was suddenly decided that, as there was plenty of room and the whole ship was at my disposal, your mother, to whom I had become officially engaged, should come too, accompanied by the wife of our local representative as chaperon. So at ten minutes' notice, without any passports, we all set off, a gay party, for Constantinople. Here I offered to recompense the many services of the British G.H.Q. Staff to the refugees and to the League Office by offering the G.O.C., General Harington, a few free holiday passages for his staff on my large and empty boat. The offer was eagerly accepted—it was afterwards amply repaid by many further services to the refugees and the League—and off I set with a mixed bag of officers. We were an amusing ship's company, and we had a pleasant time when we arrived in Cairo.

We could only stay three unforgettable days, and then we loaded up with refugees again, steamed back to Constantinople, dumped our military, and then on to Varna to off-load the refugees. When this was done I went up to Sofia, where your mother's people were already established in a funny old house in Marindrinoff Street.

I had a lot to do, in view of the establishment of the refugees and the organization of a system of relief. Sofia society was then very gay, as there were a number of Allied missions in the town, and we thoroughly enjoyed ourselves. Indeed, it was, I think, one of the happiest periods I remember. I was engaged to be married, there was important work to do and good results were being obtained. We had organized a refugee jazz band, which followed us faithfully about, so that we had music wherever we went, and on the summer evenings there were expeditions to Rila and long hours at the tennis club.

CHAPTER XVIII

REFUGEE COMMISSIONER

I

THE summer of 1922 drew thus to a close, and we decided to get married on the 15th September. It was a full-dress affair with the representatives of the King and the Government, and the majority of the Diplomatic Corps. We were married according to the rites of the Russian Orthodox Church in the Chapel of the Russian Embassy at Sofia, by one Chavelsky, who had been the Tsar's confessor, and who was the possessor of one of the most magnificent bass voices that I have ever heard. Assisting him was the massed choir of the Don Cossack regiments, and I shall never forget the wonderful singing at the services as I stood with my *kooms*—two Russian princes and one embarrassed Englishman, whose duty it was in turn to hold a crown over my head. There was a good deal of conjuring business with a ring and handkerchief, and the choir burst into a frenzied and jubilant bellow of magnificent resonance, and there we were.

There was a reception at a house which had been lent to us, with a champagne-inspired refugee band playing jazz, and on the lawn the Don Cossacks in their uniform, full of beer and melody, singing in unison. They sang about thirty pounds' worth, Ivan, and gravely embarrassed my finances. There were telegrams from King Boris, Stambulisky, Nansen and all my friends; the members of the various missions and the diplomats went down to the station, and saw us off in a hurroosh of champagne and flowers. We went on to Belgrade, and then to Budapest—a marvellous place for a honeymoon—with Tokay, gipsy violins and the Danube. The same to you, *mon fils,* one day.

From Budapest we went to Abbazia, where we sat in the sun and bathed. I wish I had the picturesque trick of contemporaneous description. I should like to be able to tell you intelligently of all the things that were happening in the world and that had some bearing on my honeymoon and its sudden end. If I had, I should paint a picture of Mustapha Kemal's hardbitten troops closing in on the fleeing Greeks in Asia Minor, of the great Polar explorer receiving in his house near Oslo a telegram from the Council of the League, of hurried consultations in Geneva, of a Hungarian telegraph-boy vainly seeking me in the Hôtel Astoria and end it all by a close-up of your mother's face when, between eating two ripe figs on the balcony of an Abbazia hotel, I opened the telegram which announced the fall of Smyrna, and recalled me to tragic scenes at Constantinople.

Back we hurried to Belgrade, where we met Dr. Nansen and the whole League Mission. Off we went to Sofia, where we were received on our way through with great ceremony, as Nansen was very popular in that country, owing to his activities in connection with the repatriation of Bulgarian prisoners of war. King Boris himself drove the engine of the Simplon-Orient Express. There were red carpets on the station which I had left only a fortnight before, and all the bells were ringing. On we rolled through Adrianople to Constantinople, which was even more frenzied than usual with crowds of new Greek refugees added to the existing Russians, Armenians, Georgians and others, and all the Army of Occupation excitedly discussing the effects of Kemal's success.

I established myself in a local office, and we hurriedly considered what we should do for the unfortunate Greek refugees. Nansen formed a committee which I attended on his behalf, known as the Greek Refugee Evacuation Committee, and on it were represented the Œcumenical Patriarch, the Greek and Allied military authorities and various charitable organizations. The representative of the Patriarch was a Greek whose lengthy name I have forgotten, but he was a most efficient individual, and so extraordinarily good at rationing Greek refugee boats with practically no money or stores at his disposal, that we always referred to him as the economical pastrycook.

The Turkish advance became more and more menacing, and General Harington, the Allied G.O.C., decided that the wives of the officers of armies of occupation should leave. So your mother was protestingly packed off to Sofia.

Meanwhile, after the sacking and burning of Smyrna—a terrible story and one which I shall not endeavour to recount—the Turkish armies were advancing and the evacuation of Eastern Thrace before the advancing gendarmerie of Refet Pasha was begun. I shall never forget the appalling sights and scenes caused by the flight of the Greek inhabitants of Thrace, who fled across the Maritza so as to get out before the avenging Turk could reach them. The Allies had arranged an armistice, but there was only a short time in which to effect the transfer of the unhappy peasants. The population of Eastern Thrace took itself up by the roots and emigrated *en masse*. Whole villages were torn up, and, with their scanty belongings piled into miserable carts, the panic-stricken peasants made their tragic way along the muddy and impassable roads in bitter wintry weather. There were a few Allied officers superintending where they could, and the Greek authorities, of course, spared no pains, though they were, naturally, completely disorganized. It was impossible for them not to be. When prefect, mayor, priest, grocer and peasant are all under the same menace of death if they do not get away in time, any organization is certain to break down. So they huddled into waggons in the winter, old and young together, and set off towards the river that goes by Adrianople. There is nothing more pathetic, I think, than to see the miserable household goods of hardworking peasants piled on a farm waggon with an aged crone of a grandmother holding the last-arrived wailing brat, surrounded by hens, chickens, goats, lambs, the dining-room furniture and gaudy daubs of royalty torn from their proud place in the best room and piled with the *ikon* on top of the crazy superstructure.

It was an extraordinary sight. As the evacuation went forward the whole country was left empty and desolate. It seemed to me, as I looked at the sight, that this was a scene which had many times been repeated in history, as indeed it had *car dans ce pays-là on viole toujours,* and as I saw the deserted farms and looked over the melancholy countryside, it began to be borne in on me that the League must be made an efficient instrument so as to stop this kind of senseless misery. No wonder that most of the relief workers who collaborated with us were pacifists of the bitter variety; there really is no fun in war seen from that angle.

From our Constantinople office we had with the utmost difficulty equipped a relief column under the command of a certain Colonel Treloar, a very striking person indeed, and a man of abounding and prodigious energy, built for stirring times rather than for peace. He did magnificent work, and I afterwards launched him into Western Thrace, where he found an excellent outlet for his energy. He was an Australian and had commanded a Guards battalion during the War. He spoke no Greek, and went round with an interpreter named Marcou, who lived in a continual state of apprehension as to what might happen to him next.

Never have I laughed so heartily as at Treloar's tales and exploits, which were always related with a picturesque vehemence characteristic of the man. "God bless my heart and soul," he would say to me, as we stood supervising feeding operations, "look at that son of a bitch of a mayor looking like a blasted stuffed monkey. He is not *distributing* the rations, he is blank blank well eating them." Thereupon he would stride off and glare at the affrighted mayor, and curse him as though he were a new recruit, whilst Marcou would make an expurgated translation to the incriminated official who, pale with rage and terror, would go off into volleys of Greek like a machine-gun.

Once I saw him stride up to a village priest who had contravened his orders about vaccination, and grasping him by his arm and greasy locks, shake him furiously, shouting, "I'll teach you to respect the League of Nations, you moss-faced scoundrel." I of course intervened and quieted things down as best I could. I always wondered what the staid officials of Geneva would have said if they could have seen the extraordinary things that were done in their name.

I was the first official of the League to do many things in its august name. I had chartered ships, I had a totally unauthorized but very useful League flag on my car, I had an enormous *Kavass* in a League uniform, which we had invented for him, based on the brighter musical comedies. I had bought flour for refugees and negotiated with officers in charge of evacuation, and all the time I must confess I only had rather a vague idea of how the League machine was supposed to work and—apart from its obvious rôle of peacemaker—what it was all about.

I read the Covenant through for the first time in a railway carriage, which was so full of bugs that I could not sleep when I was travelling one beautiful moonlight night between Dedeagatch and Gümüljina. The train stopped at a station where, in the light of the station lamps, I saw a huddled mass of dejected refugees whose faces wore a baffled, hopeless look of misery. I had an absurd and strong impulse to spring out and declaim the solemn passages of the Covenant to the patient victims of war, but I restrained it.

II

After the Thracian situation had been dealt with to a certain extent, Nansen asked Colonel Procter and myself to meet him in Sofia, where we hoped to repeat my previous success and obtain permission to send to Bulgaria a number of able-bodied Russian refugees from Constantinople so as to relieve the pressure on the resources of that unhappy town. In this our mission was successful.

There was a big dinner given by the Government, at which Stambulisky, who was then Prime Minister, was present. There were speeches. I remember that Stambulisky made a speech at the end of the dinner through an interpreter. What I understood him to say was that he was extremely tired and wanted to go to bed. But his interpreter, a charming lady who now adorns an upper stratum of Caledonian society, made a magnificent adaptation of his speech, and said a long piece about welcoming us to Bulgaria, that we must be very tired, and how indefatigable workers in the cause of peace and humanitarian efforts were certainly entitled to a night's repose! It was very well done.

Various things happened at that dinner. Nansen, finding himself next to the Minister of Posts and Telegraphs, in order to make conversation in a silent interval, asked him if he himself collected stamps. The Minister coloured furiously, and there was an agonized silence which none of us could understand, until our local representative told me in a hurried whisper that only that morning there had been a heavily documented article in the local opposition paper accusing the Minister of having stolen a colossal number of stamps.

Nansen in those days was still at the height of his powers and a wonderful example of energetic age. He would take me out for walks, and we would climb up Vitosha, the mountain outside Sofia, till I felt ready to drop, but he was apparently ready to go on for ever. He was a very great man, and it is a pity that there are not more figures in the League like him today. I shall always be proud of having been intimate with him and of having in some measure contributed to some of the results he obtained.

I saw a good deal of Stambulisky in those days. He was an extraordinary and forceful character. It seemed to me that had he lived he might have founded a Slav peasant union which would have had a pacifying effect all over South-Eastern Europe. Corrupt he may have been, and probably was, but I always found him a man of his word, if one could only manage to get the better of his peasant cunning. He passed a law preventing lawyers from becoming members of the *Sobranje* or Bulgarian Parliament. Not long afterwards he was overthrown and brutally murdered.

I well remember one incident of my negotiations with him. He had asked me to meet him at his country place at Chamkorea, on the hills outside Sofia. We went out by car, and on the way we met him and the Minister of War in a huge Mercédès car. He had two Alsatian wolf-hounds to guard him, and a police car with a gendarme and a machine-gun was following, for at that time he had displeased the Macedonians, and they never miss if they get a chance. He stopped his car and there on that country road we discussed our business, which resulted in permission for a thousand Russians to leave Constantinople for Bulgaria. This was a generous act which meant reprieve, new life and chances for hundreds of sad starving families, work for many men and release from the sapping degradation of the Constantinople cabarets for many poor girls struggling to keep body, soul and self-respect together. I tried to follow up this success by asking our local representative to get visas for a similar number of Armenians. But "No," said Stambulisky, "they will come across the frontier without permission like rain through an old coat. They do not need permission."

Later on we all had an alfresco dinner and sang Bulgarian songs in the spring-time under a flowering almond tree. Your mother was wearing that cameo brooch affair on which you used to scratch yourself when small. Stambulisky noticed it, and pointing a black and stubby forefinger, asked if it represented her mother. She was somewhat taken aback, but cleverly and quite untruly—for it represents some purely imaginary lady of Italian origin and impeccable beauty—said his supposition was correct. "That's right," he said. "I always respect people who keep their mother in memory." And then he produced from a dingy pocket a battered tin-type of his mother in peasant costume.

You must realize that he was at that time Dictator of Bulgaria. The incident put him in a good humour, and I managed to get some visas for the Armenians out of him after lunch.

The comparative frequency of incidents of that sort made that job very fascinating. One was using one's diplomatic talents for practical humanitarian problems. A timely joke and a properly studied approach might save hundreds of lives. I

studied my politicians and officials, and because I was terribly
keen and possessed experience, local knowledge and a good
cause, I was able to get things done.

III

Shortly after this I was appointed to take permanent charge
of the League Refugee Office in Constantinople. We took for
the office a large house, just near the British Embassy, which
belonged to the Catholic Archbishop of Thrace, a prelate
named Calavassy, who was only too glad under existing circumstances that we should occupy it for a nominal rent so as to
prevent it being requisitioned either by Turks or by the Allies.
There we settled down, and I spent three most interesting and
useful years. It was an extraordinary period, and one which I
think and hope is unlikely to be repeated.

Wave after wave of refugees had, since 1920, descended on
the town. When the Greeks were beating the Turks there were
masses of Turkish refugees to be fed. Then when the Greeks
began to lose they came streaming in. They had come from
every part of the Greek Diaspora, from behind Smyrna, from
Eastern Thrace, from the Caucasus and from Pontus, where the
refugees spoke classical Greek, and seemed to have retained
some of the austerity and courage of their ancestors, who, if I
remember rightly, were supposed to have been survivors and
stragglers from Xenophon's Ten Thousand. There had been
two waves of Russian refugees, one after Denikin and the next
after the defeat of Wrangel; there were Georgians who came in
after the conquest of Georgia by the Soviet; there were Armenians and Albanians. Later on there were Turks from Greece,
who arrived under the exchange of populations. There was a
band of Assyro-Chaldeans, who had come all the way from
Mosul and the Hakkiari on foot by way of Novorossisk. These

latter people had had a peculiarly tragic history: they had joined the Allied cause, and were Christians and extremely good fighters, so that the Kurds and Arabs made a point of victimizing them when possible. When the Allies left we were able to do something for them, and soon they started a little village in Mashlak, near Constantinople, and lived in houses entirely constructed from empty petrol-tins. There were Kalmucks from the Crimea, and up in Thrace and Macedonia there was an exchange going on of Bulgars and Greeks. We had various urgent tasks in connection with the delousing, feeding, clothing and evacuation to employment in other countries of all these different refugee masses, and I had a great deal to do with their leaders and those who were trying to help them.

One of our main functions was the organizing of the evacuation of the Russian refugees. In order to get out they had to have passports, visas, money for their travelling expenses, and, if possible, a job on arrival. To this task I gave all my energy and my undivided attention, and proceeded fanatically and with a great deal of success. At first sight it was a problem of seemingly impossible difficulty, as no country wished to take them; in many cases they did not want to leave Constantinople themselves, so sunk were they in misery: there was very little money available for their evacuation, and very often they had no papers of any sort on which the visa of a country willing to accept them could be placed, even when such a visa was obtainable. However, we took the thing piecemeal, and in a comparatively short space of time we had accomplished so much that my success was celebrated in a letter which appeared on the main page of *The Times* and which was most congratulatory.

It is rather difficult to describe at all satisfactorily the details of the work which we were doing at that time. It was very varied. In connection with the work of evacuation and relief, we had dealings with the Allied police authorities, and then with the Turks who supplanted them during my residence. We also dealt with the foreign embassies, the consulates and the various intelligence services, who were always carefully examining our lists, on the lookout for desperadoes, drunks, dope addicts and Bolshevik agitators masquerading as refugees. We had business with the American Relief Administration, which was engaged in feeding some of the refugees until we could evacuate them. There were the British Army authorities, the French High Commissariat, the French military forces, the Italians, the Greeks, the Turkish administration, the diplomatic and consular representatives, the relief workers and missionaries, the tourists, those who employed labour, the journalists and a great many others—altogether as varied a set of people to have to deal with as you can imagine. We managed to preserve good relations with all these diverse elements, and the work of evacuation went on successfully. No less than 30,000 refugees from Russia passed through the office individually or in small groups and were evacuated during the time I was in charge.

The organization of the despatch of a refugee convoy was no easy task. The refugees, to begin with, had no margin of resources, so that if they arrived anywhere a day late and starving, somebody had to find the money to feed them. Many of them were unable to produce any reasonable sort of identity papers, and the authorities of every country very naturally conspired to keep them waiting, while they compared our nominal rolls with the vague lists of suspects which they all kept, and which, by the way, you could buy on the market for a few piastres. Under these conditions the despatch of refugees became, from the professional point of view, a most hazardous occupation, for if anything untoward happened—and unless one personally verified everything, something was almost sure to—then one risked the loss of public money, for which a strict account had to be made, and which loss, however inevitable it might have been, was always very difficult to explain some three months afterwards to people who had every opportunity of being wise after the event.

Many a time in that period did I pace anxiously along the platforms of Turkish railway stations and the quaysides at Galata waiting for the last papers for a convoy, whilst the convoy itself stood huddled in the rain with its baggage, waiting for permission to be loaded, and the steamship agent and my assistant screamed, cajoled, implored, threatened and did everything possible to persuade some obdurate or venal old idiot of an official that everything was all right.

Gradually, however, I learned the technique of these operations, and having collected a good and efficient staff, I was able to keep myself in reserve so as to be able to throw myself in, as it were, at the last moment. When the convoy's departure was about due, I would get into the office car, driven by my Greek chauffeur Janni—who invariably addressed your mother as "Yes, Sir Mistress"—and drive down to the controls at the water-side. A prey to inward doubts as to whether everything was really all right, but ready to act as a *deus ex machina*—and for this rôle it is much better if the machine is imposing—I would order the car to advance with majestic slowness. The first thing that would happen would be a concerted rush of charitable relief workers, who would appear with blankets and baskets of provisions for those departing. "Oh," they would chorus in piercing voices, "these impossible Turks wish us to pay import or export duty on the things we have brought for the refugees, and if we do not, they won't let us distribute them; and we cannot possibly do this, as the money was not given for that at all; but you ought to be able to do something, and as an official organization, we think the League ought either to stop it or pay the money itself; and if it doesn't, we shall write to all our friends and subscribers and tell them that the League is no good." I always felt it a duty to do what I could for them, for, in spite of their fanaticism and peculiarities, they were fine people, these relief workers, and did an immense amount of good. With the official position behind me, which they lacked, I was usually able to intervene successfully on their behalf, but I should think no ambassador ever had a more exacting Government to represent than did I when I voiced their claims to their natural enemies the officials.

When this business was dealt with, usually by arranging for the distribution of donations through the British base, over which the Turks had no jurisdiction, the next trouble was usually that the Turks insisted on the payment of all sorts of taxes before they would allow the refugees to depart. I had had long negotiations with Ismet Pasha and the Turkish authorities in Ankara about this question, and they had given me an authorization dispensing us from payment, but this did not always work, for Ankara was far and salaries were not punctual. Furthermore, if the dispensation was used too openly and too frequently, all the officials concerned would pass sleepless nights trying to get it cancelled.

So, Ivan, the only thing to do was to keep it in reserve and wave it triumphantly when a reasonable bargain seemed about to be clinched. Then the stubborn official could be beaten down to what amounted to a reasonable tip for his trouble. The most difficult of all to deal with were the sanitary-control people, who were always prepared to discover a contagious disease of a completely embarkation-preventing character—as my assistant used to call it—at the last moment unless reasonable precautions had been taken to keep them sweet. There was one famous case, which I think is really worth repeating, for it seems very funny now, although it was nearly a tragedy then.

At that time relations between the Turks and the Greeks were of course extremely bad, and each side used the health regulations as much as possible to *embêter* the others. Plague was more or less endemic in the town, and always provided a good excuse for either side to hold up arrivals or departures by the production of some new and far-sweeping regulations, which were of course aimed at hampering the trade and commerce of the other side rather than making sure that plague was not distributed to the four corners of the world. On one occasion we had a convoy all ready, when suddenly a regulation was published to the effect that no refugees would be allowed to go unless they had received two vaccinations, the second vaccination having to be done a week after the first. The result of this instruction, which we obtained fifteen minutes before the convoy was due to go, meant that of course the whole thing was held up for a week. This, in turn, meant that all the members of the convoy whose camp had been liquidated, and who had packed everything up ready for departure, had nowhere to live and nothing to live on.

My two assistants conferred and went in search of those obscure individuals who, in Levantine towns, are always prepared in return for a reasonable payment to arrange anything at all with the local authorities, and produce any sort of document required, from a British passport to a duplicate bill of lading. An hour passed in frantic consultations and dashings about, and then my first assistant appeared with a relieved smile and the precious piece of paper, and announced that all was arranged. Walking up to the official, he flourished his imposing paper. The official looked at it upside down through his nose-perched spectacles, pretended to read it from right to left, and expostulated. My assistant counter-expostulated, and thrust a bank-note into the waving prehensile hand of the official, who shortly afterwards collected the refugees and marched them into the waiting tug. At this moment there appeared simultaneously, first a more senior official, and second, my junior assistant, also clutching a piece of paper. The senior official instructed the tug captain not to proceed, so I unleashed my second assistant, and the same performance took place, except that the senior official had to have something stuffed into both his hands. When the convoy was safely off, I asked my first assistant what was the nature of his paper. "Ah, this," he said, "was simply a paper from a local doctor to the effect that, owing to a suspected outbreak near their camp, all the refugees had had the necessary injection—by the mercy of Allah, exactly one week ago. The doctor also added that he had just performed the second one." I turned to the second assistant, and asked him what *he* had been able to obtain from the "Black Bourse." "Ah," he said, "my paper was one to the effect that the refugees, as a result of malnutrition and weak hearts, were physically unable to undergo any vaccination at all." Which paper finally found its way to headquarters I never knew, but I was quite anxious about it for some time.

Even when all official formalities were done, there still remained the question of the payment of the contractor, who had provided the transport from the quay to the passenger-boat waiting in the harbour. It was orientally impossible to fix a price in advance. There was one Salomon, an ancient bearded old scoundrel, who at that time was king of the water-front, and it was with him that all bargains of this sort had to be made. My rôle was to stand looking haughty and aloof, endeavouring to give the impression that I did not in the least care whether the convoy went or not, whilst my assistant conferred with Salomon. We had worked out quite a technique. On receipt of the first offer conveyed to me, I would register wrath and indignant astonishment, leap into the car and instruct Janni to drive off at top speed. Salomon would make a despairing rush forward, nearly kill himself in front of the wheels and come down 10 liras in a direct offer to me. I would refuse all direct bargaining, and wave him inexorably to my assistant, who would beat him up verbally for having dared to make a direct offer. So it would go on, and when at last a price was fixed and everything stowed away, I would summon Salomon, and from my seat in the car hand him an enormous cigar. Old Salomon would touch his head, forehead and heart with his hand, and murmur what I hoped were blessings in Turkish. The convoy would chug away, the porters would shout for no reason at all and I would descend majestically into a launch and glide over the smooth shining waters of the Bosphorus to settle the further troubles that inevitably arose when it came to transferring the refugees from the lighters to the steamer. When this was all over, and when the last refugee had been assured that he was not being consigned to slavery and that the job which was prepared for him personally was better than anybody else's, I would drive back along the swarming streets to the office feeling that really good work had been done, send a telegram to Geneva and to all the people who had to deal with the convoy *en route*, and then off I would go with your mother, drive to the Rose Noire, the Turquoise or some other cabaret along through Bebek by the coast road past the old Pasha's houses, where

> "*Dans un baiser l'onde au rivage*
> *Dit ses douleurs,*
> *Pour consoler la fleur sauvage*
> *L'aube a des pleurs.*
> *Le vent du soir conte sa plainte*
> *Au vieux cyprès,*
> *La tourterelle au térébinthe*
> *Ses longs regrets.*"

CHAPTER XIX

INFIDELS AND HERETICS

I

WITH Kemal's continued success the political situation grew worse, we had to hasten the evacuations, go in for larger operations and charter whole steamers, which we filled with refugees. Some of these operations would, I fear, have been frowned on by the Board of Trade. There was one old Yugoslav steamer, called the *Vladimir,* which we chartered and filled with Russians, who were to go to Cattaro, where we had been able to arrange for their reception. She had a mixed cargo of invalids, widows, orphans, soldiers, ex-officers and civilians. She was an extraordinary sight as I went over her prior to her departure; refugees seemed to be everywhere, cooking on the deck, smoking in the hold, playing cards in the boats; never was there such a circus. The captain, a phlegmatic Yugoslav, did not seem to mind, and was calmly waiting for the remaining people to arrive. This they did over a space of two days, and I have seldom seen such an enormous and motley collection of luggage as they had—pieces of furniture, parrot cages, small dogs, big dogs, cats, a goat, cocks and hens, trunks, baskets, perambulators, blankets, petrol-tins with ferns in them, carpets, the stock-in-trade of itinerant tobacconists, wax figures and dressmaking busts lying in abandoned attitudes, cooking stoves and sacks of onions and oranges. I had asked the British and French G.H.Q.s to lend me two officers able to speak Russian in order to convoy the ship—I thought that, if they were on board, the Yugoslavs might make less trouble about the visas if we had, as seemed probable, exceeded our allowance; these two were doing their best, assisted by my staff, to produce order out of chaos.

At last they sailed off, and eventually, after an anxious wait, we heard they had arrived safely at Cattaro. There were nearly a thousand people aboard, and it was difficult to sleep until news of their safe arrival came through.

The Greek refugee side of the work was extremely interesting. One fine day the *Gul Djemal,* a Turkish steamer of six or seven thousand tons, came in with Greek and Armenian refugees from the Pontus. She had over two thousand people on board, and they were suffering from every sort of disease—smallpox, typhus, scurvy, malaria, dysentery and many more.

The American Near East Relief, who were doing marvellous work in the feeding and epidemic line—which was their particular province, while we did transfers and evacuation to Greece in accordance with a general agreement I had made— had their hands full already with ten thousand typhus-stricken refugees in Selimie barracks. One of the most horrible sights I have ever seen were these barracks before the Americans cleaned them up. I went all over them, and realized once again what happens when the military bands cease playing. Luckily for the *Gul Djemal* refugees, a British charitable organization representing the Save the Children Fund and the All-British Appeal Fund came to the rescue and gave us the necessary money to enable us to intervene. A camp was prepared for them, and the delousing apparatus had full steam up, while a number of volunteer doctors were ready, as my American colleague put it, "all set with their bugsquirts" waiting to inoculate the new arrivals.

Everything was prepared, but the Turks would not give permission for the wretched people to land. Armed with an international mandate and an interpreter, I went to the Vali. He was not to be seen, but we saw an official in his office who was of the opinion that such a striking manifestation of the superior wisdom of Allah as the spread of epidemics amongst the Greeks and Armenians should run no risk of being interfered with by him. Let them stay where they were. If they landed, might they not infect Islam? My interpreter modified my rejoinder and the talk drifted on. I refused to budge, and disregarded all the official's efforts to signify that the interview might be considered closed.

The interpreter leaned forward and whispered confidentially in the official's ear. The expression of unbending resolve which had all along characterized his Turanian countenance slowly gave place to one of incipient benevolence dashed with greed. "Doubtless," he was thinking, "if Allah had really intended that these miserable infidels should die, He would not have plagued me with this persistent young man, of whom I am apparently unable to get rid."

Followed a further exchange between the interpreter and the official. I thought it was time to interfere, and asked the interpreter to explain. The interpreter pointed to the window through which the blue waters of the lovely Bosphorus could be seen. "The Bey think Bosphorus three hundred metre deep at this point," he said, accompanying his remarks with a wink so full of meaning that his additional gesture, which was made for my eyes alone and which consisted of rubbing the thumb and first two fingers of his left hand together, was really rendered superfluous. I decided to think that there was no doubt at all about the fact that the Bosphorus was deep at that point, but that the real question of exactly how deep it was needed further consideration.

The official, now almost completely humanized, ordered more

coffee, and we finally compromised at a depth of 250. Under the aloof regard of the official the money was placed by my interpreter on the *cafedji's* tray, as if it had been a tip for the service. The official wrote out the landing permit, and after protestations of mutual esteem we took our leave, and the only subsequent disturbances were those made by the chief accountant of the organization to whom I submitted the accounts of the operation, and who "was unable to understand the item: 250 Turkish liras for estimation of the depth of the Bosphorus." This, of course, was before the Ghazi and his men had obtained complete control and cleaned up the corrupt civil administration of the town that had survived throughout the period of the Allied occupation.

We got the poor wretches ashore and housed in the old barracks at San Stefano, where the Treaty was signed, on the seashore. But the barracks were old and fearfully ruinous, so we bought all the old tentage in Constantinople. It was a curious operation. The local Omars were a tough lot, and had they known we were in the market for all the tents there were, the price would have gone up in a wink. So we prepared a careful campaign, and went round in one afternoon buying nearly a thousand pounds' worth of tents and marquees. It was a strange and interesting performance, going through the bazaars and seeing the tents pulled out of strange sheds and old barns, and in one case from under the proprietor's bed. They were the relics of all the wars and thievery of many years, and some of them, I think, must have housed the invalids of Florence Nightingale. However, we bought them, got them disinfected, erected and filled in two days.

As soon as we had established reasonable isolation and improved the rations, the death-rate fell to ten or twelve per day.

We had had sent out urgently an anti-epidemic doctor from

the League, who had had typhus, and who was therefore reasonably immune—this I always thought the last word in organization—and what with Greek doctors and the assistance of the military, we began to get things cleaned up. Whenever we went into the camp, which was closely guarded by Turkish sentries, we had to put on white anti-typhus overalls to cover us from head to foot. Clad in these I would stalk round and try to keep the doctors from quarrelling, the delousers from bursting their engines, the Greek and Armenian priests from mutual beard pulling and the refugees from visiting their friends in the isolation-camp tents.

The camp became an absorbing interest, and the business of delousing an enthralling battle. But the louse is a terrible creeping enemy and hard to deal with. I shall never forget the condition of some of these people. I saw one pair of socks hung up on a line which was nothing but a moving grey mass. The doctors and nurses were wonderful. I think we lost eleven in all. It was a hair-raising job, but after a bit we ceased to worry about the risks. We found water in the camp; we made the refugees bathe; sports were organized—I remember a wrestling competition which looked like a frieze on the wall of a Greek temple—and at last, when the epidemic had been stifled, we got permission for them all to go to Greece. There was an old Greek nurse who worked for us whom we called the typhus hound. She was quite the bravest woman I have ever seen. Cackling away in Greek, she would dive into a refugee tent, there would be a fearful disturbance, and after a little while she would emerge with her patient on her back and carry him off to the isolation camp, replying the while to the bitter expostulations of the man's family, who were quite certain they would never see him again. How she never got typhus herself I cannot think. At last we got them all away to

Greece, where they settled down with the others. I wonder if I shall ever be allowed to do anything more useful than that?

Relief workers, the representatives of refugee organizations and private charities, and the directors of semi-public charities were difficult to deal with. They all seemed to feel that the excellence of their motive and the necessity for getting something done with a view to impressing those who produced their funds with the value of their activities, entitled them to behave *vis-à-vis* their colleagues in a way which would shock a Levantine carpet dealer. Down they would come to a convoy we were organizing, hold up the whole business, seize the nearest and most picturesque baby, have it photographed, and then, choosing a light article of refugee luggage, hump it on their backs and face the cinema operator with a tense expression. Then after this they would go away and write long articles in papers, with never a mention of anybody's activities except their own. They were not all like this, however, and a great many of them were excellent examples of unassuming charity, great courage and absolute devotion; in fact, many of them made me feel thoroughly ashamed, because I was being well paid for doing work similar to that which they did for next to nothing.

For the work in the San Stefano camp I received the thanks and blessing of the Œcumenical Patriarch. You have seen the letter he wrote to me. You should note the signature, Ivan, because Œcumenical Patriarchs are famous for their signatures, which, in accordance with the tradition of the Phanar, have to be long and extremely elaborate. This one was no exception, being about ten centimetres long, and quite illegible.

Later on during my stay in Constantinople I had to go down to visit the Patriarch at the Phanar in connection with certain League and refugee questions, one of which was the standardization of the Calendar. At the time when I visited him, rumours were current to the effect that the Orthodox Pope, as the journalists used to call him, was liable to be expelled by the Turks at any moment. I was well received by His Holiness, a most striking-looking person, who looked as though he might just have come out of a meeting dealing with the Arian heresy. I went all round the Phanar, and a most interesting place it is, redolent of theological disputes and the temporal influence of the great bishops of the period of the Arian heresy, when theology was publicly debated in the market-places and when St. Gregory of Nyssa thus described the state of the city in which I was working: "The city is full of mechanics and slaves who are all of them profound theologians, and preach in the shops and in the streets. If you desire a man to change a piece of money for you, he informs you wherein the Son differs from the Father; if you ask the price of a loaf, you are told by way of reply that the Son is inferior to the Father; and if you enquire whether the bath is ready, the answer is that the Son was made out of nothing."[1] This was the first time that the Œcumenical Patriarch had ever seen a representative of the League of Nations, and certainly the first time a representative of the League of Nations had ever been received in state at the Phanar.

I had frequent interviews with the Turkish authorities at the Sublime Porte. I used to see Refet Pasha and Adnan Bey or his Secretary, who were then Kemal's representatives, and from them I succeeded in obtaining a certain toleration for my unfortunate charges. When Refet came in from Thrace with his gendarmes and took over the town, he marched up from Stamboul in great style, and as he and his hardy gendarmes came marching through the streets, the unfortunate inhabitants vied with one another in shouting, cheering and slitting the

---

[1] Quotation is taken from *Constantinople,* by William Holden Hutton (Mediæval Towns Series, published by J. M. Dent). In this book the passage itself appears in quotes without acknowledgment of the source.

throats of sheep to do him honour. I noticed one of my Russian refugees during this performance, who seemed to be outdoing everybody in the slaughter of sheep, and I wondered why, until I remembered that he had just taken over a Russian restaurant situated on the road through which Refet had passed, and I realized that he had simply transferred his ordinary slaughter to the street. I went to his restaurant the next day and, sure enough, there was nothing but mutton on the menu.

One of the features of Constantinople at that time was the restaurant of the Petits Champs, near the British Embassy. This was an open-air restaurant frequented by a most cosmopolitan crowd. We would go there in the evenings and drink beer and watch the Ballet, which was usually followed by amazing French comedians, who used to come on in tight dinner clothes and straw hats, and sing the not quite latest songs from Paris with that marvellous rapid-fire technique which is special to French comedians and which was received with roars of delight by the mixed audience, most of whom could not understand a word of it. Then we would walk slowly back to our house by the wall of the Embassy and past the midnight market, where wrecks of humanity bought and sold strange food displayed on soap boxes lit by candles, and where ghastly druggers, pimps and prostitutes used to appear suddenly from the warm darkness, purchase phosphorescent edibles, and then crawl back to the holes from which they came, with their rags about them. In the still Turkish night we would climb on to the roof of our house, sit and listen to the strange sounds from Stamboul, and often hear the menacing cries of the *bekdjis* as they sent their cry of *"Yonginvar!"* echoing through the night to announce to absent roisterers that their houses were being burned down, a picturesque custom that, of course, has been abolished in the new Turkey.

This was a most exceptional period in the life of Constantinople, and I doubt whether its chequered history as "the stormy
bride of the Doge and the bowing slave of the Sultan" could
have produced anything more fascinating or varied. I often
think of the cypresses, Eyoub, the Sultanieh and Dolma Bagtche
mosques, of Santa Sofia, of the market and the quiet houses of
Stamboul with regret.

II

My work took me often to Greece and the Balkans. In
Greece I saw the other side of the refugee problem: for I had
been chiefly concerned in Constantinople with transit relief and
evacuation problems; here they had to deal with the more difficult question of settlement. We had a model refugee settlement in Western Thrace, and it fell to me to go there frequently and help pull it out of the many scrapes into which
it got.

I motored at that time all over Western Thrace, and a magnificent sight it is in spring with the flowers in bloom all over
the rolling plain. I saw the refugees bravely building their
lives again: I watched the squabbles of the *proedros* and the
functionaries. I saw feeding and house-building, and helped to
start village industries. One of these led me almost to the top
of Mount Olympus, where the Gods had then been replaced by
brigands. I went there in order to establish the existence of a
store of charcoal, which had figured so often in official reports
that I had almost begun to believe it was there. Of course it
wasn't, for the brigands had used some and sold the rest.

I went round the malaria areas seeing what our people were
doing and trying to compare the reports with reality so as to be
able to make the best division of our stores and resources. I
remember being shown at dusk into a mud hut not far from

Xanthe, in which an old Greek lady with malaria was lying in a moribund condition. Our indefatigable doctor struck matches, bared the poor old lady's brown body, and in an access of medical enthusiasm insisted on my feeling her enlarged spleen, which he said was a very magnificent example. I stretched out a reluctant and inexpert hand, while the old lady groaned dismally.

I was persuaded in a weak moment by a voluble enthusiast to help with the financing of an experimental machine, the object of which was to kill the mosquitoes, which caused malaria. This machine consisted of a Ford chassis, from which protruded an enormous funnel like a gramophone horn. Behind the funnel there was an apparatus for producing suction, and behind this a searchlight. The searchlight attracted the mosquitoes, which were then sucked by a sort of vacuum-cleaner arrangement into a lethal chamber. The man who drew me into this experiment was a persuasive individual, and in those times I was more open to bright ideas than I fear is the case at present. He started off by telling me that there were fifteen or sixteen kinds of mosquitoes, and that only one variety was malaria-carrying, and, as he succinctly put it, only the woman of that was fatal! Even this woman, he went on, waving his hands, had to have bitten somebody who already had malaria, and yet, he said triumphantly, the disease spreads like bad news. He was an excellent Greek, and I shall never forget the proud moment when our machine really did suck in mosquitoes. Some cold scientific brain from Geneva appeared, however, delivered statistics and lectures on methods of fixation of mosquito density in swampy areas, and proved that if the machine worked for the rest of the century, it would have made no impression at all upon the problem.

On another occasion, when I was hastening to Athens, I was

compelled to take passage in a Greek ship called the *Andros I*. She was, however, not quite so old as that. I was the only first-class passenger. I dined in state, having dressed for dinner, as I still do on such occasions as a result of having read too many magazine stories when I was younger. But also, as I have often explained to my shocked international colleagues of the Left, for the comfort of it. I was put at the captain's table, and the chief steward, a venerable Greek with flowing whiskers and the face of an Elder Statesman, dashed with a touch of the brigand, did me the honour of waiting on me.

He showed me the menu. It was in modern manuscript Greek and meant nothing to me. I endeavoured to explain in various languages that I did not want any soup. "Ah," said the head waiter with infinite sadness, "Nosup. Next," he said with an ingratiating smile, "is *horta*."

"What," I said, "is *horta*?"

At that moment the captain came in, and after the introductions were over, there followed a rapid exchange of Greek between him and the chief steward, from which I gathered that he was being put *au courant* with the difficulty. The captain turned to me and "*Horta* very good," said he, smacking his lips with exaggerated gestures of enjoyment. "Vegerable," he went on.

"Ah," said I. "What sort of vegerable?"

Here the steward, who hated to be left out of it, broke in and said, "Grass, Mossoo."

I shook my head. This caused a stream of grief and protestation. The steward and the captain wrangled and wrangled. I sat back, hoping that the incident would be settled soon, and that I should get something to eat. Pursued by the bitter criticisms of the captain, the old steward fled out of the room. I hoped that he had gone to bring in something to eat which was

not full of garlic. But I was disappointed, for he came in triumphantly bearing an enormous dictionary, which must have
been published when the ship was young. Moistening his
gnarled thumb and fixing a pair of glasses on his leathery beak,
he thumbed the pages, and peered at the dictionary with incredible concentration, while the captain looked on with the air
of one maligned who triumphantly awaits vindication. At last
he found what he was looking for. He drew himself up and
addressed me.

"No, sir, no, sir, I am damn fool."

The captain's face lightened.

"*Horta* not grass," went on the steward. "No, no, not grass,
never grass. Sir, *horta* is hay!" and so shut the book triumphantly with a bang.

After this I felt I couldn't refuse, and in trepidation awaited
the result. As far as I know, it was hay. The rest of the dinner
was eatable, but I shall never forget the captain's triumph when
the dictionary produced its verdict.

· · · ·

Soon after the evacuation of Eastern Thrace, I went over
into Western Thrace to see how our columns were getting on.
I went to see the settlement at Gümüljina. The Greek and
Turkish armies were facing each other on the Maritza. One of
my assistants had nearly caused a war because, he being on the
Greek side, his dog, imbued apparently with Turkish sym-
pathies or moved by a promising affair, strayed over the bridge
in the middle of a clear moonlight night. The Turkish sentry
saw something coming and fired incontinently; this woke up
the Greeks, who unleashed a machine-gun. The Turks replied,
and a first-class duel took place, which might have developed
into a complete breach of the armistice but fortunately died

away when, with the morning, each side saw that the other had not after all advanced from its authorized positions, but had if anything withdrawn a little.

I have vivid memories of that journey. I remember starting with your mother in the plushy luxury of the Orient Express as it glided out of the San Stefano area and on through brown scorched Thrace up to Adrianople, where we changed in the night—a dark mysterious night—in which one seemed all the time to be running on rails back and forth from Turkey into Greece with different sets of sentries and controls bullying the passengers of opposite religions; on down to Dedeagatch, whilst the carriage swarmed with bugs which we chased when they came over that part of the seat which caught the rays of the moon. Then Dedeagatch, and a long wait in a most fearsomely dirty waiting-room, a bottle of whisky and a probably germ-ridden soda. Then on to Gümüljina, or Komotini as it is now called, where we arrived in the morning, and where Treloar had the troops out to do us honour as we drove off in a Ford over to our H.Q., where the staff were living in a primitive old Turkish house which might have come down at any moment, and then dinner from tins, with everyone joyful and full of shop. One was not bored in those days, there was so much to do, so many chances of something extraordinary happening, so many jokes to make, and with it all a sense of the real vital importance of making a good show.

There was still a king in Greece in those days, and one day the G.O.C. asked us all to a great military parade service which was being held in the big church. In we went, and were given an honoured and prominent place near the general and his staff.

I wish I could describe the church to you, but all I remember is an impression of space, a smell of incense, a number of

tawdry gaudy pictures, and the rapt patriarchal faces of th
priests, with their long locks and glittering vestments. Afte
the serried ranks of soldiers, in thronged the patient and devou
peasants. Just as I was thinking that here one was probabl
more in touch with Christianity as it used to be when it wa
holding its own against the waves of Islam, and when it was
mixture of artifice and superstition and a most indomitabl
faith, an extremely nasal voice began to sing in a piercing not
part of the Kyrie, from somewhere high up behind us.
thought for a moment of the lady in the *Canterbury Tales* o
whom Chaucer wrote,

> *"Ful wel she sang the service devine*
> *Entuned in her nose ful swetely."*

The notes pierced the air with a suddenness that was startling
and the whining abandon of the voice was so indescribabl
funny that, when I caught Treloar's eye, I was in agonies les
I should be forced to laugh. All through the service we stoo
in fear of disgrace and the awful pain of throttled laughter, fo
we never knew when this amazing noise would not be repeate
suddenly behind our backs. However, we managed to ge
through without exploding, and then went off to a most pro
fuse and splendid dinner of about twelve courses, all oily!

III

In Constantinople I had my first official contact with th
Soviets, as I had to go and see about the return to Russia o
some of my old friends the Kalmucks. In some obscure wa
they knew, from their friends in Belgrade, that I had protecte
and helped their co-religionists, and I had their complete con
fidence, much to the annoyance of the professional Russia
refugee representative who claimed their theoretical allegiance

Some of them we sent to France to work on French farms, where they embarrassed everybody by camping out at the Gare de Lyon and having babies on the station. The French officials thought they were Chinese, and I received most heartrending telegrams from our delegate in France. Others thought the only thing to do was to go back to Russia. So I went to see the Soviet delegate at the Russian Embassy, to endeavour to negotiate their repatriation. I found Comrade Potemkin sitting in the office where Igantief used to have his famous drawer full of *casus belli.*

After mild protestations of official non-recognition, we discussed the matter in hand; the details were arranged, and the talk glided off into art and literature, about which Potemkin knew a great deal more than I did. At this time all sorts of stories were current about what was happening in the Russian Embassy. There were tales of murders in the basement, bombs in the attics and corpses smuggled out into the Bosphorus. As a matter of fact, I felt far more uneasy in the Phanar when I went to see the Œcumenical Patriarch, for there the place lent itself quite admirably to disappearances, and there was a musty odour which may have been of sanctity, but which was rather charnel-house in general effect.

At a time when things had got very difficult as a result of the evacuation of the Allied Armies, I went to see Ismet Pasha in Smyrna. I landed on the still desolate quay and drove through the ruined town out to a neat villa on the coast, where the Pasha had his military H.Q. We walked past smart sentries, and finally, after considerable waiting, I was admitted, and his A.D.C. interpreted for us. I had a long talk with Ismet. He was very agreeable, and said that the old Turkey was gone for ever, and that the new one under Kemal would astonish the world by developing into a modern and civilized State. I asked him if he did not regret the old days of Empire, and whether the Anatolian Turks were taking kindly to the reforms. He said that there was resistance on religious grounds, but that priests were always opposed to progress and quite willing to balk it if it threatened them. Ismet struck me then as being the intelligence behind the power of Kemal. I was able to obtain his assurance that our League refugee evacuation work would not be interfered with after the departure of the Allies, provided that we played the game and did nothing to oppose the new regime. So I left, feeling very pleased and important as the sentry saluted and I took my place in the car and drove down to the quay again.

Ismet kept his promise, we were enabled to carry on without a great deal of difficulty, and the order requiring the immediate expulsion of all the Russians, which would have meant a concentration camp for them in Anatolia, was revoked when the Turks were convinced of the fact that we were really neutral. This, I felt, was a most useful thing to have accomplished individually, and it was the result of long and patient negotiation, months of importunity and a decision to swallow a good many rebuffs to the League without loss of temper.

One last glimpse of that period, and I have done with it, Ivan.

One fine day in Constantinople I received instructions to go to a more distant country, where a considerable number of persons of a certain sect were threatened with immediate expulsion by the authorities. The persons in question had appealed to Nansen, and I was to go and see if I could not find a solution, or at least obtain a stay of execution. So off I went. When I arrived I consulted the leaders of the oppressed, and we fixed a plan covering how best to wave the international flag and use the resources I had, and then went to see the authorities and the

Chief of Police, a general, who was the person with whom I had most to do. He was a most agreeable person, and we became great friends. This was an essential part of the plan, and I spared no effort, for it was he who was charged with the execution of the decree. He was a well-meaning oppressor, and only too anxious to find a middle way out to help us. He showed me round the town, and together we inspected the haunts of all the crooks and criminals and night-lifers. Under the influence of some of the local wine, our relations soon became excellent.

As for the oppressed religionists, all was fairly easily arranged. We got the decree of expulsion stayed for a month, and at the end of that time the concentration camp was empty, while my friend the general was seen in the cabarets with a beautiful member of the sect. But, as my local delegate remarked, "It entails no real sacrifice on her part, for, as we all know, the general was an extinct volcano long ago."

When I told Nansen about it he was highly delighted. "Joost the person we need on our staff," he said. "A pity we cannot make a report of it to show how the League is subduing the militarists."

PART IV

SOUTH AMERICA

"In America the geography is sublime, but the men are not."
                    EMERSON, *Conduct of Life.*

CHAPTER XX

INTRODUCTION TO A COMPANY

I

You were put on the family estimates in Constantinople. Later on in the summer of 1925 an apprehensive couple drove over the rough cobblestones in a bouncing Serbian hack to a sanatorium in Krunska Street, from which, in the middle of the night, issued the most terrifying screams and wails. A horrifying reception. The driver crossed himself frequently, and I would have done so too if I had thought it would have helped at all. At length I discovered that the cries were due, not to tortured human beings, but to the peacocks in the garden and a forthcoming change in the weather.

Seven months later we all went up to Paris, stayed a week in an hotel, took the train to Cherbourg, were tossed about in a tender one winter's day, then a burly Dutchman picked you up, and you found yourself on the deck of a large modern liner with anxious parents fussing about you, *en route* for sun and South America—an event which you hailed by being violently sick.

The reasons for our desertion of the Near East and our embarkation for the unknown prospects of South America were many and complicated, but the general idea was that the authorities had considered that an effort should be made to see if some of the numerous refugees, whom the League was trying to settle, could not be established in that huge sub-continent.

We settled first in Buenos Aires, and from there I travelled
extensively in search of colonization and employment opportunities for the refugee immigrants who, with our help, slowly
filtered in from European concentration camps to a new life in
the new world.

Some day, perhaps, like Mr. Cunninghame Graham, you and
I will ride together across the Corrientine plain, and try to find
"the mystic Trapalanda of which the Gauchos speak at night
when seated round a fire of bones." We will struggle through
the thick forest of Misiones, preceded by Guarani peons with
machetes and red sashes, clearing away the lianas and the
hampering thorns. With oranges for bait we will fish for the
tigerish dorado on the broad Paraná. Over the Pampa will we
scurry, firing at the elusive silhouette of the ostriches. You
will see a locust cloud descend and lay bare the fertile fields,
so that nothing is left except a horrible smell and millions of
scaly brown bodies hopping and squirming where once were
the hard-earned crops.

I will go again with you to Lake Titicaca, that mysterious
sheet of blue water, two miles high, surrounded by the snowcapped Andes and navigated by the silent Indians immobile in
their *balsas* built of reeds. There we will investigate the clue
that poor mad Ivanoff, the refugee doctor, was convinced would
lead to the *Peje Grande,* the Big Fish, the enormous treasure of
gold that the Incas buried there when Atahualpa their king was
done to death by the Spaniards. We will examine the relics of
that strange Inca civilization that flourished without wheels or
alphabet in the mighty Andine valleys. We will travel up the
broad rivers, following the routes first traced by Sebastian
Cabot, Alvar Núñez and Nuflo de Chaves as they searched for
the Empire of Puztita, near the Laguna de los Xarayes, at the
very end of the earth where there was nothing but gold, gold

enough for Philip and all the maw of Spain and even then to spare.

We will visit the relics of the once-flourishing Jesuit colonies, whose idyllic state moved even old Voltaire to enthusiasm, but of which there now remain only ruins and an occasional cross with its *"Hic occisus est,"* marking the grave of some good father who died far from his native land.

Lima of the Kings will then receive us, and we shall see the bones of Pizarro, born a swine-herd, where they lie with cotton-wool in the eyeholes and the marks of the wounds of which he died. Some doubt their authenticity, but it is foolish not to believe that such dusty bones are genuine. We will look for the street called "She was great with child" and for that known as "Smite the Jews." We will see the Rimac River and the Perracholi Palace, called after a Viceroy's mistress known as "the Indian bitch" by a jealous local society.

We will climb to mysterious Tiahuanaco and so on up to La Paz, with its strange-costumed sad-faced Cholos, who chew *coca,* their refuge from all ills—from conscription, shoulder-cracking burdens, changing dictatorships and the driving American foremen in the mines. Then down along the distant Pichis trail, which begins in the Chanchamayo Valley, by the lovely Rio Perene, where once I started off to Iquitos on a mule, and where, with an Indian tribe and many wives, there lives an ex-Professor from Cambridge whose brother, a stockbroker, sends him two pounds of pipe tobacco every month.

I have no time to take you farther and tell you of all my travels, negotiations and struggles for the refugees, of how I came to take an interest in labour problems, in immigration and the like, and of how my refugee immigrant groups slowly grew and after many setbacks achieved a hard-won self-support. But come with me now to Paraguay, where began an adventure almost as strange as that of the *Lucy and Zoya,* for in it I risked and nearly lost my life and reputation.

I was in a boat fishing on the Paraná River, outside Asunción, and talking to a Lithuanian dentist named Urlaub, who told me that he had just cured himself of leprosy. He showed me a silvery patch on his arm whilst I shrank fearfully away. "The cure is to drink, to drink, not alcohol, but anything else so long as you keep on drinking," he said. "This I had," he went on, thrusting his arm nearer me, "and I cured it as I have said, and the other day I cured an old woman who also had it." The boat rocked gently, the Paraguayan sun blazed down on us, and the nightmare fish we had caught—they looked as if they had just emerged from the primeval ooze, so antediluvian was their appearance—flapped, barked and gibbered at the bottom of the boat. For weeks I was haunted by a terrible fear, and went about like Kinglake's Levantine, who thought he would surely catch the plague in Cairo, conjured up all the symptoms as a result of his terror, weakened his resistance and finally died babbling of billiard cues. However, like Kinglake, "better fate was mine," and my surreptitious examinations of my epidermis in search of silvery patches eventually ceased.

Urlaub changed the conversation, and told me of his great idea of cultivating the *guaverami.* "What is the *guaverami?*" I asked, as I searched my mind for an excuse to row to the shore.

"It is," he said, "a fruit like a small plum with a thick yellow skin and large seeds. It has a good flavour, but what would make it sell is that it has the strange property of always tasting cold, even if the thermometer is almost boiling. *Como la popa de una dama,*" he went on with a salacious grin, and poked me in the ribs, whilst I smiled uneasily. "Only the other day," he continued, "the manager of the Colonization Company that is going to start to colonize above Corumbá, and which apparently has so much money to spend, was asking me about it."

I asked him for further information about this Company, reported its existence to Headquarters, and very soon an affair had been started which spread like wildfire.

II

This South American Colonization Company, which had sprung into prosperous existence like an attractive but doubtful mushroom in the night, became more and more a cause of worry and preoccupation to me. The general position was very difficult. Far away, in my old haunts in the Near East, the refugee situation had begun to be unbearable. The refugees were threatened with internment in concentration camps in desolate areas, and though it was impossible to say exactly what this would mean, yet it was certain, to say the least of it, that it would not be healthy for the women and children. Consequently, there was a tendency at Headquarters to consider that almost any solution would be preferable to doing nothing, and when such a tendency prevails the wise official stationed on the periphery adopts a doubly cautious attitude. It was not easy to explain that, so far as I could see, the emigration of these people to any of the South American colonization schemes that I had examined would be simply a question of getting out of the fire into the frying-pan, and that as we were not responsible for the initial situation, there was no wisdom in accepting a measure of responsibility for the creation of one which might become only slightly less tragic.

So far for two years, though at times hard pressed by the exigencies of the refugee situation, I had sternly resisted any colonization adventures, and had confined myself to putting up schemes for which I could personally answer, after inspection

of the people and of the territories concerned. On the other
hand, the capital outlay required for these schemes was very
large, and the number of people whom they would have settled
very small. At this stage appeared this new and presumably
respectable Company—it had an imposing Board of fecund
guinea-pigs—which had acquired a huge concession from the
Bolivian Government in the Province of Chiquitos. It was prepared to do everything that other companies had persistently
refused to do. It would establish credits for the colonists. It
would lend the money for their voyage, it would build them
houses, it would have its own line of steamships on the Plate
and Paraguay rivers, it would organize transport, and in effect,
make the desert blossom like a rose. Subsidiary companies had
oil rights, and it would not be long before flourishing industries assured the prosperity of the towns, for which efficient-
looking blueprints had already been constructed, and an era of
development would set in for the happy Province of Chiquitos,
which only needed the magic marriage of capital and enterprise
to bring it from its unnecessary torpor to a regime of production and prosperity. There were to be trading rights, port rights
and every other sort of right, all of which were provided for in
the concession. It was reasonably clear of any frontier dispute,
and was, in fact, said the Company, the chance of a lifetime.

The Company were told that I had expatiated on the general
difficulties of such plans and had said that it was better for the
refugees to come as single spies instead of in large groups. The
Company explained that I was not a business man, knew nothing of agriculture or the possibilities of the proper application
of credit by enterprising persons. There was a tendency to consider that I was prejudiced, and this tendency was very correct.
I was prejudiced, Ivan, against these people, who had with one
fell swoop destroyed the best of most of my reports for two

years. For had I not said again and again that no company would ever do what this one had promised? On the other hand, I felt certain that I was right, and that unless they were very exceptional people, with a very great deal of money behind them and no wish to make a profit for twenty years, there must be a catch in it somewhere. I was not absolutely sure, however, and therefore I did not dare to make a report turning the thing completely down. I based myself on my experience rather more than on any logical foundation. The difference, Ivan, between the genius and the experienced person is that the genius knows that he is right, while the experienced person only thinks that he may be.

Meanwhile, the Company went on making a great splash; in fact, the only way to make you understand what sort of splash it made would be to adopt the technique of the modern radio play and let you listen-in successively to fat stockbrokers discussing the possibilities and deciding to buy 500 shares, to the tip going round the fashionable golf-clubs, to romantic young men persuading impressionable aunts to let them leave their dull offices, and with just a little avuncular capital go out to the Bolivian wilds and make their fortune, to large stockholders arranging with hard-bitten journalists for the insertion of appetizing paragraphs in the financial pages of the newspapers, to persons of consequence being persuaded, for certain considerations, to assume directorial responsibilities, and so on. In this way you might get some idea of how the affair was launched.

The Company did its business very well. It had appealed to the romantic by carefully exploiting the fact that its headquarters in Chiquitos had first been settled as a Jesuit colony. It did not add that since then nobody else had been able to do anything with the place. The romantic voyages of Nuflo de

Chaves and Cabeza de Vaca, the enthralling story of the Jesuit colonization and the visits of the Conquistadores had been cleverly written into the Company's literature, so as to appeal to the vein of romance which often lies hidden in the most hard-headed of City men. They annexed to their prospectus ancient and romantic charts of the desert lands to be exploited, and filled them with pleasing and exciting symbols of the local fauna, till the result recalled to me those attractive lines of Jonathan Swift:

> *"So geographers, in Afric maps,*
> *With savage pictures fill their gaps,*
> *And o'er unhabitable downs*
> *Place elephants for want of towns."*

For those who were not romantic there was oil in capital letters. They were told that the Americans were prospecting in the neighbourhood, and that it was a shame that they should take it all. Those who had already been bitten in oil were informed that there were mountains of gold and silver in Bolivia, that it was obviously a rich country, because of the vast mineral resources of the *altiplano*, though, of course, in reality these had nothing whatever to do with that part of the country in which the Company proposed to operate.

The Company's literature described the colonization and settlement possibilities in terms well calculated to appeal to the young and romantic cooped up in dull offices. There was, of course, it was hinted, a spice of danger and discomfort, but that after all was only to be expected. There were insect pests, but any young man worth his salt soon got used to them. There were even snakes, and here I must quote the blurb in its gem-like original—"Our colonists will, of course, wear riding-boots, *and it is a well-known fact that no snake ever bites above the knee!"*

As a basis for all this there was that mysterious and attractive concession which had been obtained by the representatives of the Company after terrible struggles with Parliaments and Governments. A concession always appeals to financiers. There is in it a hint of monopoly, a possibility that a venal Government may have been persuaded by temporary embarrassment to sell something extraordinarily valuable. It always forms an attractive basis to those who are interested in the flotation of companies. A concession can be bought and sold; it is, so to speak, a crystallized good idea. Those who have had the good idea feel that they can sell it to those who are prepared to take the more difficult job of working it out; and if these latter fail, then that is their own fault.

This concession was a good one of its kind, and it went like hot cakes. It was vague and yet specific. It talked so grandly of the land, and the rights and the ports, that it became almost impossible to believe that such things could mean anything but fat dividends and increased capital values.

Well, in any case, things developed and developed, and it was finally agreed that I, at any rate, should go as quickly as possible to look at the possibilities, with a view to sending a telegram which would enable certain refugees to be kept from their concentration camp in view of their imminent despatch to South America.

If you follow the mighty river Paraguay, Ivan, as it goes on and on for thousands and thousands of kilometres through the wild green heart of South America, you will see that after Asunción, where it joins the Pilcomayo, it goes north through Brazil and Bolivia up to Corumbá. North of Corumbá are three lakes—Mandiore, Gaiba and Uberaba. There it was, in that distant and desolate area, that the Company had its lands, and there it was proposed to colonize the refugees.

It was a far and savage land, much more so than the parts of

Paraguay which I had already visited. There were dense forests there, and the rivers were full of *piranha*. The *piranha* is an extraordinary fish with a jaw like a bulldog and teeth so sharp that the Indians use the jawbones for saws. They swim about in swarms of thousands, and as soon as they smell blood, in a few seconds they collect and destroy anything which is unfortunate enough to be within reach. They are capable in their myriads of pulling down an ox. The air was full of mosquitoes and every sort of insect. On the trees were ticks of all kinds, the *garrapata* or sticky fingers, as it is called, and the *chao*, which caused terrible festering sores. Besides this, said my more imaginative friends, there were snakes, alligators, jaguars, wild cattle, outlaws from Matto Grosso and quantities of Brazilian revolutionaries with long matted beards and lightning trigger fingers.

Others more moderate said that it was a country which was awaiting development, and that parts of the Argentine Chaco which had been fairly successfully colonized were not dissimilar, so that one might perhaps hope that in some years, if the Company lasted, something might be done.

The Company told Headquarters that it would do everything to ensure success; that it had bought two boats, one of which had already made a voyage to Gaiba, and that another was on the way. The railway would be built, and machinery for the exploitation of cotton, sugar and timber would shortly arrive.

The first voyage of the Company's steamer had taken place while I was away on my trip. The local press had been well treated, and had said that the colonists who were on board were intrepid heroes, that the shooting was good, and that reasonably risky adventures had been met with. There was a chance, wrote the well-cultivated press, that the colonists would soon find oil on their land, in which case it was assumed that everybody's fortune would be made at once.

I interviewed the local agent, a wise and careful individual, who confined himself to getting paid cash for what he did for the Company in Buenos Aires, and who would not be tempted into anything in the way of a confidential opinion.

I read the literature, all the old carefully reproduced Jesuit plans, the reports of expeditions in 1890, became desirous of seeing for myself, and finally wired Geneva that I was after all prepared to go at any moment to inspect.

I was to go on the Company's boat. This was one of the few Bolivian steamers in existence. It was shortly due in Buenos Aires from Asunción. The manager at Gaiba had been warned.

Actually the affairs of the Company were at a rather critical stage. A good many knowledgeable people had said that it could not succeed, and that the whole affair was a wild speculation, and that the knowing ones were unloading their shares. There were all sorts of rumours in the air, and, so far, only a few English colonists had actually gone up-country. On the other hand, the terms of the Company's concessions required that a certain number of colonists should be settled for the validation of the other rights granted. A number of European Governments had been approached and had been asked to allow the recruitment of emigrants for the plan. Most of these Governments were holding off, as they were eager to have the plan tried out by the other fellow whilst being desirous of not letting an opportunity slip of placing their unemployed if the affair should turn out to be a sound one. As the proposed area was so distant and inaccessible, nobody really had any clear ideas as to what the position actually was or might be. The Company monopolized and carefully controlled the information available regarding the actual state of development. They had a ready answer for all questions, and generally, of course, the tone of their *communiqués* was optimistic. They were wise enough not to overplay their hand in such a way as to make it easy to discount them, and to admit the difficulties. They said that, in effect, no colonization had ever been achieved without some hitches, *contretemps* and delays, and in this they were undoubtedly correct. But, said the Company, when our ships have arrived and our new machinery is installed, then the world will see, and those who have seized the opportunity will be the early birds and will benefit, and the others will lose.

The result of all this was that the Governments maintained an open mind and the impasse remained. If nobody agreed to go and colonize, the Company could not succeed. Nobody would agree to go until a fairly neutral report had been made. It therefore resulted that, whoever made the first neutral report, might easily make or break the Company. It was impossible for me to know this at the time, though I sensed it dimly, and it became clearer as things went on. In spite of the known urgency of finding an outlet for the refugees in danger of their lives in the Near East, I was sceptical, full of misgivings, but interested. It was just possible that this might be a great opportunity, and I did not want to risk losing it. Furthermore, the establishment of a large-sized prosperous colony of European unemployed attracted me as a constructive and useful piece of work. In addition to this, it would not help my career if always I appeared as the person who turned down other people's schemes in favour of his own more exacting ideas. On the other hand, I very much wanted to have a look at that wild land.

Supposing, for example, that one of the interested Governments, some of whom were very active, took its courage in both hands, got in first and made such a success of the thing that the

Company, being able to pick and choose, should refuse to accept our refugees, then I should find it very difficult to defend my policy. Was it fair to the refugees to turn the thing down on general principle? Obsessed by the dilemma and my responsibility, I mused and studied the affair from every angle until the Company's boat arrived.

CHAPTER XXI

S. O. S.

SHE was called the *Presidente Saavedra* and she flew the Bolivian flag. Curiously enough, I had seen her before. She had been built by the Germans during the War for the transport of munitions along the Danube. When the War was over she and her sister ship had been laid up in Constantinople, and at one time, when we were expecting to have to evacuate ourselves and large quantities of stores and refugees at any moment, she had been offered to us very cheap, and we had seriously considered buying her for the transport of refugees to Bulgaria. The Company had bought her pending the construction of the two specially designed boats for which they claimed they had placed orders. When I had seen her in the Bosphorus she had been dirty and rusty, and it was curious to see her again lying off the Boca in Buenos Aires all trim and painted. She was quite a small boat, being about as big as the larger type of tug.

I was to have gone on board one Saturday in July of 1927, but departure was delayed as the loading operations were not finished, and it was not until half-past three in the afternoon of the next day that I bid you all good-bye and, with all my kit, went out in a tug with a stiff *pampero* blowing.

The *Presidente Saavedra* was anchored out in the main stream of the river Plate some eight or ten miles out, only, of course, the Plate at that distance out is a large and spacious affair, much more like a huge lake or inland sea than a river, and from where she was lying no land could be seen.

I stowed my kit away in a small cabin which had been allotted to me. I had officially been signed on as assistant cook, for the ship was not officially allowed to carry passengers. I had dinner with the first officer, who told me lurid stories of their voyage out across the Atlantic. This had been a great feat, and they had undergone many perils and privations. I turned in early, as the *pampero* had increased its force and was now howling like seventy devils, the waves were getting larger and it was a foul night. The ship was bumping about, pitching and tossing, but as we were at anchor and had only a few miles to go next morning in order to arrive at the point where the river narrowed, I had no presentiment of danger, and I turned in more full of anxiety about what was waiting for me up-river than anxious about the immediate future.

I slept fitfully; the boat rolled and pitched, so that I was nearly thrown out of my bunk. A hurricane lamp unshipped itself and fell over, whilst my valise and baggage waltzed around the cabin. There seemed to be no point in getting up, so I turned over and ignored all the confusion about me and went to sleep.

A series of heavy bumps awakened me at about half-past eleven, and these I imagined to be due to the arrival of the lighter which we were to tow behind us, and which was to have come out with the captain in the morning. At two o'clock in the morning a very sound Scandinavian, the chief engineer, in fact, knocked on the cabin door, put a startled head round it, and told me to come up on deck at once as the ship was liable to sink at any minute.

Actually, what had happened was that some heavy pieces

of machinery had been left lying loose on the deck, and with the pitching and rolling of the ship they had started to bump against the sides of the hull. They were so heavy and bumped so often that they started a seam in the deck and the water, which continually came over the side from the waves, instead of going out through the scuppers, trickled down below, got deeper and deeper, finally put out the furnace, and made the ship settle lower and lower, with the result that more and more water came in.

It was a most unpleasant awakening. An icy fear clutched at me. This was the end then! What a fool I had been to come against my better judgment and because I wanted one more adventure! Hastily I put on a leather coat over my pyjamas, slipped on a pair of pumps, and endeavoured to stand upright in the reeling littered cabin. I was at once thrown off my feet, bumped my head and broke my glasses. Cursing in the dark, I found my electric torch and a spare pair. Then I opened the cabin door. Outside there was an alarming amount of water swishing about, which added to the general discomfort. My kind Scandinavian was waiting by the companion-way, and we went up together. As soon as I poked my nose on deck I thought it would be blown off, such was the force of the wind. There was "a dreadful noise of waters in mine ears." The rain swept down, and the sea was a fury. It was, I think, an even stronger gale than that which I had experienced off Anarpa in the small boat in the Black Sea, or when the *Lucy and Zoya* was blown into Batoum. It simply shrivelled the soul of me, and I felt that I wanted to be sick, and hoped it would be soon over.

The crew, some fourteen in all—mostly Scandinavians— the first officer, who was an Englishman, and the captain's wife were all on the upper deck huddled round the deckhouse. The ship's lifeboat was lying half on the davits and half on the deck, stove in. People were fussing about with rockets, and when he saw me, the first officer asked me if I would hold a flare which he had lighted; this I did, until the thing burned my fingers and I flung it disgustedly into the boiling sea.

There we stood and cursed our luck in the shadow of the deckhouse, whilst every five minutes a gloomy Scandinavian would come up and report that the water in the hold was still rising. Efforts had been made to keep the level down by pumping, but the pumps did not work. Lifebelts had been served out, and we were wearing them. It was bitterly cold, and the wind howled so that we had to shout at people a few inches away.

When the flares and rockets had been exhausted without evoking any answering sparks from the surrounding blackness, it was decided to open tins of petrol and set fire to them in the hope that they would be seen by the people in the port some eight miles away; but it seemed a forlorn hope.

We waited for hours, and the ship settled lower and lower as it wallowed about. Somebody cried out that he saw lights, and sure enough, in a few moments a big ship came through the wrack, making very heavy weather of it. I was the only person who could speak Spanish, so I was given a megaphone, and howled away in a cracked voice for help. I managed to distinguish a reply as the ship sailed by, and this was that she could not stop to pick us up owing to the severity of the storm, as she was very doubtful whether she herself, with her passengers, would be able to make the port. It appeared also that the captain was afraid of the water shoaling suddenly, but how this could happen I could not then imagine. But it appears, Ivan, that in a *pampero* the river Plate does shallow extremely rapidly, as the water is literally blown away in the direction of the wind. The voice continued, however, that he would endeavour to warn the port people to send someone out for us if he could get in himself.

And so he passed, with our curses, and we thought our last hope had gone. We settled down to wait for what might happen. There was nothing to be done. The water in the hold was not mounting so rapidly, but, on the other hand, the waves were still breaking right over the ship. Luckily, in the holds there was a certain amount of hay and fodder which was being sent up for the animals at Gaiba, and the air in this kept us up longer. Otherwise, we should not have survived.

At last the dawn broke, as desolate a one as ever I have seen. The wind had abated a little, but it was still blowing great guns and the sea was heavy. We breakfasted on whisky and aspirin. The ship began to take an alarming list, and it seemed probable that the end might come at any moment. The minutes passed slowly, the list increased alarmingly, until at last, two hours after dawn, one of the sailors claimed that he saw a ship approaching. It took some time for ordinary mortals to distinguish it, but soon there was no doubt that it was heading our way. It was the tug which our much-cursed visitor of the night had promised to send out. Slowly, slowly, it drew nearer, and each one smiled at his neighbour. To my astonishment, various people came to shake me by the hand and thank me for having howled so efficaciously the night before at the Argentine boat as she went by.

The tug came nearer, and after much shouting between the two boats, announced its intention of towing us back. Our officers thought that this was quite impossible, as our ship was so full of water that she was sluggish and would hardly move.

However, the tugboat captain saw a vista of salvage money and would not listen to us. Ropes came over and were made fast. It soon became apparent that we were right, for we made little progress and the ship lurched sickeningly and seemed about to roll over. Then the tow rope broke and we hoped the tugboat captain would desist, and at least save us before he tried again. But no. He threw another rope and started off afresh. This broke also. I remembered how my rope had broken off Novorossisk, and decided it was time to do something. So with the first officer's consent, I howled insults and invitations to save us, through the megaphone in agitated Castilian.

There are some people—cab drivers, tugboat captains, concierges and French motorists—who only respond to an *engueulade* and this man was true to type. He manœuvred his ship nearer and announced his intention of taking us off.

By this time the ship had a fearful list, and it was quite evident that she could not last more than a few minutes longer. We climbed on the side and waited for the tug to come as near alongside as she could.

At any moment it seemed that the *Presidente Saavedra* might tip over and precipitate us into the tossing freezing water. The first officer said to me, as the tug came nearer— at one moment level with us, at another tossed to the grey skies by a wave—"The right thing to do is to drop into the water one by one and let them fish you out; otherwise, you may be injured between the moving sides of the ships."

I looked at him dubiously. Doubtless the theory was all right. We had lifebelts on. On the other hand, I did not trust those lifebelts; they looked old and rotten. In any case, they were completely sodden. I thought I would try to jump for it when a chance came. At this moment a dark object hurtled through the air, and came down with a squashy plump on the tugboat deck. It was the captain's wife, who had been seized and hurled across the ravening waters by four lusty Scandinavians. I looked at the first officer, who grinned.

"To hell with theory; let's jump," said he.

I agreed.

"You go first," said he. "I have to wait a little."

So I stood poised, ready to jump, biding my time, while on the tossing tugboat people stood about in attitudes of expectation. I missed the first opportunity, which was taken by a sailor who leaped, just managed to fetch up on the side of the tug and was pulled in.

It was most unpleasant clinging to the side of the ship, which was now lying at about 45°, soaked from head to foot, and encumbered by a sodden lifebelt, waiting for the tug to assume a favourable position. Every now and then the *Presidente Saavedra* shivered like a sick horse. At last I saw a favourable opportunity, nerved myself for the effort, judged my time fairly well, gave a prodigious leap, and landed on the tender of the tugboat, my hands scrabbling at her sides. My arm was seized and, with a jerk that nearly broke my ribs, I was hauled over the sides and landed all sprawling on the deck.

"*Vamos, vamos, está bien!*" said the tugboat captain, and I realized that I was saved, and could pick myself up to watch the others. Over they came, one by one; some easily, some with the greatest difficulty, half in the water. The last man was so tired and frozen that he could not nerve himself to leap. Six or seven times he tried, but could not. At last he just fell in and was fished out.

Then the tug stood away and we waited. Precisely five minutes by my watch after the last man had got clear, the *Presidente Saavedra* wallowed and slid down into the sea. The first officer half sadly, half dramatically, raised his hand to the salute and said, "Good-bye, *Saavedra.*"

One of the crew said to me, "I hope I never see the bitch again."

But she did not quite disappear, which rather spoilt the drama of the moment, as the tip of her funnel and mast remained exposed. The water was shoaling, and we had been towed some distance by the tug.

I can tell you, Ivan, as I saw the waves roaring over her, I was grateful and glad to be in that tug instead of in the cold river Plate swimming hopelessly, and I warmed my hands ecstatically on the tug's funnel. The tug steamed away, and we chattered joyfully as we pitched and bounded over the dark, heaving waters of the river Plate while the *pampero* still howled like a disappointed jinn.

I went to the tug's engine-room and borrowed a pair of socks from the captain. Eventually we arrived in the port, where there was some excitement. The crew were packed off to the Distressed Sailors' Home by the port officer, an immaculate Argentine. To him I explained my position and state.

"Hm," said he, "Chief Delegate to the Refugee Service of the *Liga de las Naciones,* are you? Well, you look it!"

I had to laugh, because I certainly did have a most bedraggled appearance in my sodden coat, the tugboat captain's old boots and what had once been a straw hat. By this time it was three in the afternoon.

I asked him to let me use his 'phone, so he gave me a stiff brandy in his office, and I 'phoned your mother to tell her the news.

Back I came in a taxi, and soon was in a hot bath. I felt no ill-effects at the time. But the long hours of exposure and expectation of death amid the howling winds and furious sea had left a sore spot on my mind. I had several voyages to do afterwards, and on any ship, whenever the wind howled at night, I became a prey to a panic which I could only just stifle. For hours I would lie awake reading, unable to sleep. I would see that my lifebelt was all right and gaze through the porthole at the tossing seas, simply sweating with fear. I had been rather scornful of shell-shock before, but now I can understand it. I think that my previous maritime experiences had given me a predisposition to nervousness of that sort, and this last affair made a definite bruise in that part of my consciousness which deals with the sea. It took me about three years to get over it, and even the other day, on the enormous *Europa*, I felt it coming on me as she snored majestically through the seas, and retired to the bar, where the hotel-like surroundings exorcised the devil.

The local press made great play with the affair. The combination of a Bolivian boat and an official of the League who had signed on as cook, tickled the journalists. One artist painted an impressionist picture of a superb ship sinking amidst tremendous waves, whilst in mid-air figures were floating precariously on top of a huge roller. Underneath was a magnificent example of Spanish journalese, of which this is a rough translation: "Yesterday, on the dark boiling waters of the furious river Plate, the only ship in the world from which a Bolivian flag extended itself to the rude caresses of the salty gales, sank to its last rest, whilst from its iron decks on to a friendly local tug jumped, accompanied by the captain's wife and in the nick of time, a representative of that organization which hopes to save the world from war."

The *Presidente Saavedra* was later refloated and hauled into harbour. I went on board to see if any of my kit was saved, particularly the top-hat and ceremonial clothes in which I had proposed to visit the President of Paraguay, but there was nothing there.

What I did find, Ivan, on the floor of my cabin, was that photograph of yourself at the age of four, which had miraculously survived, and that is why it has such a washed-out appearance.

CHAPTER XXII

BUSHED IN BOLIVIA

I

AFTER this introduction to the affairs of the Company, you can imagine that I did not view its prospects with increased optimism. On the other hand, I felt bound to go on with the job because, after all, the whole affair had been an accident, and the gale had been so exceptional that it was hard to claim that the Company could be ruled out as a possible colonizing agent because of its inadequate lifeboat arrangements. Rather foolishly, it seemed to me that people would think I was afraid to go on if I used the shipwreck too much as a reason for not proceeding further with the business. Also the strangeness and isolation of that distant land and the prospect of another incalculable journey still beckoned imperiously. So shortly afterwards I took the *Mihanovich* steamer up to Corumbá via Asunción. From Corumbá, last outpost of civilization, I was to go one hundred miles up-river in the Company's yacht.

This was a very different voyage; the weather was calm, the sun shone and there was nothing to do but laze about and read about the people who had been to my destination before me. At Asunción I changed boats and set out northwards to the most interesting part of the trip. The Paraguay from Asunción to Corumbá is extraordinary and I should like to refer to it as THE RIVER and invest it with a personality—which it certainly has—as is done in the best adventure stories, but I think I will leave something to your imagination. What struck me most about it were the birds. There were egrets, *urubús,* vultures, cormorants, *carancho,* small birds, long birds, birds with queer heads and strange long-legged caricatures of birds. On the banks were the *jacarés,* the alligators, sitting on the sandbanks and sliding into the water when alarmed. Behind the sandbanks crowded the thick green jungle. There were palm trees—rather melancholy and ragged—*lapacho,* and many others brilliant with blossom. The river changed, twisted, wriggled and split itself up into main streams and tributaries, but always our boat went on, and it got hotter and hotter; at night, myriads of insects buzzed round the lamps and had to be wiped off with a rag.

On we went through the Chaco, past Puerto Casado, where the Mennonite colonists from Canada came later in order to live peaceful lives in their own way, only to become involved in the war between Paraguay and Bolivia, and then on to Corumbá.

On either side of the river stretched the forests, full of every sort of tropical tree and plant: *cuchis, quebrachos, tajiboa, curupaus,* cedars, *higueras,* and many others of beautiful foliage, romantic names and incredible hardness.

I left the *Mihanovich* boat at Corumbá—a curious town upon the Paraguay River, just close to the Brazilian Paraguayan frontier. Corumbá is hot and full of tarantulas.

The Brazilians have made a surprisingly modern town, with electric light and good roads—the whole entirely surrounded by very wild country indeed. The main hotel is called the "Galileo," and as I settled down to sleep I lit the lamp, inspected the sheet, said to myself "*Eppur si muove,*" and regretted that there was no one there to appreciate the aptness of the allusion.

The next morning I enquired for the manager of the Company, who was to meet me in "the Company's yacht," of which I had, after experience of the Company's "steamer," a most lively apprehension. I was told that he was expected down from Gaiba in a few days' time. I was not sorry to have a day or two in which to look round and gather general opinions about the Company in this, the last town I should see for some time. I saw the Company's agents—a German and a Belgian, who ran a general business. They, like their colleague in Buenos Aires, were hard-bitten persons, and not giving away much information. The sum of their opinions was that the affair might easily succeed and could indeed be brought to a profit-making stage, always provided that their invaluable services were retained and remunerated.

I had seen and reported on a good many land-settlement and colonization propositions, and the position was always the same. Those interested in the affair always said that it was a wonderful opportunity, whilst those with alternative lands to propose invariably stated that it was the local death-trap, and that it would be impossible to plough the fields on account of the bones of those who had perished there—so I reserved judgment.

Then I met the local British Consular agent, who reported to the Consul at São Paulo many hundreds of miles away. He was of the great race, kept a hardware shop and was very glad to see me there. I sat with him behind his hardware counter for two entire mornings, and he told me his views of the affair, whilst an occasional customer dropped in and the hot sun climbed round the sky. He was a character, and had been an Intelligence agent during the War; he told me lurid tales of the bitter struggles that he had waged all over South America with the German agents. He had started life in the textile trade in the North of England. He was a kindly and courageous Israel-

ite. A complicated series of adventures had brought him to
Corumbá, and he informed me that a partner of his had been
up in the Gaiba country on a cattle deal. From him I learned
a good deal of the previous history of the affair I was investi-
gating and something of the curious adventures of the British
colonists who were alleged to be established there. It was the
presence of these presumably flourishing colonists that had
made it very hard for me to turn the whole thing down incontinently, for, as the authorities remarked, if British colonists,
accustomed as they were to a fairly high standard of living,
could flourish in the area, it seemed absurd for me to say that
the conditions were too difficult for refugees who were being
charity-fed in the Balkans or who were liable to be put in
Anatolian internment camps at any minute.

The British Consular agent's advice was indeed invaluable,
and I was extremely grateful for his kindness. "Vy," said the
British agent, waving a saucepan lid so that it glinted in the
Brazilian sunshine, "I dunno vat the League of Nations vants
to do, but if it listens to the Company it is listening to some
pretty good liars, and, believe me, I am a judge. Look at this,"
he said, depositing the saucepan lid and taking up some of the
Company's literature which he had kept inside a dusty tin bath
—"it talks about 'a railway in course of construction from
Santo Corazón at Gaiba,' Vy, I vish I may die if there is a
single rail there at all. Mind you," he went on, "I do not say
the scheme's impossible. Nothing is impossible. But not the
vay they are doing it."

The next day the energetic and forceful manager arrived,
and I acquainted him with the criticism that had been made.
He explained that most of the adverse comments were due to
jealousy and disappointment at not having received lucrative
orders from the Company.

I made as many other enquiries as I could, and then prepared to go up-river on the last lap of the journey. With the manager I went to see the Company's yacht. This was a powerful launch with a large 100-h.p. motor. It had a battered appearance and a big hole in the side just above the water line. But it offered ample accommodation. Like all the launches I have ever had to do with, there was something wrong with the engine, and it took all the manager's energy to galvanize the local mechanic into making a job of the repairs. At last, however, all was ready, and we set off on our hundred-mile journey up-river, well provisioned and with a crew of three.

It was a curious journey. There was always at least a foot of water in the launch and a good many of the moving parts of the engine seemed to be under water. However, she was not uncomfortable, and we made steady progress. As the river opened out it provided some marvellous views. It was deserted, except for an occasional Indian canoe snaking past with a silent figure paddling.

During the first part of the voyage one could sometimes see a straw hut on the banks in a clearing, but soon these ceased and there was nothing. We went on till the sun went down and the moon rose.

The manager talked and talked about his early adventures and about his great dream of developing the Concession. It soon became evident that there was more in this man than mere greed of money. It would, I think, have been better for him had he been but the ordinary speculator, ready to take his profit and get out in search of another opportunity. But no. He saw himself confounding his critics by creating a great colony and making money as well. He was bluff and hearty, a persuasive, energetic talker, a virile personality and, it seemed to me, incredibly obstinate. He explained the perils of the river, talked of the *piranha*, the man-eating fish, of the alligators and the great *pantañal*, or swamp jaguar, that sometimes swims across it. He told me of the Indians and their queer habits, and of the best way to deal with the abounding insect plagues from which he himself had suffered, as I could see from the scars on his legs. He said that the mosquitoes of the river were probably the most dangerous of all, and related to me how people who had been wrecked on the banks had been practically bitten to death by them.

The banks of the river, Ivan, were narrow, and on either side in certain parts there stretched trackless swamps which at times were submerged, and which were nearly always impassable, so that wrecked persons could take their choice either of walking along the narrow paths till they could walk no more, or of sitting where they were, on the chance that something would pass along the river whose attention they could attract. Before the Company had begun operations, boats on the river were very infrequent, and a month might go by before there was a chance of rescue; whereas, now it would only be a fortnight. A grim prospect for the wrecked, thought I, and eyed the water in the launch.

On we went and came to an attractive place called Mandiore. Here, I learned afterwards, we had a narrow escape without my knowing it. The Company, or one of its subsidiaries, had erected a sawmill there, and a dour individual had been put in charge and left for many weeks without news or supplies. His wrongs and hardships, and the forest in general, had got on his nerves to such an extent that, hearing that the manager was passing that way, he had sat up for a week with a loaded Winchester on his knees on a bluff overlooking the river, intending to shoot at the occupants of the launch until his ammunition was exhausted. Happily for us it was he who became exhausted and we passed whilst he was sleeping.

However, it did not diminish my general anxiety as I lay down to sleep on the deck of the launch, to think that the atmosphere was obviously a somewhat desperate one, and it would be perfectly easy to arrange for me to be disposed of "accidentally" if it was thought that my report might be unfavourable.

This may sound somewhat alarmist and seem rather farfetched, Ivan, but I assure you that, in that wild part of the world, and with people wrought up by hardships, oppressed by the forest and the general difficulties, and surrounded by an atmosphere of ruthlessness, the thing seemed very likely. In fact, my friend, the British Consular agent, had gone so far as to say that he knew of many cases where this had happened, and offered to take out a special insurance for me in a company which he represented. However, I pushed these preoccupations from me, and settled down to enjoy the scenery, which was marvellous, and the experience, which certainly promised to be unique.

We had a whole armoury on board, and I amused myself shooting at alligators and some animals that appeared on the banks in the evening. The climate was most agreeable at that time of the year, and not at all unpleasant as I had been led to believe, though the crew, with whom I had some conversation under the suspicious eye of the manager, told me that in the rainy season it was a very different question, as I could well imagine.

At last, after passing through some rocky gorges, we came to Gaiba Lake. We went across with a brisk breeze blowing, which made the waves splash about us. Then we came to a landing-stage, and there we landed. Close to the landing-stage there was a number of buildings, groups of people were standing about, whilst some horses and other animals were feeding in a sort of paddock. I felt as if I had surprised the Swiss Family Robinson. The most curious feature of the little settlement was a radio station whose aerials were suspended between two very tall *Motacu* palms. The power unit of the radio station was a Ford tractor, which was standing rusty and immobile between the palms.

I met the manager's family, his wife and his son, an attractive boy whose boyhood dreams were well realized, for he was walking about with a fowling-piece, a fishing-rod and riding-boots, and must have been overjoyed that someone from the outside world should be able to see him thus. For the rest, there was a girl secretary, a young wireless operator, a Norwegian agricultural expert who looked as if he might die at any moment, and a number of individuals with long matted beards, ragged clothes and enormous revolvers. These latter were the Brazilian revolutionaries who belonged to the Revolutionary Forces of General Prestes. General Prestes was there himself, a curious-looking person who looked like a cross between Rasputin and Buffalo Bill. He had just led the Federal troops a terrible dance during a bitterly fought revolution in Matto Grosso and São Paulo. There was also a Delegation of the Government of Bolivia.

I settled down in these strange surroundings, and spent the first day or two looking round the port and environs, perched insecurely on a horse, the more comfortable mule which I had demanded being refused me as not consonant with the dignity of a distinguished stranger.

At first, my impressions had not been unfavourable; a tremendous lot of work had been done, the people did not seem unduly dissatisfied, the climate was not inferior to that of Misiones in the Argentine, where Europeans lived more or less happily, and the scenery—particularly in the early morning and late evening—was of a most satisfying beauty. I talked with one or two of my Russians, who had filtered through to this distant spot, attracted by hopes of jobs with the Company, and in this way managed to learn a good deal of what had happened.

The material difficulties with which the settlers had had to contend had obviously been enormous, and they had had to begin without properly established communications on that uncompromising river. This was evidently the crux of the question, and it was certain that, unless something was done to improve the existing situation in that respect, the whole enterprise could not last long. On the other hand, if it could succeed in establishing reasonable transport facilities between Corumbá and Gaiba, it was possible that the little settlement might consolidate its position and perhaps even develop. The Company had had very bad luck with their boats; one had been wrecked, as you know, in the Plate, and the second, which had started off across the Atlantic from Tilbury with stores, had last been heard of emitting S.O.S. signals somewhere off Santos, so that the only transport at the disposal of the Company was the Company's "yacht," and what was usually referred to as the "gasolina," which was a largish lighter on which a Ford engine and a propeller had been grafted. There was also an occasional Brazilian boat which went through the lake without stopping, about once or twice a month—if it did not break down or run aground—on its way to Cuyabá, a long way up the river. As nobody knew when this boat might be expected, it was not really of very much use.

Stores were not too plentiful, and there were times when the colony was reduced to living on a strange diet of tinned Norwegian fish-balls, a quantity of which the Company had bought up cheap on the advice of a food expert, who maintained that they were the most suitable diet for persons living in semi-tropical surroundings, and *charqui,* a local form of sundried meat, and a most unpleasant variant, I can assure you.

II

We decided to go out and see the colonization area and the much-discussed British colonists. A rough road known as the *Picada* had been hewn through the forest; one branch of this went to a place called San Carlos, where the colonists were; another, in course of construction, was destined to arrive at a name on the map—there was very little more there than that—called Santo Corazón. It was some 70-odd kilometres through the forest, and the road, which was very rough-looking with stumps of trees and occasional branches lying across it, represented a very real achievement under the circumstances. It had been hewn on a geometrical straight line by the Brazilian revolutionaries whom the enterprising manager had been able to enlist under their leader. Along this road our expedition started. Mules, oxen and horses had been sent on thirty-six hours before, and we started by night in a motor-car.

It was a weird journey over that forest road, and we bumped along through the silence for hour after hour in the cool night. On either side of us the forest seemed full of animals. The headlights of the car made their eyes and those of the birds glow and show up like points of fire, and sometimes they would run for miles in front of us while we took potshots at them with rifles. I shot at and wounded a large animal which probably was a *tigre,* but it disappeared snarling into the forest.

In the early morning, just as the sun came up, we came to an opening in the forest, a large ant-eater went slowly across our path, parrots flew overhead and the scene was one of brilliant beauty, though on the trees, which formed the main background of the scene, were blood-thirsty ticks waiting to dig themselves in on anything with blood in it.

Finally we got to San Carlos, changed our car for horses, and rode on towards the settlement where the British colonists were to be found. The country was open, with high rank grass and a few dissipated palm-trees; tongues of forest reached out hungrily from the main dark forest. Overhead the sky was brazen. Inside a large *rancho*—which is a roof on four posts— were four or five disheartened people. There was one who had been somebody and who was no longer anybody any more. Another had been an officer in the R.A.F.; there was a Canadian farm-labourer named Christmas, who had lost his false teeth, and who greeted us with a disarmed and disarming grin. There was a dark strong boy of Anglo-Bolivian extraction and a good-looking youth who had been a professional dancing partner at a large London hotel and who still, in the middle of the wildest part of Bolivia, retained a certain attractive and insouciant elegance which went well with his picturesque attire and which made me wish for both their sakes that I had been accompanied by a wealthy female explorer. They all wore revolvers, khaki shirts, riding-boots and breeches, and, except for the ex-dancing partner, a sullen expression, which hardened into one of definite hostility when the manager appeared.

This incongruous group had been attracted by the Company's literature, had dreamed of a colonial life and the control of peons from a long chair with a long drink waiting on a camp table, the wearing and tapping of riding-boots, of hunting, shooting, comic revolutions and a joyous return to London with an aura of adventure and the proceeds of a successful crop available for mild debauchery. After a great deal of hardship they had fetched up at San Carlos, and their introduction

to colonization had really been rougher than even their gulli-
bility could have justified.

At the moment of my arrival the situation was curious.
The Company could not afford to let them depart, for if they
got home, the publicity attending their return as failures would
have reacted most unfavourably on the Company's prospects.
On the other hand, they had no practical knowledge of farm-
ing, except Mr. Christmas, and he was a wheat farmer and
knew nothing about semi-tropical products. They were unable
to go, unable to succeed, wanting to work, and indeed working
at times very strenuously, but inexperienced and ill-equipped
for a proposition which might well have beaten the most experienced South American colonist. So there the poor symbions
stayed and lived on tinned Norwegian fish-balls, stewed parrots
and boiled mandioca. Mandioca, Ivan, is a distressing form of
starch somewhat like a potato without any taste. They worked
in a desultory fashion on their plots and clearings, and had
begun to build palm-tree houses for themselves. They lived
huddled together meanwhile, and under the circumstances it
was no wonder that they cordially detested each other, so that
when I asked one of them where the other lived, he said wearily, "Oh, a long way away," and pointed to the opposite corner
of the hut.

It was a strange night that I spent with them. There was a
certain strain. We could not talk freely in front of the manager, who could stop their food supplies and in whose hands
they were. They most obviously resented my appearance to see
their nakedness and failure, and they probably felt that, coming in the way I had, I could not possibly appreciate the appalling difficulties with which they had been faced, nor their
weariness and boredom. They did not wish us to see the unfinished houses, on which they were working desultorily, and I

sympathized with them. The greatest injury you can do to an artist is to show his unfinished work to a stranger, and I thought that the manager would certainly be shot in the back as he overbearingly and contemptuously pointed out their mistakes to me as we went round. The gayest and most successful of all was the late dancing partner. Buoyed up, perhaps, by his previous success in wringing sustenance from the wealthy ladies who had previously patronized him, many of whom must have appeared even more desiccated and uncompromising than the parched prairies of Bolivia, he had decided to go in for pigs, and these had increased and multiplied surprisingly, and like lean and wiry greyhounds, swarmed over the half-hearted clearings of his comrades, so that as soon as their shy crops thrust green sprouts up towards the burning Bolivian sun, they were immediately devoured.

I was grateful to these people for one thing, for when I saw them, I decided that under no circumstances would I permit any of the refugees for whom I felt responsible to come out to a situation of that sort.

The only thing to do in the face of this obviously disconcerting situation was to say little, be as sympathetic as possible and, in the rôle of the visiting inspector who has to be placated, insist upon everybody having as good a dinner as could be obtained, coupled with as much alcohol as was necessary to dissolve the present. This I accomplished, though the manager did not like it, and under the influence of food and wine, a little better spirit appeared at last, and we told stories cheerfully until a late hour, when I went to sleep in a corner of the hut, somewhat perturbed by the last round of local snake stories.

The next day we arrived at the semi-open zone at Santo Corazón to see the lands that were destined for the proposed colonists. I should mention that, whilst at Gaiba, I had received a wire from headquarters saying that they wished to send immediately a refugee group which was ready and waiting. I replied at once on no account to send anybody until I had reported. There was, however, a certain urgency and the Company were exercising great pressure.

The next day we rode through pleasant open country. It was wild, but there was a semblance of a track at first, and for a time we followed the banks of a stream. We rode all day, and in the evening arrived at a lonely *rancho* inhabited by a Bolivian cattle farmer with his wife and family. It had been a tiring day. We had seen some wild cattle and some game. Once we had come upon a deer, a pretty graceful animal. It was so close that one could hardly miss it. I levelled my Winchester, but I had not the heart to slay it as, though I have killed a good few animals in my time, I always have a qualm and feel like a sportsman turned into an assassin as I look down at something I have killed and its glazing eyes look up at me reproachfully—so I fired high and watched it bound away in freedom, which more than rewarded me for the manager's look of incredulous disgust. Of course, if I had been hungry, these considerations would not have availed.

We slept at the *rancho,* and I thought over the events of the day. I had thoroughly enjoyed riding over the Bolivian parklands, complete with gun and horse, in what was really a very desolate spot, seeing that after the *rancho* there was nothing in front of us for many miles. Gradually, in spite of the attractiveness of the country, my opinion crystallized against the whole business. It was all very well, I thought, for me to look on the bright side with everybody trying to show me the best of things, and what was more important, getting quite a different angle to that of the colonist, in view of the fact that I was reasonably sure of being able to get away and not having to stay and fight with the inexorable forest. Everything, it seemed, depended upon the Company, and I was not convinced. It seemed impossible to turn the whole thing down at once, and if I did, it might be that I should encounter difficulties in returning to civilization; so I determined to temporize and string things out, while making sure that none of our people should be sent, at least, until the fortunes of the Company had taken a definite turn one way or the other, which it seemed to me could not be long delayed.

We had an excellent supper of roast cattle, as one of my Russian refugees once described it, and after searching my skin for *garrapatas,* a necessary daily performance, I went to bed on a mattress spread out in a corner of the *rancho* which was innocent of walls.

Just as I was dozing off I saw something large and ratty jump about by the side of my bed. I moved suddenly and it bounded away. After this there was no rest for me. I lay with one eye open and saw two more of these apparitions. They kept coming and going as I lay and dozed at intervals. They seemed very large for ordinary rats, yet somehow it seemed to me that in the wilds of Bolivia, rats might very well be outsize. I hate rats, ever since one bit me in the ear in an Arabian fort; so I lay quite still and helpless, not daring to wake the others for fear of being laughed at. Next morning, when dawn came, I satisfied myself that I really had seen something. I had. But to my disgust they turned out to be, not rats, but piglets, a few days old and quite pink! Their squeaks were ratlike, but I was very annoyed with myself. The *ranchero* allowed them in—he had, in fact, no means of keeping them out, as there were no walls, and they cruised around, squealing and looking for pieces of food from our supper.

The next morning we were in the saddle early again and rode around for miles. It still seemed theoretically possible that success might be made of the scheme, as the land was fairly fertile and the *ranchero's* crops were good and his animals not too unhealthy.

The manager was insistent with his questions as to my opinions, and I fenced with him as best I could. This part of the country was much wilder and full of game. I saw many parrots or macaws, an ant-eater, an animal that looked like a wolverine, some deer and many sorts of birds. Once we heard what the manager said were monkeys, but I did not see any. That evening the *ranchero* said that he had been worried by a huge wild bull which came persistently round his *rancho* and attacked the other animals. Most of his cattle were semi-wild, and he asked us to shoot this one, which was becoming a nuisance. I asked him why he had not shot it himself, seeing that he had quite an efficient-looking rifle and an imposing general armament of guns and revolvers. His motives were mixed. He had heard that Englishmen always liked to shoot things, but on the other hand, ammunition was expensive, and he was rather short of it. This seemed a reasonable excuse, so we agreed. That evening we sallied out, lay in wait and filled the bull full of lead, when it finally crashed out of the scrub into view. It took eleven .405 Winchester bullets to kill it, and it weighed about a ton. The dogs worried it as it died. Not a very thrilling slaughter, as we had plenty of cover from which to shoot.

The next morning we set out early on the way back to San Carlos, as we intended to do two days' ride in one. The baggage had preceded us by a longer route. On we rode, the manager setting a good pace. I had been very non-committal as to the possibilities of immediate colonization and he was in a somewhat sullen mood as we set out. In any case, during a hard day's ride in the sun, conversation is unwelcome, so after a little we rode on for hour after hour in sweating silence whilst the sun rose higher and higher. The going became more difficult, and at times one had to brush lianas and other obstructing plants from before the horse's nose. The manager's horse seemed much fresher than mine, and soon I found that he was getting rather too far ahead for me to be able to follow easily. The track had completely disappeared and I had no idea where we were going. I shouted to my companion to wait for me, but there came no reply. I fired my revolver, but still nothing happened, except the echoes and the scream of a disturbed parrot. I suddenly realized I was lost.

My pony stood disconsolate with a stupid expression on its equine face. I waited and gave up shouting, for this was only a waste of strength. I had been riding for about five hours and it was then ten o'clock in the morning. I had no water with me and very little idea where I was. It soon became obvious that I was quite alone. I sat down and considered the situation carefully, while horrid fears grew. What a fool, I thought, not to take the obvious warning of the shipwreck and the alarming tales in Corumbá and desist from this absurd affair! I saw myself wandering round in circles and perhaps being found covered with flies and insects three weeks afterwards by a search party. Would they put a cross with *Hic occisus est,* as the Spaniards did for the Jesuit missionaries that were killed by the Indians or who died in the Chaco? Or perhaps there would be no search party and only the insects and carrion birds.

Then it came to my mind that perhaps I had been intentionally abandoned, as the British Agent in Corumbá had foretold, but I dismissed this possibility as absurd because, after all, the publicity attendant upon my disappearance would be definitely injurious to the Company. If that had been their game they

would probably have adopted some other method. I decided to
wait where I was, in the hope that the manager would notice
my disappearance fairly soon and retrace his steps along his
route.

So I waited for an hour by my watch, but nothing came but
more and more mosquitoes and insects. It got hotter and hotter
and I grew thirstier and thirstier. When the hour was up I
decided to get on my pony and let it take me where it would,
in the hope that it might know the road; but it knew absolutely
nothing and was quite disinclined to move at all without guid-
ance. Then I sat down in the menacing silent heat and endeavoured to think before thirst and panic should destroy my
sense. I tried to recall the route by which we had come, but as
we were returning by a different one there seemed to be no
point in this, and I found that I could in effect remember very
little of it which seemed at all different to the country which
surrounded me.

The first essential, I decided, was to get to water, and then I
remembered the stream which we had crossed on the way up
and which must be somewhere not very far away. I decided to
try to get to this, for I reasoned that anybody coming to look
for me would certainly cast along the stream for lack of a better
plan. I decided that if ever I found it I would stay by it, for at
any rate, the question of water would be solved, and it seemed
to me that, though I might last a day or two without food, I certainly could not do so without water. So I reasoned and sweated,
and every now and then was almost overcome by futile rage
over the whole absurd situation.

What was I doing, I asked myself, lost in the wilds of Bolivia, hundreds of miles away from civilization? I mused sadly
of pitchers and wells, for a well was just what I needed most.
Then I began to look for the river. I wandered about trying to

keep in one general direction by using the sun as a guide, but I was often diverted by belts of forest. Marks that might have been paths, that developed, became promising and that finally *were* paths unmistakable and beckoning, filled me with hope, and then just faded away into absolute nothingness.

On one occasion I came to a place which I had visited but five minutes before! I felt so thirsty that I began to conjure up a vision of all the drinks I had ever had. My horse began to show signs of fatigue. It had seemed fairly jaded when we started, as did many of the animals round there, for most of them were suffering from a peculiar disease brought on by eating some injurious Bolivian root.

I began to notice tracks of animals, and then I struck a general line of reasoning, of which I have never ceased to be proud. Why, thought I, if there is a river it must be the only water for miles, and the animal tracks must eventually lead to it. The next problem was to decide whether the tracks led to the river or away from it. It seemed, as so often happens in life, that there could be two distinct schools of thought, and that the chances of either being right were absolutely equal. However, I began to feel that human reasoning might eventually triumph over all this Bolivian foolishness. Firstly, said I to myself, aloud, raising an argumentative finger to an unresponsive equine gaze, it is probable that, as far as wild cattle are concerned, they at any rate would probably go together to drink, or at least join up on the journey at some point not far from the river, whereas, when coming back they would be more inclined to separate. When I examined this idea a little further it seemed to be based on no sound reasoning at all. I looked at the horse for inspiration, and the sad animal hung its head. Surely, thought I, there ought to be something more that one could deduce, for really, Ivan, it was very difficult to know what to do, the country being only semi-open, with great blocks of forest which obscured the view and which made it very difficult to keep a straight course anywhere. Suddenly I had a better idea. The stream was probably the lowest point around, and where I should find sloping animal tracks I must go downhill, and that would be the nearest way to the water. So, on this basis, I moved suddenly on at random, passing the tracks and calculating my general direction on the basis I have explained to you.

To cut a long story short, after what seemed like many hours but was actually a little over two, I came into some open country, and there in front of me, about 2 kilometres away, I saw a winding line of green, which must mean the river. Breathless with excitement, I pressed my unwilling horse into a trot and went towards it. The horse, like a perplexed Civil Servant badgered by an indecisive politician, concurred, and seemed overjoyed that the fool on his back had at last made up his mind. I came at last to the bushes that were growing round the stream, which was about 10 feet wide and 2 or 3 feet deep. It flowed sluggishly through steep banks. I went upstream a little, until I found a place where the water was flowing a little faster, and tying my horse, I clambered down the bank. Lying at full length, I lapped up that muddy water as if it had been iced lager. It was about the same colour, but I didn't mind. As I lay on my stomach, relieved and satisfied, watching the water go by and waiting to drink again, I looked up at the opposite bank, and there I saw two gleaming eyes looking at me and the tip of a twitching tail. It was a small jaguar dotted with black spots, and it sank into its surroundings in such a manner as to be almost completely invisible except to someone very close by. Heavens, thought I, will this day never end? I lay perfectly still for the moment; then my hand crept to my revolver while the big cat kept on looking at me and did nothing but twitch its tail. On second thought I decided not to fire, as it seemed to me unwise to start an offensive from the prone position. If I only wounded the beast I might be mauled by it, as it certainly looked as if it would make light of the leap across the stream. It was not one of the large *pantañales*—which are often as big as Bengal tigers—but I had been told that the smaller ones were often the more dangerous.

I could not make up my mind whether to fire or not. So there I lay and sweated until my glasses became covered with mist! My heart ticked crookedly, Ivan, as you said when you trod on the snake. There we lay for what seemed quite a long time, but was probably only a few seconds. Suddenly I was overcome by an irresistible desire to laugh. It arose from my remembering that stuff which as a boy I used to read in books about the power of the human eye over wild beasts. It sounds incredibly stupid now, but I wondered then, as I lay, whether this alleged power had ever been tested by anyone wearing glasses before. These, I reflected, were not usually worn by lion-tamers or other persons who might have perfected the method. What, I wondered, would be the effect on this supposed power of a powerful lens? Would it so magnify the effect—as seemed stupidly logical—that the animal would think it was being glared at by Napoleon or Charlemagne or Attila, or a sergeant-major in the Guards, or would . . . Here it was that I felt I must laugh, or burst. Anyhow, I decided suddenly to move, emitted a shout, and with a convulsive movement, leapt to my feet and scrambled backwards. This was too much for "spots," who turned tail and crashed off into the undergrowth, hastened by a vainglorious shot from my revolver.

I stood for a moment, feeling rather weak at the knees, and then I made my way back to where the horse was tethered. It was shivering with fright, but finally it staggered down to the water and began to drink. I tethered it to a tree, then I strolled down to a part of the bank which commanded a fine view of the countryside, and sat down to consider the position again under the shade of a flowering tree. It was then about three o'clock in the afternoon and very hot. I sat for half an hour, smoking my last pipe of tobacco, and feeling rather pleased with myself, as I felt that sooner or later, now that I had attained this vantage-point, someone would turn up to look for me. I decided to wait till evening before trying to shoot anything for dinner, and made a smudge fire which I thought might be useful at night both for mosquitoes and as a means of showing where I was. As I was gathering the sticks I saw some figures approaching about a kilometre down the stream. "Act Three," said I to myself, "the arrival of the hostile Indians," and watched them carefully from behind a tree. Then I told myself that my suspicions were absurd, for though there were Indians in the neighbourhood, they were supposed to be some fifty miles away, and in any case preferred to keep to the thick forest. Soon I saw that it was the ox-waggon from the *rancho* and a man on a mule with our stores, which had left the day before. I rode out to meet them.

"Que suerte tiene Vd., Señor!" said the man who rode on the mule when I had told him all about it. "You are lucky, for if you had missed us, nobody else might have passed for a week, and to those who do not know it the way is difficult to find."

There were stores on the waggon, so I organized an enjoyable meal of biscuits, sardines and warm beer. Then we started off slowly and I rode alongside quite contentedly. We got into San Carlos at about half-past seven, just in time to stop a relief expedition which was setting out to look for me. Everybody had been greatly disturbed, but the excitement soon subsided. The manager explained that he had endeavoured to retrace his steps, but fearing to get lost himself, had finally decided that the best thing to do was to push on to San Carlos and organize a search party from there.

That night we set out on the Gaiba road and shot gaily at the animals as they appeared in the searchlights. I stayed at Gaiba a day or two to write my report, and thought things over. There was fishing in the lake and shooting in the forest. I caught some most extraordinary fish, some of which ate fruit with every symptom of relish. At night we played bridge or listened to the radio. It was extraordinary to go out into the primeval forest and listen to the negro jazz music coming over from Charleston.

As regards the main problem, I had decided on my policy. There seemed to be no reason why I should be the person to make startling disclosures and bring the whole business crashing to the ground. I decided finally to set out certain essential conditions the fulfilment of which I thought would prove an acid test of the Company's bona fides. Instead of two ships they must have four and of an efficient type; houses and buildings must be built before the arrival of the colonists, crop prices guaranteed, doctors provided and so on and so forth. I worked out a whole list of provisos which would cost them a very large sum of money indeed to satisfy. I intended to supplement this by private communications to headquarters as soon as I got back to civilization.

After some difficulty I left one morning in the Company's yacht. With me, down river, came the sick Norwegian agricultural expert, who was almost too weak to stand, and the crew of the launch. But although out of the wood, we were not yet done with the river. The launch leaked, the motor failed continually, and there was always about two feet of water in the boat. In spite of these anxieties we made slow yet not unpleasant progress. One night the motor failed, a storm blew up, and we spent a miserable mosquito-bitten night under a tree on the bank, to which we had tied up until the storm had exhausted itself.

The next day we chugged on. I shot some birds, which we ate, and a huge alligator. I caught a glimpse of some monkeys in the trees on the river's edge. They are called *luju*, a good name for a monkey, I think. In the evenings they roar loudly, stirred thereto, it is alleged, by the terrible goitres from which they suffer. The Indians kill them and make guitar strings from their intestines. The crew took the dinghy out to bring my alligator in, and when they had got it over the side it came to life again and nearly wrecked the dinghy with its tail, which continued to flap about even after its head had been almost blown off by a close-range bombardment. We ate its tail, which is the only eatable part, and the skin was scraped for curing. We had some trouble with the crew on various small points, but managed to overcome it.

The Norwegian agricultural expert confirmed my general impression of the impossibility of successful colonization under existing circumstances, and told me some of his own experiences, which had been even more alarming than mine.

At last, on the fourth day out from Gaiba, we saw in the distance the bluffs of Corumbá, where I landed and went up to the Hotel Galileo with a sigh of relief.

I was welcomed by my friend, the British Consular agent, and sat down to send a confidential report to headquarters. I stayed two or three days in Corumbá, got some jaguar shooting, and went to a magnificent Brazilian circus which was visiting the town. The best part of the performance consisted of an old-fashioned play, in which the devil came on with horns and a tail and seduced the daughter of a rich coffee planter.

Then I travelled slowly back to Buenos Aires via Puerto Esperança, São Paulo and Santos.

From the point of view of adventure the episode of the Company was ended, as I never returned to Gaiba. In fact, there can be but few relics left there of the whole affair, which, of course, was eventually liquidated when all had been lost. Administratively, however, it was still destined to cause me much anxiety. When my stipulations were received, the Company trumped the trick by promising to do all, and more than I had asked. They would have guaranteed the moon if I had asked for it. On the other hand, my suspicions were now more or less confirmed. It was merely a paper acquiescence and they were incapable of a real reorganization, for too much money had been lost at the beginning. Their second boat had a terrible voyage across the Atlantic and finally stuck for six weeks on the banks of the Paraguay.

Eventually, to my relief, the whole scheme was abandoned as the result of a wise decision at Geneva, and I breathed a sigh of relief.

After this affair it became fairly clear that not much more could be done in South America than had already been accomplished. A good many refugees had arrived, been more or less comfortably settled, and were attracting a slow but steady stream of relations and friends. I began to devote a good deal of attention to social, industrial and political problems, and acted as the correspondent of the International Labour Office for its general business in South America. I went to Geneva for a Conference in 1928. On returning to Buenos Aires, I found myself on the tender at Cherbourg with Anna Pavlova and her *corps de ballet,* Dr. Voronoff and a consignment of monkeys for Buenos Aires, a negro bishop, the Uruguayan football team, which had just won the Olympic Games, and was told that the presence of an international official would do little to allay the superstitious fears of the crew concerning the probably disastrous effect of such a cargo.

At the end of 1929 I was transferred to a permanent post at Geneva.

ENVOI

"But in spite of all temptations
To belong to other nations,
He still remains an Englishman."
Sir W. S. Gilbert, *Pinafore.*

CHAPTER XXIII

GLIMPSE OF GENEVA

IF THE past is difficult to describe, Ivan, the undigested recent is far worse. When I came to Geneva to occupy a permanent position at the headquarters of one of the organizations of the International Civil Service, I was fresh from the outposts, where I had had definite responsibilities; where my activities had been, as it were, individual and complete, instead of auxiliary and collective, and I felt that I had indeed come to a strange world.

There was the question of languages. Used as I had been to working in an international milieu with people who had been "at a great feast of languages and stolen the scraps," yet I found the continual day-to-day use of two official languages and two more subsidiary ones somewhat strange. I found it very hard to preserve the normal use of my mother tongue and strange picturesque expressions would intrude from other languages. Most of us here sooner or later get into the habit of translating French idioms often quite literally as a result of being too lazy to find the correct English equivalent, and of course the French and Swiss frequently adopt English expressions.

I wonder if you will remember how one day we asked the way when we were out in the car just over the frontier near Annecy. We had interrogated a French gentleman with a beard, which was so huge that it looked as if it would inevitably be caught up in the wheels of his diminutive car—it must be an obscure manifestation of the law of diminishing returns that the larger and the more bearded a Frenchman, the smaller his car. His proximity to Geneva and the Anglo-Saxon *cara* as the Spaniards say—which has clung to me through all my vicissitudes—resulted in this gentleman scorning to reply in French, in which language I had addressed him.

Said he, removing a small hat from a large bald head, "No, gentleman. This is not a National Road, but one of common interest. It is, however, a good road, a veritable billiard."

It is probable that you will also recall from this period the case of the small Swiss hotel in the mountaineering resort where, in order to protect the parquet floor, a notice in "English" had been put up to the effect that "It is forbidden to circulate in the boots of ascension," whilst downstairs in the bar the same painstaking translator startled and raised false hopes amongst the thirsty clients by a notice saying in neat block capitals that "Drinks pay for themselves at the moment of ordering." This was why we always called it the magic hotel. To appreciate these examples one must have lived bilingually and internationally. This aspect of life at Geneva amused me greatly when I first arrived.

It was not long, I admit, before I made the acquaintance of the cranks, the professional defenders of strange obscure causes and the enthusiastic protagonists of logical, desirable but quite impossible reforms and learned to avoid them as—

> *"Fire in each eye, and papers in each hand,*
> *They rave, recite and madden round the land."*

At the beginning, I must say it seemed to me that I had left the real world and come to an artificial one, a world of papers and speeches. By papers I do not mean only newspapers, though I had to read far too many of those. It seemed to me that I was being drowned in papers—documents, minutes, drafts, treaties, conventions, recommendations, blue and grey reports, white papers, yearly reports, biennial, monthly, daily, weekly, and verbatim reports, letters, telegrams, memoranda, forms, questionnaires, annexes, despatches, publications, graphs, charts, pamphlets, précis, notes, carbon copies, condolences, congratulations, lists of staff, lists of vacancies, *notes verbales,* fan mail, indeterminate indescribable *papiers,* observations of Governments and observations of idiots. They rained upon me, and sadly I endeavoured to read and deal with them, pass them on, digest them, speed them up, put them away with honours or get rid of them in some other way. While I struggled with them my colleagues would dash in through the door with more. *"Regardez-moi cela, mon vieux,"* they would say, *"c'est tordant"*; or *"Que barbaridad, amigo!"* and depositing their offering on the already alarming pile, would go off satisfied at having got rid of a difficult one.

In addition to the written words, there were the spoken. In order to familiarize myself with the international democratic method I attended assemblies, conferences, large committees, small committees, committees of three, finance committees, committees on wages and hours, on industrial hygiene, on child welfare, on public works, on statistics, on costs of living, on lead poisoning, on the hydraulic resources of Mongobarbaria, on labour conditions in Candy (Isle of), on the Kikuyu, on conditions of sponge fishers, on the fumigation of steamships, on the standardization of sexual hormones, on child labour in the Sudan, on coal, on steel and iron, on wool and jute, on rags and bones, on whales, on lighthouses, on gold and silver, on recruiting in Liberia, on over-production, on under-consumption, on glass workers, on phossy jaw, on notification of industrial diseases, on accident prevention and compensation, on emigration, on reorganization of the office and on methods of fixation of almost everything.

After papers and words came people, and I was interested in the continual procession of the famous of all countries across the Geneva stage. I will not bore you with the names of all the personages I have met nor tell you with a wealth of detail how I played bridge at a reception in a four composed of the Prime Minister of Moldo Wallachia, the Marquis of L., who played very well, and the Neopomponian Lady Delegate to the Conference on Calendar Reform, nor how on the second tee at Onex I drove through the Aga Khan and Douglas Fairbanks, whilst famous and warlike Japanese peered smilingly over the top of every bunker and along a distant fairway the raven silhouette of Robert Cecil—looking with his caddie like good King Wenceslas—stalked slowly over the sodden rough towards the international flag which had just been replaced by a Montenegrin economist wearing nether garments of the variety you once described as *petits fours!* In a short time I became accustomed to the fauna, and would "talk as familiarly of roaring lions as maids of thirteen do of puppy dogs."

As things went on, however, I began to see my way about more clearly, to understand the real and vital interest to millions of people of questions which at first had seemed to me as dry as the "remainder biscuit" and so uninteresting that to deal with them in any form was an effort. In other words, I began to develop a social sense and to understand something of the way in which the slow movement of public opinion produced reforms through the tiresome but inevitable method of international co-operation.

I began to realize the devotion of the people who had invented the complicated and delicate machinery of which we were in charge and the ability and energy with which they made it work in spite of the horrid difficulty of reconciling conflicting interests and of dealing with national prejudices.

I began to understand that beneath the spate of speeches and the deluge of documents, something very great and fine and on a larger scale than has ever before been attempted was being accomplished for those who work. As I travelled abroad to Spain, to Mexico, to the United States, to Egypt and elsewhere, and met people who were dealing with industrial and labour questions in the various countries, I saw that it was not all talk and empty resolutions but that the international standards set up and the studies devoted to the problems of international competition in industry had favourably influenced the national legislation, had given the workers greater protection, had given the ministries in the new countries dealing with the workers a prestige and importance which they certainly would not have obtained without international support, and had set up a system of control and obligation internationally accepted.

At first I missed in international work at headquarters the intense satisfaction of direct results personally accomplished for good; I missed the stimulus of a direct link between activity and result such as is experienced by the national officials who set in action national ameliorative machinery. Yet, as time went on, I began to feel that the future organization of a better world must and can be accomplished only by some such technique and experience as that which is being carefully and painfully elaborated and obtained at Geneva. It seems to me now, that the cause is good and worthy of anyone's brain and experience, though the methods used may not always succeed. There are many difficulties, and often I wonder whether we shall succeed or whether obscure forces will get the better of us and bring us again to a state of stupidity deserving of another and more terrible lesson of anguish and woe than that of 1914, the memory of which, alas! is gradually fading from men's minds.

The next twenty years will show, I think, for, as I write, it seems to me that prospects are not too promising. It would appear difficult for things to go on as they are at present, without some sort of explosion. Whether it will be possible to limit this explosion—as it was not, in 1914—is hard to say. One may perhaps hope that so much has been achieved. One thing seems to me certain, and that is, that in the present year of grace the immense ground gained by the lovers of peace—I use the phrase in preference to the word pacifists—after the War and which was gained owing to an inevitable revulsion at such stupidity, is in danger of being lost. From 1921 to 1932 the ideas of peace seemed to be in the ascendant, and it really did seem as if war might be avoided. Now, at the most, the scales are balancing, and already the conviction of the inevitability of war is becoming more and more vocal. The smiles of the sceptical become more and more overt when questions of peace and disarmament are discussed. The militarists and technical experts in destruction are beginning to face their fellow-men bold and unashamed, and the ordinary common-sense opinion of the man in the street seems to be hypnotized by the serpent gaze of approaching mutual destruction. Already a great many quite sensible people consider the recognition of the inevitability of war as a return to wisdom and common sense after a period of hallucination. Gradually, people are becoming accustomed to this idea, and pre-War mentality, which admitted mutual destruction as regrettable but normal, seems all over the world to be gaining ground. As disarmament begins to fail, rearmament proceeds apace. It is very difficult to say why this is.

"Why do the nations rage?" Probably because "the people imagine a vain thing."

However, I have done. For the moment I go on with a busy

and interesting life. I am gradually beginning to feel—though with frequent lapses—that to fight against unemployment and social injustice is as interesting as war, adventure and refugee work, and that the obtaining of information and the work of conciliation which enable a reasonable and rational international convention on an industrial question to be formed and ratified is really as romantic as Secret Service or the seeking of wealth by commercial activity, and—most difficult of all—that it is possible to admit a feeling for all humanity, not instead of, but side by side with—ranking equally but below, in my case, to use a Chinese hierarchal distinction—that love of country which was inborn in me, which is obvious in you, and which—as it is foolish to ignore—still remains the strongest force in the world to-day.

It may be that by the time you read this all will have been settled. Peace may have been guaranteed and the problems of social progress solved. Or there may have been another Great War, in which case it seems doubtful if you will ever read it. Meanwhile, there are family interests. There is the grinding machinery of international collaboration and its precious infrequent satisfactions. There is crisp snow under smooth ski and mountain sunshine. There is striving for peace. There are balls well hit and hands well played. There is friendship and feud. There is an unregenerate plan—oft discussed with a kindred spirit—for a tour, before we are both forty-five, to Afghanistan and points East, for alas! as you may have observed, like the Mandarin in the story of Wong Tsoi and the merchant Tien King, I also "am of a straggling and romantic nature, though the dignity of office makes it impossible for me to go very far in any impropriety."

So that sometimes when I gaze at international Conferences, upon the "grim Geneva Ministers" and listen to their statistical eloquence, I feel with Kinglake—for, alas! I am not yet quite resigned to all the victories of peace—"If a man and an Englishman be not borne of his mother with a Chiffney-bit in his mouth, there comes to him a time for loathing the wearisome ways of society—time for not liking tamed people—a time for not sitting in pews—a time for impugning the foregone opinions of men, and haughtily dividing truth from falsehood—a time, in short, for questioning and scoffing and railing. . . ."

．　　．　　．　　．　　．　　．　　．

So now, Ivan, we have come to the present. At the moment you are feeding the chickens in a temporary Geneva garden, whilst your mother and I are wondering what on earth we shall do about your education.

The second half of my life and the first of yours lie before us. For the moment, so calm and fine is this summer day, so peaceful the hen cluckings and garden noises, so drowsy the noonday, so distant the squabbles of peace and the speeches, that I feel as though we were all resting for a moment *sur l'océan des ages.*

But maybe the weather will change, the fleecy clouds will darken, events will crowd thick and fast, the winds of chance will blow and the squalls will push us *vers de nouveaux rivages,* and then will come the day when, like Jim Hawkins of whom you now love to read, you will steal out in Ben Gunn's coracle by yourself to try your luck with Israel Hands, Long John Silver and the rest. I wish you wit, health, pieces of eight and, most especially, as good a companion as mine.

> *"With sail all set go beating forth*
> *To what anchorage or bay*
> *No chart tells. But sail thee on*
> *Dear Admiral or stowaway."*

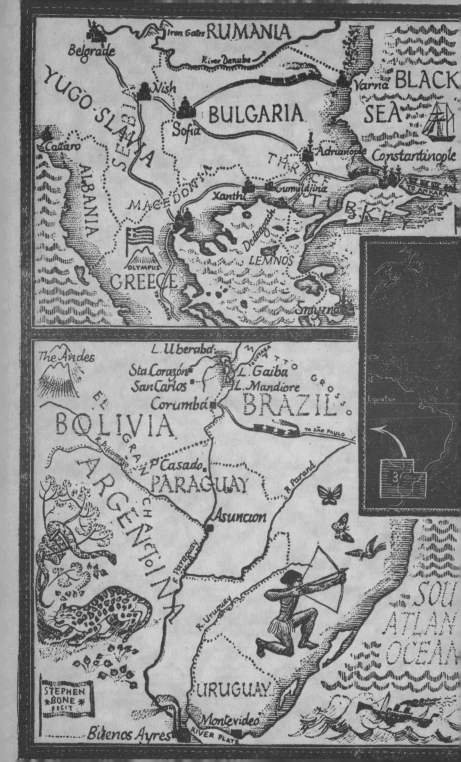